CAREER DIRECTIONS

Consultants

Patricia L. Burch
Guidance Counselor
Binghamton City School District
Binghamton, New York

Richard Campbell
Director, Cooperative Education/Youth Employment
Nebraska Department of Education
Lincoln, Nebraska

Ruth-Ann Jones
Career Investigation Teacher
Crockett Junior High School
Irving, Texas

Mamie Hardy
Director, Professional Service
Changing Times Education Service

Robin Rudicell, Ph.D.
Curriculum Consultant
Bureau of Career Development
Florida Department of Education
Tallahassee, Florida

Developed by
Changing Times Education Service
EMC Publishing
Saint Paul, Minnesota
and
Visual Education Corporation
Princeton, New Jersey

Program Editor: Eileen Slater

Project Editor: Frances A. Wiser

Assistant Editor: Risa L. Cottler

Writers: Natalie Goldstein, Galen Guengerich, Cheryl Morrison, Linda Strickland

Special thanks to: Ellen Soloway, Bob Waterhouse

Production Supervisor: Anita Black

Text Designer: Howard Petlack

Text Illustrator: Bill Colrus

Photo Researcher: Toby Mosko

ISBN 0-8219-0661-5
© **1991** by EMC Corporation

Published by EMC Publishing
300 York Avenue
St. Paul, Minnesota 55101

Printed in the United States of America
0 9 8 7 6 5 4 3 2

Preface

Career Directions has four principal aims. The first is to help you learn more about yourself. Understanding yourself is the first step in choosing a career that is right for you. The second aim is to give you information about jobs and careers. The more you know, the better equipped you will be to choose among the options. The third aim is to show you how to set goals and make plans for reaching them. You will learn how to develop a career plan and get the qualifications for that career. The fourth aim is to help you learn about your role in the American economy.

Career Directions is divided into 4 units and 16 chapters. Each unit is concerned with one of the text's principal aims. Unit 1, for example, focuses on you as an individual. The first chapter introduces you to the concept of your future career. Each of the next three chapters concentrates on characteristics that will affect your choice of a career.

Unit 2 concentrates on work. The first chapter of this unit explains how jobs are structured. You also will learn about entrepreneurship as an employment option. Chapters 6 and 7 introduce you to sources of job information for planning a career and looking for a job.

In Unit 3 you will learn how to plan a career strategy. Chapter 8 shows you how to draw up and execute a plan. In Chapter 9 you learn how to build qualifications for a career. The next two chapters tell you how

to go about finding a job and meeting with employers. The final chapter in this unit gives guidelines for success in any workplace.

Unit 4 focuses on workers' roles in the American economy. The first chapter introduces you to money management, including banking and budgeting. Chapter 14 explains the basic principles behind America's economic system. In Chapter 15 you will explore how entrepreneurs contribute to the economy. The final chapter summarizes the steps involved in choosing, planning, and building a career.

Career Directions has a number of special features that enrich the material presented in the chapters.

❑ A photo essay in each unit focuses on a key concept in the unit.

❑ A first-person feature in each chapter relates an individual's experiences in a job or in developing a career.

❑ Twenty two-page features describe jobs in specific occupational categories.

❑ Full-color photographs, cartoons, and charts illustrate key points.

Career Directions provides an opportunity for you to learn about yourself and to explore numerous careers. By doing so you can begin to plan one of the most important parts of your life—your career.

 Brief Contents

Table of Contents

Chapter 3 Your Attitudes, Habits, and Personality 44

Chapter 4 Your Developing Skills 60

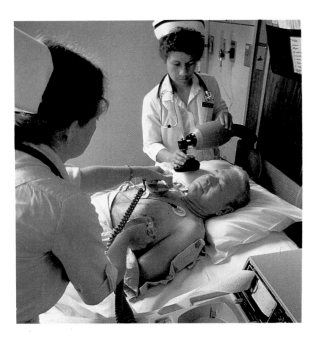

Cluster Feature Contents

First-Person Feature Contents

UNIT 1

FOCUS ON YOU

▼

▲

Do you enjoy
taking care of
animals, such
as horses,
cats, or dogs?
If you do, then
you may want
to use your skill
in handling animals
to become a
veterinarian or an
animal breeder.

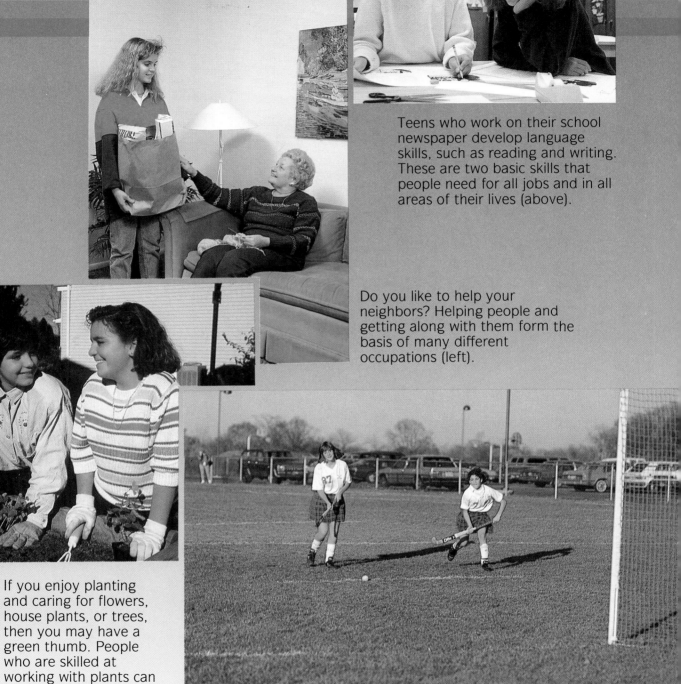

Teens who work on their school newspaper develop language skills, such as reading and writing. These are two basic skills that people need for all jobs and in all areas of their lives (above).

Do you like to help your neighbors? Helping people and getting along with them form the basis of many different occupations (left).

If you enjoy planting and caring for flowers, house plants, or trees, then you may have a green thumb. People who are skilled at working with plants can use their abilities to become landscapers or nursery workers (above).

Playing a team sport is a great way to learn how to work as part of a team. Throughout your life, you will find that teamwork is a necessary part of many activities and most jobs (above).

If you like to listen to music, you may want to try playing an instrument. You will not only acquire musical skills, but also patience and discipline.

Some people view painting as a chore, whereas others see it as a challenge. If painting is one of your favorite activities, then you may want to become a professional painter or start your own painting business.

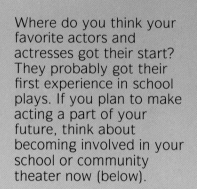

People can express creativity in many ways. This teen is making pottery, and in the process he is developing his artistic abilities (right).

Where do you think your favorite actors and actresses got their start? They probably got their first experience in school plays. If you plan to make acting a part of your future, think about becoming involved in your school or community theater now (below).

Joining a club is a good way to develop an aptitude or interest you have. These girls belong to their school's computer club. There are many settings in which they will be able to use their knowledge of computers (above).

These two young teens are working together to make a model. They are developing patience and concentration as well as coordination (below).

This girl likes to spend her spare time helping her sister work on her car. People who like to work on engines have mechanical abilities that can be utilized in many occupations (left).

Being able to teach other people is a skill that can be used in schools and in businesses. This girl is developing her teaching abilities by tutoring a younger student (above).

These junior volunteers learn how to help others, and they get to take a firsthand look at the health care field. If you enjoy taking care of others, then you might be interested in a career as a doctor, nurse, or orderly (above).

Babysitting is an excellent way to acquire skills. You learn how to be responsible and how to take care of children (above).

9

1
You and Your Career

When you have studied this chapter, you should be able to:

➤ Judge the present state of your career plans

➤ List the main steps you have to take to progress further

➤ Explain what is meant by objective thinking, and why it is so valuable in making career decisions

Vocabulary Words

Occupation

Goal

Interest

Values

Job

Career

Objective

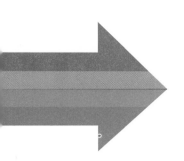

When you go to school or wait for the school bus, you probably see dozens of people going to work. You might even see hundreds if you live in a city. You may not pay much attention to all these people. After all, they are just part of the morning scene. Tomorrow morning, take another look and try to imagine what sort of jobs these people have. Do you think they are glad to go to work? How do you think they feel? Why do you think they feel the way they do? If you could talk to them, you would hear a different story from every person. Some of their stories might sound like the following ones.

Take Janice, for instance. She is a social worker who runs a center for senior citizens. She loves being with people. She enjoys creating new programs for the center. Most of all, Janice likes helping those who need assistance, whether she is counseling them or helping them get government aid. In other words, she loves her job. Even when she is not at work, she thinks about her job.

Hank is quite different. He works for a health insurance company as a claims examiner. He examines and checks health insurance claims that people file. He also investigates claims and approves payments. He does the job well, and he likes it, but he would be an equally happy and competent worker in a bank or helping to run a business. Hank rarely thinks about his job when he is away from it. He likes the steady income because it enables him to pursue hobbies outside of his job.

Jen finds her work rather dull. She is an accounting clerk for a small company. She spends most of the day recording payments and receipts on a computer. She does not find her job challenging. She wishes that she could be doing the more complex accounting work that her manager does. She can accept the boredom because she has made plans to get another job. Jen is going to night school and in a few years will finish her training as a certified accountant.

Tom is a truck dispatcher at a shipping company. He assigns drivers to trucks and stays in touch with them while they are on the road. He also handles any questions or problems customers have with the freight that has been delivered. Because the company is expanding, Tom has to deal with a lot of pressure. He often is tired from working extra hours. Tom really dislikes his job. He feels that the only good thing about it is the paycheck.

How will you avoid finding yourself in a situation like Tom's? Will you be more like Janice or Hank? Will you find the right job in two or more stages, like Jen? Right now you probably cannot answer these questions. In fact, you may find the whole subject rather scary. Do not worry. You do not need to make final career decisions at this point. What you *can* do is to start learning how to make those decisions. That way, when the time does come, you will be prepared. This book can help by showing you what you need to know about career decisions now and in the future.

More and more jobs are becoming high-tech jobs. These jobs often require advanced math skills.

Where Do You Stand Now?

If you had to choose an **occupation** right now, what would it be? An occupation is the work a person does to earn a living. Some of you might answer confidently and surely. You believe you know exactly what you want to do. Others of you probably will have some idea of what you would like. More than likely, however, most of you would have a hard time answering that question at all. Which of the following groups do you feel fits you?

Knowing All Along

Kevin has wanted to be a firefighter since he was three. Over the years, he has learned a lot about the job because his father is a firefighter. At first, Kevin simply was fascinated by fire engines. Now he knows about the realities of the job. He knows that the job includes physical danger, waiting for long periods with nothing to do, close friendships with other firefighters, and the good feeling that comes from helping out in a crisis.

Kevin still believes that firefighting is the job for him. He may be right. People who care that much about a job usually enjoy it and do it well. Some people, like Kevin, stick to having one **goal** all their life. A goal is an aim that a person is willing to make an effort to achieve. There is, however, another situation that he should consider. Kevin may not develop the physical build that helps his father to be such a skilled firefighter. There also is a chance he will change his mind in four years' time, only to find that he knows nothing about other occupations.

If you are convinced that you have a firm career goal, take a good look at yourself to see if you really are suited to the work. Even if your answer is yes, you should continue to learn about other occupations. Not only may you simply change your mind, but the occupation itself may change to keep up with technology and

Some people enjoy manual jobs, or jobs that require them to work with their hands.

People who enjoy working with children must have special skills and abilities.

you may decide it is no longer what you want to do. In addition, think about skills that can be transferred to other jobs.

Having a General Idea

Sally is very good at math and knows she wants a job in which math plays a part. However, she has no clear idea what that job might be. She knows that plumbers, surveyors, and engineering technicians use math, but she has not looked any further. Sally should be careful not to narrow her choices too soon, though. People who are good at math often find that they are equally good at computer programming, for instance. Also, the number of occupations that require math is growing rapidly. In fact, Sally will be able to choose among a very large number of jobs.

Children often learn about jobs from their parents and other adults in their lives.

For some teens, going to college is part of their career plan.

Derrick's situation is a little different from Sally's. Derrick knows he wants to do something to help protect the environment. He does not know much about job possibilities, but he thinks he would like to be a forest ranger in a national park. Derrick does not know that most people who work to protect the environment are employed in offices. They may do studies of the environment, design systems to monitor the environment, or work with others to help write and pass laws that protect the environment. That would not be as appealing to Derrick as working outdoors.

Derrick also needs to learn that there are more young people who want these types of jobs than there are job openings. He may not even be able to get a job in this area. Derrick may feel he has made his basic career decision and does not need to know much more. If he did more research though, he might decide that he would not like the occupation after all.

Having No Idea

Brad has not thought too much about the future as yet. His grades are all pretty good, but there is no one subject he really likes. Although he knows he could never be a professional athlete, he is more interested in sports than anything else.

Brad probably is more typical than either Kevin, Sally, or Derrick. If Brad were asked to make a career decision at this time in his life, he would have a very difficult time doing so. There are, however, many things he, and you, can do now to make it easier to reach that decision in a few years' time.

(continued on page 16)

Review Questions

1 ▶ Why should you learn about other occupations even if you have a firm career goal?

2 ▶ What do people who know what their strong talents are need to be careful of?

3 ▶ Why is it important to research jobs you think you might like?

FOCUS ON YOU

WHEN CHOOSING IS NOT ENOUGH

Whenever my dad says to me, "Hey, McWiz, can you spare some time?" I know that his old car is broken down again. McWiz, short for mechanical wizard, has been my father's nickname for me since I was about seven. I have always loved working with motors and engines and fixing them.

The only person I have ever met who is as crazy about engines as I am is Dale. Every Saturday we rent a lift at a garage so we can fix cars or rebuild engines.

One Saturday last May, Dale and I were fixing a fantastic '57 Chevy and daydreaming about owning one. We realized that if we wanted to buy one, we would have to get jobs so we could earn some money.

Dale and I are alike in our mechanical-wizard way. In other ways, though, we are different. Right up until the end of June, Dale put off looking for a summer job. He said he was sure he would not have any trouble finding work at a local garage. I did not want to take that kind of chance. I am the kind of girl who plans ahead.

I talked to everyone about finding a job. One night a neighbor called and said there were summer jobs at the airport for kids who wanted to learn about jet engine mechanics. It sounded so interesting I went to the airport the next day. I got the job.

I spent the summer learning about jet engines. The work was challenging, and I really liked it. At the end of the summer, my supervisor recommended me for a scholarship at a school for aviation career training. He said that he believed I had a great career ahead of me. I feel that way too.

Dale did get a job at a local garage. Whenever I asked him about it, he would change the subject. He later admitted he was ashamed to tell me he had pumped gas all summer. He was upset and angry with himself because he had not found a better job. I think from now on, planning will become part of his McWiz strategy, too. ■

Brad's parents are both very happy with their occupations. Even though Brad is not interested in any particular occupation, he hopes in the future to be able to choose a career that is right for him. One of his goals is to be as satisfied with his occupation as his parents are with their occupations.

There are certain steps you can take now to help make decisions later. Those steps include knowing yourself, learning about as many jobs and careers as possible, practicing making plans, and taking into account the "big picture."

Know Yourself

You cannot fit a square peg into a round hole. In the same way, you never will be happy in a job for which you are not suited. The more you learn about yourself, the more likely you will be to choose an occupation that is right for you.

How can you know yourself better than you already do? The first part of this book will help you think about yourself by asking you to answer questions about yourself. When you answer these questions, you will learn more about what you like and dislike, and about what really matters to you.

Part 1 also will help you develop self-knowledge by showing you what you can and cannot change about yourself. Your **interests** are bound to develop further. Interests are activities that a per-

If you need help sorting out your feelings, your friends may be able to help since they know you well.

It is important to find out as much as you can about careers that interest you. For example, if you want to be an athlete, you might read about other athlete's lives.

son especially likes. Your present skills and abilities will improve and you will develop new ones. You will continue to change in both of these areas. However, there are some things about yourself you cannot change. For instance, if you enjoy being a leader, you will not suddenly change and prefer to have other people take the lead. Recognizing which characteristics you can change, and which ones you must accept will help you become more knowledgeable and more self-confident.

As you move toward becoming an adult, you will continue to develop your own outlook on life. Many things, such as **values**, will become a part of your outlook. Values are all the things that people consider important in their lives, such as friends, security, and education. Part 1 will help you recognize your outlook and your values and show you how they relate to career choices.

Learn About Jobs and Careers

Up to now, you have been reading about **jobs** and **careers**, but do you really understand how a job is different from a career? A job is a position that a person holds to earn a living. A career is a planned sequence of jobs.

Do you remember Jen, the accounting clerk? When she becomes a certified accountant she will get a new job. She will, however, stay on the same career path. At the college where she attends night school she has been given credits for previous training and experience in beginning accounting. If Jen had decided to go to school to learn about a completely unrelated field, she would be switching career paths. The path you take will be influenced by the decisions you make now and in the near future.

Part 2 will help and encourage you to learn about as many jobs and careers as possible. After all, the more knowledge you have about jobs, the more options you will have. You also will learn how to make the research task manageable. You will look at jobs as they are grouped together by similar abilities, interests, and level of education. You will learn about these groupings in two-page features that are included in each chapter. Each feature is different and is centered around one particular grouping of jobs. There are 20 of these features in the book.

You will learn to ask a few questions when you examine a job. You might make a list of the following questions, since they will help you review jobs in which you are interested. How is the job defined? What are the main activities? What abilities are required? How much responsibility is involved? Would you work with other people? In what type of environment would you work? What are the average levels of pay and prospects for promotion? What is the outlook for the occupation as a whole?

A good way to know whether you might like a particular career is by getting a part-time job where you can use the same skills.

Making Some Decisions

It may surprise you, but you can begin to make important career decisions now. It does not matter whether those decisions are large or small. What matters is that by making choices you will be gaining the confidence to continue making more choices in the future. A career decision is not a single, giant step. Rather, it is a series of many steps, some small, some large.

Part 3 of this book will show you how to select part-time jobs and other activities to broaden your knowledge of yourself and of different work settings. You also will learn how to set short-term and long-term goals, and how to review them periodically and change them when necessary.

For example, Elizabeth is interested in becoming a college professor but she is not sure that she will be able to speak well in public. She has decided to join the school debating team. If she finds that she dislikes public speaking, she will switch to her second career preference—librarian.

By the end of Part 3, you will have learned how to look at occupations from two points of focus:

☐   What is the occupation like?

☐   How would it suit me?

See the Big Picture

In Part 4 you will learn how important it is to take a look at the big picture where occupations are concerned. For example, some jobs are challenging and pay well. Other jobs may pay less, but may be extremely rewarding and fulfilling. These are things to keep in mind when you make your decision.

Getting the big picture has another value. Occupations are continually shifting in response to change. For instance, jobs in physical fitness have increased because the adult population has become more concerned about being fit and healthy. With a little research, you usually can tell whether a job is secure or endangered. This will help you choose an occupation.

The big picture also will show you how trends may affect different occupations. For instance, the introduction of personal computers has started a trend toward people working in their own homes. It is now possible to work at home for a mail-order catalog company, a computer software company, or the editorial department of a newspaper. Computers have made it easier for individuals to start their own businesses as well.

Review Questions _____

1 ▶ Which personal qualities can you develop further?

2 ▶ Why should you learn about as many jobs and careers as possible?

3 ▶ Why should you start to make career decisions now?

Be Objective

Julie always has wanted to be a professional golfer. She loves golfing and watching it on television. She dreams about someday being good enough to play in a professional match. According to Julie's coach, however, she is not being **objective**. That means she is not looking at the situation without emotion. She is allowing her feelings to distort reality. Her coach believes that if she were being objective, she would realize she is not talented enough to be a professional golfer.

It is very important to train yourself to be objective about career decisions. If you want to be an actor, for instance, try to figure the odds of your being a success. Ask yourself such questions as: Do I have the ability? Am I willing to work hard?

You also should take an objective look at any industries that have jobs in which you are interested. Some industries, such as the travel industry, have been growing fairly steadily. Others, such as the building industry, tend to experience highs and lows depending on how the economy is doing.

Being Objective About Yourself

It usually is very difficult to be objective about yourself. It is hard to evaluate yourself without emotion. You probably see yourself differently than your friends, parents, or teachers do.

An advisor who listens to you and is objective can help you plan your future.

It may be easier for you to be objective if you try to look at yourself as though you were another person. Try describing yourself as you think others see you. Ask teachers, good friends, and relatives to suggest careers they think might suit you. Then, after you listen to them, ask them why they made the suggestions they did. Think about whether any of them sound interesting.

Getting a Sharper Focus

If you have taken the first steps—of knowing yourself, of learning about lots of jobs, of practicing making decisions, and of looking at the big picture—you may want to talk things over with your school counselor or with an advisor. This person can help you think more clearly by asking you the right questions.

Christine decided that she wants to go into the army. Her advisor asks her why. Was she persuaded by a recruiting film? Is it a family tradition? Christine replies that her mother dreamed of being in the army. In her day, however, women in the army were given very restricted duties, so she decided against it. The advisor then asks Christine if she is trying to fulfill her mother's dream. When Christine cannot answer that question easily, she realizes she needs to examine her choice more objectively.

Alex likes cooking and often prepares dinner at home. A friend of his parents manages a local diner and has offered to train Alex

You can get advice from advisors, family, and friends, but it is more important to listen to your own inner voice.

to be a short-order cook when he finishes high school. Alex has researched other occupations but has not found one that interests him as much. Before he accepts the offer, he asks his uncle for advice. The uncle questions Alex and discovers that Alex likes to make complicated and imaginative dishes. He asks Alex if he would not rather be a chef. Alex says he did not consider that because of the cost of the training. His uncle convinces him to talk to his counselor about financial aid.

Listen to Yourself

Review Questions _____

1 ▶ Why is it important to be objective about yourself?

2 ▶ If you take the first steps on your own, what can you do next?

3 ▶ In addition to an advisor, who can you listen to?

Advisors cannot help you much if you do not listen to yourself. Alex had an inner voice that was trying to tell him he might not be happy as a short-order cook. He was not listening to that voice, though, because he thought he could not afford to pay for the training that would be involved in other options.

Sometimes the wisest thing to do is to stop thinking about a problem and just see how you feel about the main decision. For instance, if you have just made a career decision, do you feel excited or slightly depressed? How do you imagine you will feel after one year in the job you have selected? How will you feel after 10 years? Try to determine what your gut reaction is even as you think about yourself objectively.

When you make decisions about occupations, you should ask yourself two questions: What is the occupation like? How would it suit me?

Summary

- [ ] You can begin to make career plans by examining where you stand right now.

- [ ] To move further along, you need to learn more about yourself.

- [ ] The next step is to learn how to research information on jobs and careers.

- [ ] You can practice making career decisions now.

- [ ] You need to look at the big picture when considering any occupation.

- [ ] When it comes to career decisions, you need to be objective about yourself.

- [ ] An objective advisor can assist you in seeing yourself clearly.

- [ ] You need to listen to your inner voice when making career decisions.

Vocabulary Exercise

occupation	values	objective
goal	job	
interest	career	

Write a paragraph in which you use all the vocabulary words in original sentences.

Discussion Questions

1. Where do you stand right now with your career plans? How can you improve the plans you have made? How can you begin to develop plans if you have not made any?

2. Do you think you need to learn more about yourself? Why, or why not?

3. Do you think some people have a better outlook on life than others? Explain your answer. How would you describe your outlook on life?

4. Who do you think would make the best objective advisor for you? Why?

Thinking Further

1. (Speaking) Describe yourself as you think others see you. Then suggest careers for yourself based on those characteristics.

2. (Reading) Read a current newspaper and try to locate any articles on trends that would affect jobs. Think about how those trends might affect the whole job market.

3. (Writing) Take a folder and label it *Career Plans*. Then take a sheet of paper and put today's date at the top. Describe your career plans as they are right now. Are you more like Kevin, Sally, Derrick, or Brad? Put the sheet in the folder.

   Now take a second sheet and date it. List your current hobbies and interests. Take a look at it. What do they say about you?

   Date yet another sheet, and put down all the jobs that have ever appealed to you. Start the list with jobs that interested you when you were small and work up to today. Include all jobs, even those that may seem funny to you now. Then look at the list. Can you see a pattern in it?

   Finally, take a fourth sheet and date that, too. Write down all the jobs you have done. Unpaid jobs, such as those you do at home, count, too. Look at the list. Which of these jobs, or which parts of each job, did you like best? What new jobs would you like to try for a different experience?

   Clip the sheets together and put them in the folder. After completing this course, look at the sheets you have filled out. Have you changed your mind? Is there any new material you could add? If so, add it.

4. (Reading) Read the following feature to learn more about jobs.

WHO PROVIDES ADMINISTRATIVE SUPPORT?

To complete a complex task you often need other people's help. This also is true in business. It takes the assistance of many workers for a business to run smoothly.

Rico works as a word processor through a temporary employment agency. He works in a different office every few weeks. He has worked for many kinds of organizations, including large corporations, small businesses, schools, hospitals, and government offices. He enjoys the frequent changes of scenery, and his interpersonal skills help him to get along with the many different people he encounters on the job.

After high school graduation, Rico attended classes at a local business school to improve his ability to use computers and software. He also has well-developed skills in spelling, punctuation, and grammar.

Even though Rico enjoys his work, he plans to make a career change in a few years. He can get plenty of job assignments now, but advances in office technology are expected to decrease the demand for word processors by the turn of the century. Moreover, working through an agency limits his income and provides little opportunity for advancement. To prepare for a career change, Rico is attending classes part-time at a nearby college.

Right now, Rico works the day shift at a law firm. He spends most of his time typing and revising legal documents, which are often lengthy. He also types correspondence.

Marilyn is a secretary at the same law firm. While Rico does typing for all of the firm's lawyers, Marilyn works only for two of them. She screens their telephone calls and incoming mail, maintains their files, prepares their expense and billing reports, and helps them assemble legal documents. She

occasionally helps with legal research. Because the firm has a word processing department, Marilyn does not do much typing. Typing, however, is an important part of some secretaries' jobs.

Marilyn uses a personal computer for many of the tasks she performs at work. Like Rico, she took specific classes after high school graduation to learn to use different kinds of computer software.

Marilyn's income is higher than Rico's, but her job carries more responsibility and is less flexible. She works from 9 a.m. to 5:30 p.m., five days a week, with two weeks off each year for vacation.

Marilyn and the other secretaries take turns filling in for Judy, the receptionist, when she leaves the office for lunch. Judy's primary duties are answering telephone calls and directing them to the right people, greeting visitors, and notifying others in the firm when visitors arrive to see them. She also sorts the incoming mail.

Receptionists need pleasant speaking voices, good language skills, and calm dispositions. They must dress neatly, too. Receptionists usually are not supervised closely, so they need good judgment and common sense to deal with situations as they arise. In general, though, receptionists do not need as many skills as secretaries do, and they earn less money. The employment outlook for receptionists is excellent, partly because of business expansion but mostly because receptionists tend to move on to other occupations after a short time.

In the *Occupational Outlook Handbook,* you will find the jobs of word processors, secretaries, and receptionists in the cluster called Administrative Support Occupations, Including Clerical. Other jobs in this cluster include:

❏ bank tellers

❏ bookkeepers and accounting clerks

❏ computer operators

❏ file clerks

❏ insurance claims and policy processors

❏ postal clerks and mail carriers

❏ shipping and receiving clerks

❏ stock clerks

❏ teacher aides

❏ telephone operators

❏ ticket agents

2

Your Needs, Your Interests, and Your Principles

When you have studied this chapter, you should be able to:

➡️ Discuss where your principles come from and why they are important in choosing an occupation

➡️ Identify your most important needs and wants

➡️ Explain how you can define your interests and preferences, and suggest how they relate to your choice of occupation

Vocabulary Words

Principle	Lifestyle
Consumer	Self-esteem
Need	Preference
Want	Volunteer
Producer	

How choosy are you about buying new clothes? Different people have different standards. Janet, for example, is happy with any clothes that feel comfortable and do not look too baggy. Peter, on the other hand, likes bright colors and spends a good deal of time shopping for clothes that give the effect he is looking to achieve. (He has even bought uncomfortable clothes because he likes the way they look.) Astrid adores fashion. She makes many of her own clothes so she can afford to keep up with the trends.

Although it is more difficult and more important, choosing a career is something like choosing clothes. A job that makes one person feel great may be unbearable for another person. Careers, however, are different from clothes in a very important way. You can change clothes whenever you please, wearing one outfit one day and another the next. A career is something you work at five days a week, and hope you will not have to change too often.

This chapter is the first of three chapters that can help you identify a career you can enjoy. It begins by asking the question: "What can a career provide for me?"

Your Principles

Principles help us make many decisions in life by setting standards for our behavior. When we make decisions based on these standards, we feel good about ourselves and our lives. If, on the other hand, we make decisions that go against our principles, we often feel uncomfortable or unhappy.

You may wonder what your principles have to do with your choice of occupation. John did not see the connection either, until he had to decide between jobs with two different airlines. One airline offered him a job as a passenger agent at the metropolitan airport near his home. There, he would work with other ground personnel, helping to manage the arrival and departure of passengers at the gates. The other airline offered him a job as a flight attendant. He would be responsible for making the airline passengers' flights as comfortable as possible. His trips would take him to many interesting places, perhaps even overseas. Which should he choose? What should he consider when making his decision?

John thought carefully about the options he had. He knew he would enjoy working in both positions. However, he realized that as a flight attendant there was a strong possibility that he would be away from home for several days at a time. Because John was the oldest son, his brother and sister relied upon him to help care for their invalid mother. For that reason, John felt that being at home each night was extremely important. That is why he decided to take the job as passenger agent. Since he would still be working for an airline, he would benefit from the free travel offered to airline employees anyway.

What Are Principles?

John decided that his relationship with his family was an important thing in his life. Helping his family was one of his principles. By recognizing that he would be happier if he could be at home each evening, John was able to make the decision that was best for him. If John had chosen to become a flight attendant, his time away from home probably would have been a source of frustration. As a result of that frustration, his job would have been less fulfilling and less rewarding.

Recognizing Your Principles

Where do your principles come from? How can you identify them? As you grow, you learn from your parents or guardians what they believe to be important in life. Their principles, in other words, form the basis for your own principles. As time goes on many other influences enter your life—teachers and friends at school, religion, books, magazines, other things you read, television, and movies. These may influence your principles as well.

You can recognize the principles you have come to hold when you face decisions or conflicts in your life. For example, imagine you are at home one evening studying for an algebra exam the next morning. The telephone rings. Your best friend asks if he can come over to talk to you. He has just had an argument with his parents and is very upset. You need to make a decision. If you talk with

People frequently owe their principles to the teachings of religious organizations.

Principles will influence your choice of a career. For example, some people believe the environment needs to be protected, and they work toward that goal. What are some things you believe in?

your friend, you will not be able to study for an exam that is important to you. On the other hand, if you tell your friend to wait until tomorrow to talk he may become even more upset, and your friendship may suffer.

This kind of conflict reveals two important principles that you hold. Your friendships mean a lot to you, and your schoolwork means a lot to you. You value both of them.

Principles and Occupations

Principles can play an important part in your choice of occupation. For example, Lynda enjoys working as an engineering technician for the Air Force. She chose to join the Air Force because she believes a strong military is necessary to the country. Lynda's friend Jill also works as an engineering technician. In fact, the two women went through technical school together. Jill, however, chose to work for an engineering company. Although she wanted to work with Lynda, she did not want to be in the military.

Both Jill and Lynda made occupational decisions based on principles that are important to them. Both are happy in their jobs, but neither could be as happy in the other's job. You probably can think of other occupations that some people might choose and others might reject based on their particular principles. Thinking about your principles is an important part of deciding which kinds of occupations you should pursue.

Review Questions ——

1 ▶ How are principles related to decisions in life?

2 ▶ List two influences on your principles other than your family.

3 ▶ When can you recognize principles that you have come to hold?

Your Needs and Wants

If you buy and use products, then you know what it means to be a **consumer.** As a consumer who is spending money, you probably have thought about the difference between **needs** and **wants.** Needs are things you cannot do without, like food or shelter. Wants are optional. Although you can live without them you would like to have them anyway. Wants include such items as compact disc players, concert tickets, an extra pair of jeans—anything you enjoy, but could do without.

It is because of principles that people's needs and wants differ. For example, skateboarding is very important to Chaz. Therefore, he considers his skateboard a need. Stan has many other hobbies, so he thinks of his skateboard as a want.

At present, a parent or guardian probably provides you with many of your needs and wants. Your meals, your bed, your clothes, and your allowance come from their earnings. When you become an adult, you probably will provide for yourself. Then you

People's lifestyles are different because they have different interests and preferences. Your lifestyle reflects the things that matter most to you.

People with high self-esteem have confidence in themselves. That confidence is evident whether they are working or having fun.

will become a **producer** as well as a consumer, contributing to society and earning your own money. Your needs and wants, and perhaps those of your own family too, will be paid for from your own wages or salary. Your job, however, can provide other satisfactions that do not come from the money you earn.

Material Needs and Wants

All of us have certain material needs that must be satisfied in order for us to stay alive: adequate food, water, shelter, and clothing. These needs take priority, since you have little choice about whether or not they are met. Your occupation must provide money to meet these needs.

That is not all. You will surely want more from your job than just enough money to survive. Take Sarah, for example. Her income as a physical therapist allows her to live in a comfortable apartment. She often buys new clothes and eats at her favorite Mexican restaurant once or twice a week. She also wants to buy a new television set, a new car, and go on vacation to Florida or California. The decisions Sarah makes about fulfilling her material wants determine her **lifestyle,** or the way she chooses to live and spend her time and money.

A few Americans, of course, do not need to work in order to meet their needs and wants. Harry started his own catering business when he left college and got lucky. The business not only pro-

(continued on page 32)

WHAT AM I GOING TO DO WITH MY LIFE?

During my junior year of high school, my friends began talking about what they were going to do when they graduated. I did not join in any of those conversations. You see, I did not have any idea what career I was interested in.

Sure, I thought about my future. I had taken classes in plenty of subjects in school, but I did not like anything in particular. I knew I would have to make a decision soon, especially if I planned to go to college or get training after high school.

After a few weeks, I guess my worrying started to show. A friend finally talked to me and got me to tell him what was wrong. He suggested I go to the school's career counselor to see if she could help. At first I rejected the idea. I saw myself as independent. I always met challenges on my own and figured things out my own way. After a few more weeks of useless worrying, however, I decided to try the counselor.

I talked to her for about half an hour. We discussed my interests, preferences, and skills. Then she handed me a test booklet. I told her that I was not prepared to take a test. She explained that this was more like a survey that would clearly show what my interests and abilities are. It would help me recognize what is important in my life. I opened the booklet. Sure enough, the questions all asked how much I liked or disliked all kinds of things. I had to think hard about some of my answers. What did I really like and want?

The next day I met with the counselor again. She talked to me about my love of mountain climbing. I told her how I loved the challenge, the beauty of the rock formations, and the wonderful solitude. She asked me if I had ever thought of studying geology. She described career opportunities in the geology industry such as locating and extracting natural resources, planetary history, volcanoes, earthquakes, and teaching. She gave me pamphlets about geology careers, a book list, and a list of courses I might want to take.

Sometimes getting professional advice makes sense —even if you are very independent. Now I am studying earth science in college. Even though I do not know exactly what area of geology I will go into, I am not worried. ■

vided a substantial income for him while he still owned it, but five years later he sold it to a national chain for a very large sum of money. Harry, in turn, invested this money and it provided him with enough extra money to cover all of his needs and most of his wants. Harry, however, soon became bored without a job and opened a restaurant. Now, he once again feels the satisfactions his previous business provided.

Being Accepted and Respected

What Harry's story shows is that an occupation can satisfy more than your material needs and wants. It can satisfy emotional needs and wants too. Harry does not need the money, but still feels the need to work. Work gives him a sense of satisfaction that he does not want to lose. Of course, not everybody who makes a fortune decides to go back to work.

Sarah, the physical therapist, enjoys her relationships with her co-workers and with her patients. All people need to know that the contribution they make is valued. It helps fill an important emotional need common in everyone—the need for **self-esteem.** Self-esteem is a healthy confidence in yourself and your ability to achieve your goals. With a high level of self-esteem you feel better and are more likely to perform well on the job.

Feeling Fulfilled

It is easy to become totally absorbed in a job you enjoy and find fulfilling.

Have you ever heard people say they enjoy their job so much they would go to work even if they did not get paid? On the other hand, have you seen the bumper sticker that reads, "A bad day fishing is better than a good day at work"? What is the difference between a person who does not look forward to going to work and one who almost forgets to go home at the end of the day? One finds work fulfilling. The other does not.

People whose occupations are fulfilling often can become completely involved in what they do. Their jobs are like hobbies to them. They are fascinated by their work and believe it accomplishes something worthwhile. For example, a person who believes children need to be mentally challenged may become totally absorbed in designing educational toys.

This level of fulfillment, however, is not for everybody. If your entire life revolves around your work, you may spend long hours trying to reach difficult goals. You may neglect other aspects of your life that are important to your overall well-being, such as family, friends, and leisure activities.

Review Questions

1 ▶ Describe the difference between needs and wants.

2 ▶ Name an emotional need that having a job can fill.

3 ▶ Name three signs that people's occupations are fulfilling.

To achieve fulfillment in your life you need to find your own ideal level of involvement in your work. Sarah, for example, like most physical therapists, values her profession for more than money and respect. She feels dedicated to helping people and knows she would be less satisfied with her work if she was not helping. This does not prevent her from having fun outside of her work, though. She takes time to plan a vacation with her friends and to enjoy her apartment.

You too can look for a career that will provide you with satisfactions besides money. After all, you will spend close to one-quarter of your adult life at work. It is worth taking time to make a careful choice. What activities give you the most pleasure now? Do you enjoy sports and physical activities? Do you enjoy using your mind? Do you enjoy most activities, as long as you are with friends? Your answers to these and other questions can help you find the kind of job that will give you the greatest satisfaction.

Your Interests and Preferences

Have you ever made a list of your interests and **preferences**? You probably can name several of your interests without much thought: playing volleyball, making pizza, and listening to big band jazz, for example. Could any of these point the way to an occupation you would enjoy? Identifying your preferences, your basic likes and dislikes, may take a little more thought. Would you rather work indoors or outdoors? Do you prefer working with words or machines? These types of questions also can help to steer you toward an occupation that would satisfy you.

Have you ever heard someone say, "You learn by doing"? It is true—the more experiences you have, the better able you are to decide what you like and dislike.

You will make many choices when selecting a career. One choice will involve the type of environment in which you will work.

A Job that Interests You

One of your goals in choosing an occupation should be to find a job that will interest you. Say, for instance, ever since you can remember you have been interested in computers. It would certainly make sense for you to think about a career in computers, perhaps as a software technician or as a computer programmer.

What if you think you have had no career-related interests, or if, like Michele, your ambitions have changed many times. When Michele was six she wanted to be an animal trainer at the circus. Between the ages of seven and eight, she decided that she would rather be a horse jumper. At 12, she changed her mind again; she liked the idea of running a kennel. Right now, at 14, she imagines herself in many different roles, such as a news reporter, a veterinarian, or a physicist.

If your interests are not very clear, or if they have changed several times, you may find it helpful to think about your preferences, because they usually are less changeable than your interests. It is common for interests to change.

Defining Your Preferences

Suppose you were asked, "What are your interests?" You probably could list four or five topics, though not all of them would relate to jobs you could get. If someone were to ask you about preferences, though, you probably would ask, "What do you mean?" All of us have clear preferences that relate to jobs. Preferences are the choices you make about all the aspects of working and lifestyle.

Here are some questions you can ask yourself to uncover your own job preferences:

- [ ] Do I prefer a job working with people, or would I rather work alone?

- [ ] Do I want a challenging job or a safe and secure job?

- [ ] Would I like to work indoors or outdoors?

- [ ] Am I more interested in working with machines or working with words?

- [ ] In my spare time, do I prefer to read a book, make something with my hands, go to the mall with my friends, play a fast-paced ball game, or watch TV?

- [ ] At school, do I generally prefer math, English, science, or social studies?

- [ ] Am I ready to work variable hours, or do I like a set schedule?

If you take a career assessment test, you will see that there are no right answers. Those tests measure how you feel about certain things.

□ Do I work best under pressure, or do I work better when I have plenty of time for each task?

□ Would I rather work in a city or in the country?

□ Would I prefer a job that involves travel, or would I rather stay in one place?

Answers to these types of questions can help you define more clearly what kind of job would suit you. For example, Michele was thinking about several careers and these questions helped her decide for which ones she was better suited. She said *yes* to working with people, a challenging job, and working outdoors. She also picked science, a variable schedule, working under pressure, being in the country, and doing some travel. Of her three occupational interests, Michele decided that being a veterinarian suited her preferences better than either of the other jobs.

Help from the Guidance Department

What if, after thinking about your preferences, you still are unsure about what interests you? Your school guidance counselors have many different ways of helping you define your interests and preferences. Among these are some surveys that can help you identify your interests.

These surveys are based on years of research and testing. Because they are objective they can be very helpful. They do not start with any fixed ideas about the kind of person you are. In fact, they have been designed to separate what people *really* want from what they think they *should* want. Your answers to these surveys, along with the help of your guidance counselor, do more than identify your interests and preferences. They also suggest specific jobs or job areas that might suit you.

For example, you may be given a survey that reveals patterns in the things you like and dislike. You simply indicate whether you *prefer, do not mind,* or *dislike* each of the activities listed on the survey. Your response patterns not only point toward certain occupations, that may interest you, but also reveal preferences for particular lifestyles as well. Surveys also are available that focus more on interests than on specific occupations.

Emphasizing Career-Related Interests

Why, you may ask, should you now spend so much time thinking about your interests and preferences? The answer is simple: so you can make full use of the time between now and when you begin your career. As you and your guidance counselor work on identifying your interests, you will begin to see interest patterns devel-

The best way to know whether you will like something is to try it. That is how you can learn more about your likes and dislikes.

1 ▶ Name two careers that might be of interest to a person who likes computers.

2 ▶ Identify three career-related preferences that might help you define your interests.

3 ▶ How are the surveys used by guidance departments helpful?

4 ▶ Why is it useful to you to explore your interests and preferences now?

oping that point toward possible occupations. You can begin to choose those courses and extracurricular activities that explore the various interests you have identified.

For example, if you look for a part-time job when you are older, look for one that is connected with an occupation in which you are interested. Be careful, though, not to limit yourself too much. Think in general terms, and be open to many possibilities. You may want to be a **volunteer.** A volunteer is a person who works without pay. If you enjoy helping people, think about being a volunteer at an organization that delivers cooked meals to the elderly, or provides similar care. Such a job will not only help them, but it will also help you. It could confirm for you that this is a job area that could provide lasting satisfaction for you.

Even if your feelings about a part-time job are negative, you will have learned something important about yourself. Emily, for example, enjoyed taking care of her baby sister and was thinking of a career in the area of child care. She decided to babysit for neighbors in the evening and on weekends. Before long, she realized that she did not enjoy caring for other people's children. She was glad to discover that now, rather than halfway through training as a child care worker!

It is important to identify your interests and preferences before you choose an occupation.

Summary

- [ ] Knowing what principles are most important to you can help you choose an occupation in which you can believe.

- [ ] Parents or guardians take care of your needs and wants now. When you become a producer and start providing for yourself, you will be responsible for meeting your own needs and wants.

- [ ] Like everyone, you have material needs and wants that help you to stay alive and develop a particular lifestyle.

- [ ] A well-chosen career also can fulfill your emotional needs and wants—for example, self-esteem and a feeling of fulfillment.

- [ ] Defining your interests and preferences can be very helpful for selecting a career that will satisfy you.

- [ ] With the aid of objective surveys, a guidance counselor can help you to identify your interests and preferences and link them to possible occupations.

- [ ] Through coursework, work as a volunteer, and part-time jobs, you can start to explore jobs you think might appeal to you.

Vocabulary Exercise

1. Write a meaningful sentence about yourself using these three words.

   needs   self-esteem   producer

True or False?

2. Principles are beliefs that act as standards for our behavior.

3. Job-related preferences include working outdoors or indoors, working variable hours or regular hours, and having a job that involves traveling or staying home.

4. Wants are those things you cannot do without.

5. Your wants and your needs are what determine your lifestyle.

Discussion Questions

1. Principles may differ between people, even between close friends. List some principles you think everyone in your class holds.

2. Why do you think self-esteem is a need and not a want? How is self-esteem a part of your life?

3. Do you think people can gain self-esteem without having a job? How?

4. Why might some people be unfulfilled in their occupations? Would the world be better if they were fulfilled? Why?

5. If some of your interests are not met by your work, name some other ways they can be met.

Thinking Further

1. (Writing) Write a few paragraphs in which you compare and contrast the lifestyles of two people you know, writing about the different wants they appear to have.

2. (Listening) Ask three adults you know to talk about three of the most important principles in their own lives. Make notes *after* you have talked with them, indicating whether you agree with the points they made, or if not, why not. How do their principles appear to relate to their jobs, or to other aspects of their lives?

3. (Speaking) There are many products available in modern life, such as cars, television sets, refrigerators, and air conditioners, that some people might say are wants. Others, however, will argue that they are needs. Choose one of the products above and prepare a debate. You take one side and find a friend to argue the other side. You may choose a product other than those on the list if you wish, but you must find someone to argue the other side.

4. (Math) Do a survey of your classmates. Ask them whether they think principles, interests, or preferences are most important when choosing a career. Then prepare a report presenting a tally of how many students selected each and indicate what you have learned.

5. (Reading) Read the following features to learn more about jobs.

WHO HANDLES NATURE'S RESOURCES?

When you pick up a piece of paper or sit on a wooden chair, do you ever think about how many people work to bring you these products? There are many people involved.

Brent, Fred, Charlayne, and Phil help harvest the timber that serves as the raw material for many products you use, from paper to furniture. They spend their work-days in the woods, performing difficult jobs under hazardous conditions.

Brent, who studied forest harvesting in a community college and has many years of experience as a forester, works for himself as a logging contractor. He obtains contracts from big logging companies to cut timber at their logging sites throughout Oregon. Like other successful people who own their own businesses, he has management skills and is willing to take risks. For example, he uses his own money to purchase the saws, cables, and other equipment that he and his crew use on the job.

Fred, Charlayne, and Phil work on Brent's crew. They got their training on the job. They continually learn new forestry skills from Brent and other more experienced loggers. They work hard most of the year, but winter weather often brings logging to a halt and leaves the crew members without work—and pay.

Fred works as a faller, using heavy chain saws to cut down trees that have been marked for harvesting. In his first forestry job, he worked as a brush clearing laborer, preparing the ground for logging.

In her job as a bucker, Charlayne uses several kinds of saws to trim the tops and branches from the fallen trees, and then to cut the trees into logs of a specified length. Brent hired Charlayne because of her experience as a carpenter. This is her first forestry job. She hopes someday to work for a big logging company as a cruiser. In that job she would hike through the woods to logging sites to check out the working conditions and

to estimate the value of timber that can be cut. She is taking night classes in math to become better at estimating job costs.

Phil is a choke setter. His job is to fasten steel cables and chains around the logs Charlayne has cut, so tractors can drag them away from the site. He wants to become a tractor operator.

Brent works alongside his crew and supervises. He fills in as an extra faller, bucker, or choke setter when necessary. Brent worked for a big logging company for several years before he became an independent contractor.

All loggers must be able to work as part of a team. They also must be healthy and strong, with enough stamina to do heavy labor for many hours. Most importantly, they need good judgment for making quick decisions when dealing with hazards.

Brent and his crew face a variety of hazards. They constantly must be alert for trees and branches falling in unexpected directions, especially on windy days. They also must avoid slipping on muddy ground and tripping over hidden roots and vines. They get scratches and skin rashes from brambles and poisonous plants. Years of exposure to noise from the chain saws can damage their hearing. Protective equipment, including hard hats, safety glasses, and heavy boots

and clothing, is extremely important for all loggers.

Due to improvements in logging equipment, logging slowly is becoming a safer occupation. However, the new equipment also is reducing the number of logging jobs, especially for fallers, buckers, choke setters, and others who do manual labor. Workers who operate tractors and other heavy equipment will be less affected by the changes. The need for forestry workers whose tasks are more mental than physical, such as those of cruisers, is likely to remain about the same as now.

Loggers' jobs are in the Agriculture, Forestry, Fishing, and Related Occupations cluster of the *Occupational Outlook Handbook*. Other careers for people who want to work with trees and other plants include:

- ❏ farm operators and managers
- ❏ forest technicians
- ❏ gardeners and groundskeepers
- ❏ horticulturists
- ❏ landscapers
- ❏ soil conservationists
- ❏ tree-farm workers
- ❏ tree trimmers

WHO COMPLETES THE BUILDING?

Do you ever think about all the people who built your home or school? Each person used a special skill without which these buildings would not be complete.

Armando, Brian, and Toby build houses. They work with other members of a contracting company's construction crew. For the last year, they have been putting up a new housing development. Later they may work on another development, or they may build houses on individual sites throughout the area.

Armando is a concrete mason. He and

his helpers build the foundation of each house. They also build sidewalks and patios. During the winter, Armando and his helpers look for other work, because concrete cannot be poured when the temperature falls below freezing.

Before the concrete for a house foundation is poured, Brian and the crew's other carpenters must build the wooden forms that define the shape the foundation will take. Armando measures the forms to make sure their dimensions are correct. Then he supervises the laborers who pour the concrete and spread it with shovels. Armando and a helper then finish the concrete by smoothing its surface.

Once the foundation is set and the forms are removed, Brian and the other carpenters frame the house, or erect the outside walls and the roof. Next, they build the supports for the inside partitions. After the electrician and the plumber have run the pipes and the wire through the supports, the carpenters nail drywall panels to them. They install counters, cabinets, and interior trim when the house is nearly complete. Unlike most masons, carpenters can work throughout the year. They generally frame houses only during warm weather, but they can erect the partitions and do finishing work

inside the house at any time of the year.

Toby, a drywall finisher, goes to work on a house as soon as the carpenters nail the drywall panels in place. Her job is to prepare the panels for painting. Using a putty-like substance called joint compound, she fills all the gaps between the panels. Then she covers the joint compound with strips of perforated paper tape and applies a little more joint compound. She also fills nail holes and dents or other imperfections in the panels. When the joint compound dries, she sands all the drywall panels so the paint can be applied to a smooth surface.

Armando, Brian, and Toby all learned their trades on the job. Their jobs do not require education after high school, but they all need basic skills. Math skills are very important to Brian and Armando, who measure the materials they use.

Virtually all construction jobs are physically stressful. Armando, for example, must bend and kneel as he works, which is hard on his knees. Brian and Toby spend most of their time standing, often in awkward positions. In addition, they all face hazards from the materials and equipment they use. Brian and Toby are prone to lung problems from breathing sawdust and plaster dust. Armando sometimes gets chemical burns

from wet concrete. Injuries and job-related physical ailments cause many construction workers to seek other occupations by the time they reach middle age.

Brian, Toby, and Armando earn about the same income. Some highly specialized construction workers, such as stone masons, earn higher wages. Many construction workers belong to unions, which determine their wages. The number of jobs for construction workers is expected to increase at about the same pace as for other occupations over the next several years.

In the *Occupational Outlook Handbook*, the jobs of carpenters, masons, and drywall workers are grouped in the Construction Trades and Extractive Occupations cluster. Other jobs in this cluster include:

- ❏ carpet installers
- ❏ glaziers
- ❏ insulation workers
- ❏ painters and paperhangers
- ❏ plasterers
- ❏ roofers
- ❏ roustabouts
- ❏ tilesetters

Your Attitudes, Habits, and Personality

When you have studied this chapter, you should be able to:

▶▶ Identify good attitudes and habits that help people achieve success in their work

▶▶ Explain how bad attitudes and habits can be changed

▶▶ Discuss aspects of your personality that you should consider when choosing an occupation

Vocabulary Words

Attitude

Supervisor

Habit

Courtesy

Personality

Introvert

Extrovert

Joe works on an assembly line in an automobile factory. His paycheck allows him to meet his basic needs and many of his wants. He enjoys his job installing muffler systems.

Joe's co-workers would say that he keeps to himself. Joe rarely is in a bad mood. He has a positive attitude and works hard to do his job well. He arrives at work on time and treats people with fairness and kindness.

Joe has found a job that suits him. His tendency to keep to himself could make some jobs difficult, but not this one. In this chapter, you will look at people's traits, whether they can be changed, and how they can affect job satisfaction.

Your Attitudes

Some people looking at a half-full glass of water see a glass that is half full. Others see a glass that is half empty. It all depends on the **attitude** of the person. Your attitude is your typical way of thinking and feeling—your outlook on life. Attitudes are evident in everything you do. Your attitude affects how you react to people and how you deal with situations. Some people see the best of the world around them. Other people have a negative attitude, making life harder for themselves and others.

Your Attitude Toward Work

Attitude plays a large part in your getting, keeping, and enjoying a job. While meeting with a potential employer at a clothing store, one applicant may say, "I like to work with other people, and I think I can help your customers find the clothes they want." Someone else could take another approach, saying, "I do not like standing on my feet all day, but at least the job does not sound too boring." If you were the employer, which one would you hire? You would doubtless choose the first person, who sounded positive about life and work. A person with that kind of attitude would work hard for his or her employer.

The second person sounds interested in doing as little work as possible. That would be unfair to the employer, who has a right to expect a day's work for a day's pay.

Your Attitude Toward Authority

Your most important work relationship on the job probably will be with your **supervisor.** Supervisors are the people who give you your work orders, answer many of your questions, and check your

When people work together as a team, both the people and the organizations benefit.

work. They also have an important say in whether you are promoted, or even fired. Having a positive attitude not only toward your work, but also toward your supervisor is, therefore, a key to your success at work and your enjoyment of it as well.

As you get to know your supervisor, you need to remember that nobody is perfect. If you find yourself complaining about your supervisor's faults, try to seek out some good points and focus on them. Seeing the good instead of the bad is what is meant by the glass being half full, instead of half empty.

Diane started out very badly with her supervisor at the phone company. He reminded her of her grandfather, who had always bossed her around when she was young. She found herself gritting her teeth whenever he spoke to her, even if it was praise for a job well done. She tried, however, to see him in a positive light. She realized that he was well organized and that, in spite of his manner, he tried to praise something in her work every day. This made her see him in a more positive way.

Your Attitude Toward Others

Attitudes toward your co-workers also are important, as are attitudes toward customers. If you are critical of the people you deal with at work, chances are you will not be very happy at work. Paul

Often, people view the same tasks in very different ways.

felt that the other tellers at the bank were far more careless on the job than he. They definitely were faster than he was. Paul grew angry with them because they could deal with more customers. He felt that made him look bad. He also felt bitter toward many of his customers, who seemed to have more problems than the customers with whom his co-workers dealt.

Paul was very nervous when his supervisor suddenly called him in for a talk. She had noticed how upset he seemed, even with his customers. Instead of getting angry she simply asked him if he was having a problem.

Working on Your Attitudes

A large part of Paul's problem was his attitude. He had developed negative feelings toward the other people with whom he worked. This actually caused him to slow down, and it also made him behave angrily toward his customers.

Although his supervisor pointed this out, she also was encouraging. She praised him for his careful work, reassured him that care was the most important thing for a beginner and that speed would come later. She said that many of her best tellers had started out slower than average. This greatly reassured Paul, and as his self-esteem improved, he began to see his co-workers in a new light. He began to watch how they worked, even picking up from them a few timesaving tricks.

When you become aware of having a bad attitude, try to focus on the positive. Find a good point to counter each bad point that is upsetting you. View the person or task with an eye toward the good

Review
Questions _____

1 ▶ Why is your attitude toward work important?

2 ▶ How can you change your attitude toward someone at work if you start by feeling negative toward him or her?

3 ▶ What is the best way to settle a problem with someone if you think changing your attitude will not solve it?

Work is more enjoyable when you get along with your co-workers.

points. Developing a positive picture of someone often changes your attitude toward that person.

Of course, there will be times when one of your co-workers, or your supervisor, is truly making your life difficult. Even then you can look for a positive solution. Your first step could be to discuss the matter directly with the person who is causing you trouble. If this fails to work, many companies have a special person or department to deal with these types of problems. In both cases, however, it is better to focus on solving the problem than expressing anger at the person who is causing the problem.

▌Your Habits

Maria turns into the parking area next to the site where workers are building a new highway bridge. She checks her watch and notes that she has 10 minutes to look over her notes before her meeting begins. Maria, a civil engineer, designs bridges for the state highway department. Her job is important to her, and she finds it fulfilling. She has been working on this bridge for two years, and yet another problem has developed. This time it is with the guardrails. She hopes that today's meeting will solve the problem so construction will not be delayed.

As Maria steps out of the car, she puts on her hard hat and work boots. She knows construction sites can be dangerous places, so she always wears the required protective gear. Maria waves to the construction supervisor, then makes her way to the small construction office where the meeting will take place.

(continued on page 50)

TESTS CAN BE FUN

(Lauren loves her job as a teacher—but she was not always so happy at work. She owes her happiness now, she says, to a personality test she took.)

When I started out, I had the idea that whatever job I chose would be *it*. I might get promoted, but I would always stay in the same line of work. My first job was bank clerk, and I liked the idea of moving up—first to bank teller, then to service representative, and maybe to branch manager. I thought my career was set. If I did my job okay I could make it to the top. That is not what happened, however.

I made teller after only three months, and I really liked meeting the customers. Unfortunately, it was always "Have a good day," then on to the next person. I did not realize how fed up I was until they talked about promoting me again. Looking around, I suddenly knew that I did not want to move up—the jobs just were not me.

My friend Dana suggested employment counseling. As I said, I had never thought about changing careers. Dana told me about a friend who had been down on his job just like I was and went to a job counseling service. That person had found the ideal job in, guess what, a bank!

So I went to the counseling service, and talked to some counselors. I told them my feelings about the bank, and they gave me a personality inventory. It was like a test—126 questions to answer—but it was fun. I was writing what I thought and felt, not what I knew (or did not know).

The results were a revelation to me, but they fit perfectly with what I had been feeling. Apparently I had answered the ques-

tions not as bankers do, but like a schoolteacher would. The test results were in a *profile*. They showed a set of scores for different personality traits. For example, the scores said I tended to make judgments based on my feelings rather than my thoughts. I also had a high concern for other people and was interested in helping them develop. It was amazing. The test seemed to know me better than I did.

My aunt thought I should stay in banking. I figured, why be unhappy? I enjoy teaching. Each student is like a different challenge and each day brings new problems to solve and new satisfactions. ■

Once inside, Maria sees that the representative of the guardrail supplier already has arrived. Maria has worked with him in the past and knows he can be a difficult person, but she speaks pleasantly with him until the other people arrive. She has learned that being friendly toward other people makes everything go more smoothly.

As she arrived for the meeting, Maria displayed a number of good **habits**, or things she does over and over again. Of course, just as people can have bad attitudes, they also can have bad habits. Habits, like attitudes, can be changed for the better. Look at some of the good habits displayed by Maria and see how they are important in the workplace.

Arriving on Time

Maria made certain she allowed enough time for travel so she would arrive before the meeting began. Punctuality, or being on time, is a habit you must develop before you begin working, if you have not done so already. Most employers stress being on time.

In some jobs politeness and courteousness are more than just good work habits—they are prerequisites.

They rarely put up with employees who arrive late or take longer breaks than they should.

If you find it difficult to be on time, ask yourself why. Have you developed a lazy attitude? Are you so disorganized that you cannot find what you need? Do you oversleep because you go to bed too late at night? Once you discover the problem, work hard on making changes. It may take a lot of willpower; however, you will find that being on time makes your life easier all around.

Courtesy

Maria showed a cheerful and friendly attitude toward everyone she met. Even though she did not particularly like the guardrail firm's representative, she knew that acting pleasantly toward him would make the meeting go more smoothly.

Courtesy is the ability to be thoughtful and considerate of other people. When you are at work, treat your co-workers and the public politely. Greet people pleasantly when you meet them in the office or speak with them on the telephone. Thank people when they complete a task particularly well or in good time, even if it is part of their job.

Some people think they should act politely only if they feel like being polite. These people believe it is better to show their moods, whether they are in a good mood or a bad one. This approach can cause serious problems for them at work, as well as elsewhere. No one likes being around a sour, grumpy person, especially not for eight hours a day! Take a lesson from Maria and learn to be courteous and polite. You will be much more successful at work, and your mood will improve, too!

Persistence

Maria had been working on this bridge for two years. Many times she became discouraged, wondering if it would ever be completed. Once she even thought of asking to be assigned to a different project. In the end, though, she decided she should keep working on the bridge until it was finished.

Persistence, or the ability to stay with a job, is a habit employers look for in their employees, because it demonstrates a good attitude toward work. Some jobs, like Maria's, may be difficult and frustrating at times. Others may involve tasks that are boring or may need completing in a very short period of time. When you find yourself in one of these situations, what should you do?

So that you do not become discouraged at work, you need to set short-term goals for yourself. What can you achieve in the next

Experienced workers know that it is important to follow safety guidelines on the job.

hour? What progress can you make at work today? Even if the goals you set are not large ones, you will feel good about reaching them. Try to focus all of your energy only on one thing at a time. If you try to do several things at once, you probably will accomplish very little. By sticking to one task, you will develop the habit of working on a job until it is finished.

Safety Consciousness

Before Maria went near the bridge, she made sure she was obeying the safety rules. She knew the construction site was full of potential dangers, and that the rules had been made to protect her and the other workers. Safety is important in all workplaces, not just at construction sites. Good safety habits will help prevent accidents on the job, whether you work at a desk in an office or set steel beams for highway bridges.

Begin to develop safety habits now by training yourself to be aware of your environment. Look around you when you are at home, in school, in a store, or on the street. What potential dangers can you spot? How careful are you when you cross the street? Do you know where the nearest fire extinguisher is? Do you know the telephone number to call if you need an ambulance? Do you read the directions carefully when you use household cleaners or lawn products? Do you observe safety precautions when you operate machinery? If you make safety a habit now, you will be more safety conscious when you are on the job.

Review Questions

1 ▶ Name three habits that are good to have in the workplace.

2 ▶ Name three possible reasons people are late for work.

3 ▶ Is it better to show the kind of mood you are in at work? Why or why not?

4 ▶ How can you keep yourself working at a job that seems difficult or frustrating?

5 ▶ What is the key to developing good safety habits?

Your Personality

So far, the past two chapters have identified several factors that can help you find a rewarding and satisfying job. You have thought about several things that contribute to the kind of person you are—your principles, needs, wants, interests, preferences, attitudes, and habits. These all have become aspects of your **personality**, or the individual quality that makes you act differently and be different from everyone else. There also are other very basic traits that contribute to your personality. For example, some people react to situations with great emotion, while others appear not to react at all. Because these personality traits are a part of us from the time we are very young, they can be difficult, if not impossible, to change. So think carefully about them, because they will affect how happy and successful you will be in a particular occupation.

Emotionality

Every person experiences the same basic emotions, but each person has a different way of expressing those emotions. For instance, you might show excitement by jumping up and down. Your friend, however, might simply smile and look pleased.

Do you express your emotions openly? Do you quickly become excited and enthusiastic about things that interest you or do you have a calmer approach to life? Do you remain cool and level-headed no matter what happens? Recognizing how emotionally

Some jobs require people to make on-the-spot decisions, sometimes in life or death situations.

Do you spend a lot of time doing things by yourself? If so, you might like a job that allows you to work on your own.

involved you become in situations around you will help you choose a more satisfying and rewarding occupation.

People who openly display a wide range of emotions often are well suited for certain occupations such as telemarketing and recreational work. Musicians and other artists also have a high level of emotional involvement in their work.

Other occupations require coolness under pressure. Emergency medical technicians, ambulance attendants, and air/sea rescue team members must stay calm and in control even in a life and death crisis.

Many people find that having a sense of humor can make tense times at work more bearable. A good laugh at the right time can relieve the stresses that accompany any work situation. You do not need to have a ready supply of good jokes in order to have a sense of humor. You can take your work seriously, but still find time to laugh and enjoy the lighter side of your job.

Assertiveness

Being assertive is like swimming. It is smart in some situations, such as when you are in the deep end of the swimming pool. It is not very smart in other situations, such as when you are in a wading pool. Public relations workers must be assertive in representing their company, but kindergarten teachers need to take a gentler approach. Some people become assertive when they get angry. In the workplace, angry assertiveness almost always spells disaster. Positive assertiveness can help you perform well on the job; that is, if you choose the right occupation for your level of assertiveness.

Think about how you work with other people to find solutions to problems. This will help you recognize whether you are assertive. Do you try to get what you think is right by confronting other people quickly and purposefully? If you do, you probably would find success as an FBI agent, security guard, advertising executive, or stockbroker. These jobs require people who are bold and forceful. If you prefer to consider a situation carefully before you take any action, choose an occupation that requires less assertiveness. You may be happy working as an economist, a chemist, or a machine tool operator.

Just as with other personality traits, it is not necessarily better to be one way or the other. Each trait, like assertiveness, is simply better suited for particular occupations.

If you consider yourself a "people person," you probably would enjoy a job that allows you to interact with people.

Introverts and Extroverts

A third personality trait that seems hard to change is sociability. Abraham, according to most of his friends, spends a lot of time alone. He reads books, listens to music, and takes long walks in the park near his home. Being on his own seems to suit Abraham, his friends and relatives say. It gives him time to think and to enjoy all of his favorite activities.

Krista is the exact opposite. Her focus is on other people and the activity around her, and there always is plenty of that, since she is president of her class, a member of the honor society, and co-captain of the basketball team.

Psychologists would say that Abraham is an **introvert** and Krista is an **extrovert**. Abraham is happiest working on projects by himself, and it is possible that he might enjoy working as a statistician. Krista prefers working with people. A job in occupational therapy or in acting might suit her.

Time, however, may cause changes. Introverts often become more sociable as the years go by. Extroverts, on the other hand, may find they want more private time. Since plenty of jobs are available to suit all kinds of people, each person can focus on finding an occupation that matches his or her level of need in terms of being with other people.

Review Questions

1 ▶ Name three occupations that require levelheadedness.

2 ▶ Name four occupations that require assertiveness.

3 ▶ What is the difference between an extrovert and an introvert?

Summary

❏ Positive attitudes toward work, authority, and other people can make your work more satisfying and rewarding.

❏ A person can develop a positive attitude by finding and focusing on good points.

❏ It is better to focus on problems than on people when trying to improve a work situation.

❏ Punctuality, courtesy, persistence, and safety consciousness are important habits to develop before you begin working.

❏ Habits, like attitudes, can be changed if you are determined enough.

❏ How openly you express your emotions, how assertive you are, and how much you need to be with people are personality traits that should affect your choice of occupation.

❏ Some personality traits are hard to change.

Vocabulary Exercise

attitude   habit   personality   extrovert

supervisor   courtesy   introvert

Insert the appropriate words from above in the spaces below:

Trudy is an (1)_____ who prefers to work on her own. Because this is one of her (2)_____ traits, it would be very difficult for her to change. Even though she seems shy, Trudy always responds with (3)_____ whenever some- one speaks to her. This is a good (4)_____ that she has worked hard to develop. Her (5)_____ , who is more of an (6)_____ who cares greatly about those who work under her, has helped Trudy develop this posi- tive (7)_____ .

Discussion Questions

1. Describe a situation in which attitudes could conflict and contradict each other.

2. How could the habits mentioned in this chapter improve your life now?

3. What other habits can you think of that would be valuable to an employer?

4. Explain the connection between being extroverted and being assertive.

Thinking Further

1. (Writing) Describe three people you know and indicate your attitude toward them. Try to explain why you have a positive or negative attitude toward each of them.

2. (Listening) Listening is something we can improve by making it a habit. Make a list of resolutions that you think might improve your listening skills.

3. (Speaking) There is an old saying, "Sow an act, reap a habit; sow a habit, reap a character; sow a character, reap a destiny." Explain what this means to you, and say whether you agree with it. Does it support what is said in the chapter?

4. (Reading) Read the following feature to learn more about jobs.

WHO PLANS AND BUILDS... EVERYTHING?

Have you ever wondered who designs the cars, trucks, trains, and planes that take you where you want to go? Take this chance to meet some people who do that.

As engineers, Jason, Gary, and Dina are all involved in the design and development of passenger jets and their components. Each of them has had a hand in helping the Mercury Aircraft Corporation get its new XTX supersonic jet off the ground.

Jason and Dina both work for Mercury, but they work in different departments and have different specialties. As a mechanical engineer, Jason is part of a team that designs and tests jet engines, such as the one for the XTX supersonic jet.

Dina is an electrical engineer. She supervises the installation of wiring systems in jets like the XTX. These wiring systems were designed by other electrical engineers. They provide power for the aircrafts' outside lights and the controls in the cockpit, as well as for the lighting in the passenger cabins and the equipment flight attendants use to prepare meals.

Gary works for a company that sells parts to the Mercury Aircraft Corporation. He is a ceramic engineer. He designed a crucial part of the XTX jet engine called a ceramic insulator.

The mechanical, electrical, and ceramic

engineering specialties include many subspecialties. Mechanical engineers work with the production and use of power and heat. Jason's specialty is jet engines, but mechanical engineers also specialize in motor vehicles, climate control systems, and other kinds of projects. Gary specializes in jet engine components, but ceramic engineers also specialize in glassware, tiles, and other products. Dina's specialty is power distribution systems, but electrical engineers also specialize in areas such as robots, computers, and stereo equipment.

Engineers in all specialties need aptitudes for both science and math, because solving scientific and mathematical problems is an important part of their jobs. Engineers also must write reports and discuss projects with other engineers, so they need well-developed language skills as well. Other qualifications include creativity, good analytical skills, concern for details, and an ability to work as part of a team.

Jason, Gary, Dina, and most other engineers have bachelor's degrees from colleges where they studied engineering. Dina, like most engineers in supervisory or managerial positions, also holds a master's degree. Jason, Gary, and Dina occasionally attend classes at engineering schools to keep up with the latest technology.

Job opportunities for engineers are expected to increase more rapidly than for other occupations in the next decade. More engineers will be needed to help meet the increasing demand for goods and services. Engineers also will be needed to develop better transportation systems as well as weapons and other products for the military. In addition, employers are expected to continue hiring engineering graduates for sales and management jobs in which engineering backgrounds are useful.

The employment outlook for electrical engineers is even better than for engineers in other fields. However, shortages of teachers and equipment may force universities to limit the number of students admitted to their electrical engineering programs. The great demand for these graduates may lead to higher starting salaries.

Engineers in the aerospace and electronics industries could lose their jobs if the federal government reduces military spending or if corporations cut back on research and development. In general, though, engineers' jobs are more secure than those of workers in many other occupations.

In addition to mechanical, ceramics, and electrical engineers, occupations in the *Occupational Outlook Handbook*'s Engineers, Surveyors, and Architects cluster include:

- ☐ aerospace engineers
- ☐ agricultural engineers
- ☐ architects
- ☐ biomedical engineers
- ☐ chemical engineers
- ☐ landscape architects
- ☐ nuclear engineers
- ☐ petroleum engineers
- ☐ surveyors

Your Developing Skills

When you have studied this chapter, you should be able to:

▶▶ Explain why basic skills are important for working in all occupations

▶▶ Describe the importance of learning other essential skills

▶▶ Define aptitudes and identify some different ways to recognize them

Vocabulary Words

Interview

Skill

Resume

Aptitude

Aptitude test

Achievement test

Occupational ability pattern

Think about what your first job **interview** might be like. An interview is a formal meeting between an employer and a job applicant. Imagine that you are applying for a part-time job as a cashier in a large sporting goods store. The man who interviews you asks what type of activities you enjoy and how you became interested in the job. He wants to make sure your personality and interests match the work you will be doing.

He has another concern as well. Do you have the **skills**, or developed abilities, necessary to do the job? He wants to know what skills you already have mastered. Will you be able to read instructions quickly and accurately? Can you calculate prices without difficulty? If someone has a question, can you listen carefully and answer effectively?

He also wants to know which skills you could easily develop. Will you be able to learn how to use the computerized cash register and take inventory?

Your interviewer knows you are not an expert in all of these areas, but he does expect you to have some basic skills and he wants to be sure you can learn to master others. In this chapter we will discuss some of the skills employers look for in the people they hire and how you can develop those skills.

Basic Skills

When Kara was very young, her mother often sat with her looking at books on numbers and the letters of the alphabet. As Kara worked through the alphabet and tried to count from one to ten, her mother coaxed her along. She corrected Kara when she was wrong and praised her when she started to improve.

The skills Kara learned as a child were the foundation for the most basic skills that are taught in school—math and language skills. Ever since you learned to count and to read, you have been developing math and language skills. You already use those skills in many areas of your daily life. It is no wonder that all the basic skills—math, reading, writing, listening, and speaking—are essential for most occupations.

Math Skills

Today we live in a society filled with the wonders of technology. Computers are used to check out groceries, diagnose automobile engine problems, write documents, and keep track of credit card bills. A small calculator performs tasks that would have required a huge computer only 30 years ago. Our telephone conversations pass as light beams through fiber-optic cables. We can send letters around the world in a matter of seconds by using facsimile

It will be to your advantage to have good math skills since they are necessary in almost every job.

machines. With all this new technology, businesses can operate much more efficiently than in the past.

Since computers and calculators can do so much of our math for us, you might think that the growth of technology has reduced the need for math skills. However, just the opposite is true. As technology advances, people need more math skills to design, maintain, and operate these machines. As a result, employers look for employees who have developed their math skills. This is especially true of employers in technical fields related to computers, communications, engineering, and medical technology. The number of jobs in these high technology fields is growing very rapidly.

This emphasis on math skills, however, does not mean that everyone needs to be brilliant in math. It does mean that everyone should develop certain basic math skills such as the ability to think through math problems logically and to perform calculations accurately. In addition, because most occupations involve some use of a computer, everyone should have at least a basic knowledge of how to operate a computer. In the past, for example, a store would keep its sales figures in a ledger book, which was then either added up by hand or by calculator. Today, many businesses have computerized those financial records and even the cash register has become part of a computer system.

Written Language Skills

Otis is an electronics technician who repairs two-way radios for a small communications company. After graduating from high school, he attended a vocational-technical school for two years to learn how to repair electronic equipment. When he was in school, Otis did not think reading and writing would be very important in his chosen occupation. He thought he would spend all of his time working on electronic equipment.

Otis soon found that reading and writing are very important to his job. He has to read the repair manual for each piece of equipment on which he works. He also has to read letters from electronics manufacturers describing changes in equipment and in repair procedures. When customers attach notes explaining the problems they are having with their radios, Otis must read them, too. Otis also is required to write a report on each radio he repairs. In the report, he must describe the problem he found with the radio and explain how he fixed it.

As you can see, reading and writing are important even in those occupations that do not put special emphasis on written language skills. Any occupation you pursue will require good written language skills. After all, the first impression your future employer will get of you will come from an application form or from your letter and resume. A **resume** is a written account of a person's previous jobs and skills that is sent to a potential employer. Evidence of good writing skills on a resume can mean the difference between getting the job you want and losing it because you made a bad impression.

The working world relies on people who can communicate effectively in writing. Whether the information appears on a slip of paper or on a computer screen, it must be written clearly and read carefully. People who have developed their written language skills are more productive employees than those who struggle to read instructions and write notes or reports. Regardless of the occupation you choose, you will make a better employee if you can read and write well.

Spoken Language Skills

Listening and speaking are just as important in the workplace as reading and writing. You probably do not study spoken language skills in the same way you study math, reading, and writing. However, you use them constantly in school, at home, and everywhere else you go. Developing your ability to listen carefully and speak clearly will help you perform well on the job, regardless of the occupation you choose.

If you have excellent spoken language skills, there are many interesting jobs in which you can use them.

Review Questions

1 ▶ Why are basic math skills important today, both at work and elsewhere?

2 ▶ How will an employer get an impression of whether or not you have good writing skills?

3 ▶ What are some of the benefits of good spoken language skills?

When you begin a new job, your supervisor or a co-worker probably will explain your duties to you verbally. They may not be available to repeat the instructions several times, so it is important that you understand what they say the first time. Workers who do not listen carefully, or who allow their attention to wander when they are being given instructions, often do their jobs poorly because they do not understand what they should be doing. A good listener, who focuses on what the other person is saying, can learn new tasks easily and quickly.

Speaking is an important skill as well. Your job may involve speaking to your co-workers and supervisor, or it may require you to make presentations before large groups. Many workers who are experienced in a particular task become involved in training other people how to do the work. In each case, the goal of good communication is to make your point clearly and concisely, so that others will understand what you are saying.

People who take the time to develop their spoken language skills appear more knowledgeable than those who do not. Because they can communicate their ideas effectively to other people, their supervisors and co-workers usually are willing to listen to their ideas and opinions. As a result, they have a greater influence on the decisions that are made in the workplace. These people are more likely to advance quickly in their occupation, perhaps eventually becoming supervisors or managers themselves.

(continued on page 66)

SKILLS FOR THE REAL WORLD

When I got a cooperative education job in landscaping, my first thought was, "This will be great—I will only be in school part of the day next term." I figured that I would be out in the real world learning practical skills instead of useless information.

Well, things turned out a little differently than I had expected. The first day on the job, Mr. Taylor, my boss, had me prepare a solution of lawn fertilizer. "Just be sure you use the right ratio," he said.

"Sure," I said. "I know about ratios."

Then he left. I studied the directions and calculated the proportions of each ingredient in the solution. I could not believe I was doing work based on what I had learned in math and chemistry classes.

"You have good math skills," Mr. Taylor said. "Try some seed counts."

This assignment was like math class. Every square yard of lawn required a specific number of grass seeds. Mr. Taylor had given me a list of the lawns we would be seeding, specifying the lawn size and type of grass wanted. I had to figure out how many pounds of seed we would need for each lawn. First, I panicked. Then I remembered similar problems I had done in math class. I began to calculate and put together the pieces of the puzzle. When I had finished, Mr. Taylor checked the figures briefly.

"It looks like you have done a great job," he smiled and said.

The first day was just a sampling of the knowledge I use on the job. The second week I had to read reference books to learn which plants and trees were suitable for the soil conditions in our region of the country. That was like biology and geography class!

The third week I worked on the grounds of a huge estate. Mr. Taylor told me the owner wanted a Victorian garden. Mr. Taylor said. "Look up what Victorian-style plants we can use." I had to think back to history class to remember what time period was Victorian. Then I went right to a book on late 19th century English gardens.

Every week that I worked I found myself using more skills that I had learned in high school. When I finished my cooperative education job, Mr. Taylor told me to study hard because he wants me to have a lot more skills to use when I start working for him full-time after I finish high school. ■

Foreign language skills can be very valuable in many jobs.

Essential Work Skills

All workers need to have basic math and language skills to be successful in any occupation. People also need to have certain other skills to enter given fields. For instance, if you intend to work in a foreign country you need to learn the language of that country. Because learning these essential work skills can take a long time, you should begin studying them while you are in school. Now is the time to explore a wide variety of skill areas, so you can concentrate on developing those that interest you most.

Keyboarding and Computer Skills

Twenty years ago, it was unusual to find a computer in workplaces not directly related to finance or scientific research. Today, it is unusual to find a workplace that does not have a computer of some kind. Computers are even being used in factories, restaurants, grocery stores, and automobile repair shops. Evening classes at local colleges are full of people who need to learn to use computers. If you take the opportunity to learn how to use a computer while you still are in school, you will be prepared when you need to use one in your future occupation.

Computer and keyboarding skills are particularly important for anyone planning to work in an office. For example, after Robert graduates from high school, he wants to train to be a medical records clerk. He knows that medical records clerks use computers almost constantly. They retrieve patients' records and print out reports using computers. He also learned that people with computer skills often have more interesting jobs and advance more rapidly than those who do not. Robert is taking as many computer courses as he can in school, so he will be well prepared for his future occupation.

If you plan to go to college, you may need to know how to use computers for some of your classes. Many students write their papers and do their science projects on computers. In fact, some colleges require all students to buy their own computers. If you learn how to use a computer now, you will be able to use this valuable skill in college and in your occupation.

Other Skills You Can Learn in School

Have you ever sat in class, staring at the book in front of you, and asked yourself, "Why do I have to learn this? What good will it ever do me? Why will I need to know this once I get out of school?" Sharon asked the same questions in her French class when she was in school. She did not like memorizing the vocabulary words or listening to French tapes in the language lab. She was much more interested in her math and economics classes.

Today Sharon is glad she spent time learning French. She works

Computer skills are necessary in many of today's jobs.

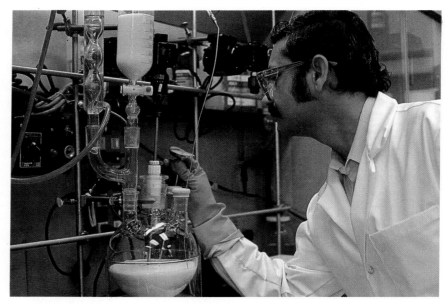

The science background you acquire in school can serve as a foundation for many jobs.

for a large bank as a financial analyst, deciding to which companies the bank should loan money. Recently, the bank has started developing its business in Europe, and especially in France. Because Sharon already knows how to speak basic French, after a short refresher course she will be given the job of managing the bank's operations in France.

Other skills you can learn in school are essential in certain occupations. Art and drafting classes teach you skills you can use as a graphic artist or a facilities designer. If you take classes in basic automobile mechanics and electricity, you will learn skills necessary to becoming an automobile or airline mechanic. In geography class, you will learn how to read detailed maps and charts, an essential skill for geologists and surveyors. You can use general skills like these from the first day you begin your new job. You will show your employer that you have the skills and abilities necessary to do your job well.

Essential Background Knowledge

While you are in school, you should learn basic math and language skills as well as essential work skills, such as operating a computer and speaking a foreign language. What about some of the other subjects you study in school, though? How will they help prepare you for occupations? Rather than teaching you a specific skill, many subject areas provide basic knowledge you must have to become an expert in a particular field.

For example, you may not learn to be a laboratory technician by taking classes in biology and chemistry. However, the science background you develop in these classes and the scientific method that you use to complete your lab assignments are useful for all laboratory technicians. Learning about different parts of the world will not give you all the training you need to be a travel agent, but your knowledge of geography and history will help you serve your travel customers well.

A background in social studies will prepare you for any occupation that involves interaction with other people, especially jobs in admissions counseling, purchasing, or personnel. As you can see, every subject you study in school can prepare you in some way for a future occupation. By studying hard now, you will be gaining skills and abilities that are necessary for you to be successful in a variety of careers.

Review Questions _____

1 ▸ Why should you learn keyboarding and computer skills now?

2 ▸ Why are other skills you learn worthwhile?

3 ▸ How can basic knowledge help you in occupations?

Discovering Your Aptitudes

Even though you can learn some work skills in school, many other work skills can only be learned in specific occupations. For that reason, employers provide training so that new workers can develop the skills necessary to do their jobs properly. Imagine that Alexis wants to become a jeweler. How can she and her future employer tell whether she will be able to easily learn the necessary skills? What they both want to know is whether Alexis has an **aptitude** for working with small pieces of jewelry and tiny watch mechanisms.

Having an aptitude for something means it is easy for you to learn how to do it well. Alexis might eventually learn to be a jeweler, even if she does not have the aptitude. However, it probably would take much longer for her to learn the trade and she would never be as good at the job as someone with an aptitude for doing it. How can she learn whether she has an aptitude for learning jewelers' skills or any other skills?

If her hobbies include building small models or making pieces of jewelry, Alexis probably has an aptitude for working with watches and jewelry. In addition, she can find out what aptitudes she has by taking a special test, which you will learn about later in this chapter.

Employers often provide training for their employees when they purchase new equipment.

Aptitudes Employers Seek

People are hired for work because employers have tasks that need to be done. In the hiring process, employers look for indications that potential workers have aptitudes for learning how to do these tasks. In this way, no money is wasted training people who are not

Some people's aptitudes become the basis for their careers.

suitable. Matching a job applicant's aptitudes with the tasks that must be done also protects the applicant from wasting time trying to learn tasks that will never come easily.

As employers evaluate potential employees, what aptitudes do they look for? The following list contains a number of general aptitudes that may interest an employer. The list also has examples of occupations in which each aptitude would be helpful.

General Aptitude   Occupations

Working with numbers: statistician, actuary, bookkeeper
Working accurately and systematically: drafter, auto mechanic
Working with hands: woodworker, machinist, assembler
Working with words: reporter, editor, writer
Working with children: child-care worker, teacher, pediatrician
Working with animals: veterinarian, zookeeper, animal shelter worker
Studying scientific subjects: researcher, geologist, physicist
Thinking logically: repair technician, philosopher
Listening to others: minister, social worker, personnel manager
Being creative: artist, advertising copywriter

Identifying Your Aptitudes

You probably already know a lot about your own aptitudes. You may have heard a parent or friend say something like, "She argues so well that I bet she would make a great attorney," or, "With his drawing ability, I think he has the makings of an artist." In saying these things, they are referring to aptitudes you already have shown. By listening to people around you, you can begin to identify your aptitudes for learning job-related skills.

What have other people said about your abilities? Now is the time to take a close look at the things you enjoy doing and the things you dislike doing. You probably will discover that you are interested in doing the things for which you show an aptitude. For example, if you have an aptitude for working with numbers, there is a good chance you will enjoy your math classes.

Of course, you do not always enjoy doing the things you do well. Just because you are an expert at cutting the grass does not mean that activity brings you great satisfaction. Thinking about the things you enjoy doing is one good way to identify your aptitudes. Look at the list of aptitudes in the previous section and check off the activities you enjoy. In doing so, you probably have identified some of your aptitudes as well.

Taking Aptitude Tests

After thinking about the activities she enjoys and looking over the list of aptitudes, Stephanie realizes she enjoys doing a lot of different things. Does that mean she would be able to do many different jobs well? How can she be more certain which of her many interests are also aptitudes? Stephanie decides to ask her school guidance counselor for help in identifying her aptitudes.

The guidance counselor suggests that Stephanie take an **aptitude test**, which measures a person's ability to learn something. Aptitude tests are very different from **achievement tests**, which measure your skill and knowledge in certain subject areas. Aptitude tests help people discover which occupations match the skills they can develop easily. These tests are commonly used by both career counselors and employers to evaluate aptitudes.

One aptitude test, the *General Aptitude Test Battery* (GATB), is used by many state employment agencies. It tests:

- general intelligence
- ability to work with words
- ability to work with numbers
- ability to see the relations between objects
- ability to distinguish between different shapes and forms
- ability to perform clerical tasks
- hand/eye coordination
- ability to work with fingers
- ability to work with hands, arms, and legs

After you finish the test, your guidance counselor can compare your aptitude profile with **36 occupational ability patterns**. These

Thinking about what you enjoy doing is a good way to identify your aptitudes.

basic sets of abilities cover several hundred different occupations in all fields. Your guidance counselor can then suggest in which occupational areas you might do well.

Some tests, like the *Differential Aptitude Tests*, combine both achievement and aptitude tests, while others specialize in one particular skill area. The *Bennett Mechanical Comprehension Test* measures a person's aptitude for work in the mechanical trades. Employers often use the results from specialized tests to help them place new employees in the training program or position for which they are best suited.

If you take one of these tests now, your guidance counselor can assess the results and help you find out more about the jobs in which you probably will do well. You also can use that information to make good choices about part-time and vacation jobs while you still are in school. Finding out what skills you already have, and which ones you can easily develop, will put you on the path toward a successful, fulfilling occupation.

Review Questions

1 ▶ Why will your future employer be interested in your aptitudes?

2 ▶ How are your interests and your aptitudes related?

3 ▶ How can aptitude tests be helpful to you now?

Summary

❑ Basic math, written language, and spoken language skills are necessary for your success in any occupation.

❑ Computer skills, mechanical skills, foreign language skills, and other general work skills that are needed in different occupations can be developed while you are in school.

❑ Employers look for people whose aptitudes show they can develop job skills quickly.

❑ You can discover your aptitudes by looking at your interests and by taking aptitude tests.

Vocabulary Exercise

interview	aptitude	achievement test
skill	aptitude test	occupational ability pattern
resume		

Write a complete sentence using each of the vocabulary words above in its correct context.

Discussion Questions

1. Why do you think it is important to develop your basic skills, even if you do not have a high aptitude for some of them?

2. What are the differences between essential work skills and aptitudes?

3. What are your favorite subjects in school? Name some occupations in which you could use that knowledge.

4. Think of the interests you have. How could they be translated into aptitudes? In which occupations might you use those aptitudes?

Thinking Further

1. (Writing) Select a book from your file of career resource books. Find a description of an occupation that interests you. Write a paragraph that answers these questions:

   ❑ What basic skills does the occupation emphasize?

   ❑ What general work skills would it require?

   ❑ What aptitudes would an employer look for in an employee in that occupation?

2. (Math) Your aunt's employer has offered all employees a 2 percent raise if they complete a computer course at the local college. Your aunt earns $575 a week. The course costs $320. If your aunt uses her raise to pay for the computer course, how many weeks would it take her to pay for it?

3. (Reading) In your library find information on adult literacy. How many adults in the Unites States have a reading problem? Does your community have any programs to help them? How could you help out with these programs?

4. (Reading) Read the following feature to learn more about jobs.

WHO HELPS LABORERS?

There are workers in almost every field whose role is to help others complete tasks. That is true even in the construction field.

Rachel is working on a construction crew earning money for college expenses. This is her third summer on the crew. Luke, her friend, got a job on the same crew this summer. He needs to earn money for a training program.

Construction crews employ a variety of unskilled laborers to do work at building sites. These workers do chores for the electricians, carpenters, plumbers, masons, and other skilled crew members. They also do general labor, such as hauling materials, cleaning up rubble, and digging trenches. Because this is Luke's first experience with construction work, he is given simple tasks.

When shipments of building materials arrive, Luke helps unload the trucks. He also helps clean up scraps of lumber and wire, broken bricks, cement bags, and other debris from around the construction site. Sometimes he runs errands, such as picking up lunches for the other crew members.

Rachel did these simple tasks during her first summer working with the crew. In addition, by observing and talking with some of the skilled construction workers, she began learning about the methods and materials they use.

The second summer, because of what she had learned, Rachel was given a job as a hod carrier. She helped the bricklayers and plasterers. Her duties included cleaning and organizing their tools and equipment, mixing plaster, and helping to set up the scaffolds they stand on to reach high places. She is working as a hod carrier again this summer.

Rachel expects to return to the crew next year—probably for the last time because she finishes college the following June. As a construction helper, Rachel earns more money than she could at most other summer jobs that do not require formal training. She gets to work outdoors, too, which she likes. Rachel also enjoys physical activity, and that is a big part of the job.

Each summer when she returns to the crew, Rachel recognizes most of the skilled workers. A few of them, in fact, were unskilled helpers like herself when she first met them, but they have advanced into skilled jobs. For example, Thad, now one of the bricklayers, worked as a laborer operating a cement mixer during Rachel's first summer on the job. To learn bricklaying skills and to qualify for this higher-paying job, Thad attended an eight-week training program. The program was co-sponsored by the bricklayers' union and the contracting company that employs the crew.

While she recognizes most of the skilled workers, most of the unskilled helpers and laborers Rachel works with each summer are new on the job. People often work at these jobs only long enough to raise money for tuition or other specific purposes. Another reason for the high turnover is that many people who take construction jobs discover they do not like the work enough to continue doing it.

Luke is not sure he will continue working on the crew. He finds the work dirty, difficult, and boring. His muscles ache from all the heavy lifting he does, and at the end of each day he seems to have a new collection of scrapes and bruises. He also dislikes working in the sun, especially on the hottest days of the year.

Because of the high turnover rate among unskilled construction workers, job openings are likely to remain plentiful over the next several years. Contractors increasingly are using machines for simple tasks traditionally done by people, however, so the employment outlook for unskilled laborers is not as bright as for skilled workers. Construction laborers also tend to lose their jobs whenever business declines in the building industry. However, growth in population and economic activity will cause construction work to grow in the years ahead.

In the *Occupational Outlook Handbook*, unskilled construction workers' jobs are included in the Handlers, Equipment Cleaners, Helpers, and Laborers cluster. Other jobs included in this cluster are:

❑ gas station attendants

❑ machine feeders

❑ parking lot attendants

❑ refuse collectors

❑ shipping packers

❑ vehicle cleaners

UNIT 2

FOCUS ON WORK

▼

▲

OCCUPATIONS IN THE 20 CLUSTERS

Telephone operators need to be pleasant, courteous, and patient because they must deal with many different people every day. They are included in the cluster titled *Administrative Support Occupations, Including Clerical* (left).

This nursery worker is overseeing the production of nursery products grown in greenhouses. Her job is part of the *Agriculture, Forestry, Fishing, and Related Occupations* cluster (right).

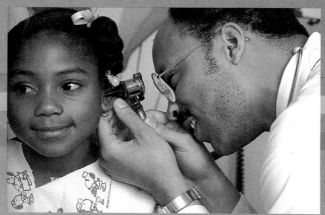

This physician's specialty is pediatrics, or caring for and treating children. His job is part of the *Health Diagnosing and Treating Practitioners* cluster (left).

These roustabouts are part of a crew that works together drilling oil. The *Construction Trades and Extractive Occupations* cluster is where their jobs are listed (right).

NORTHERN

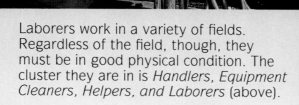

Laborers work in a variety of fields. Regardless of the field, though, they must be in good physical condition. The cluster they are in is *Handlers, Equipment Cleaners, Helpers, and Laborers* (above).

This surveyor is being assisted by a technician who is operating an instrument called a theodolite. Their jobs are included in the *Engineers, Surveyors, and Architects* cluster (right).

Medical technologists perform complicated medical tests in laboratories. These workers are included in the *Health Technologists and Technicians* cluster (right)

Accountants play a key role in the management of all types of businesses. This is one of the many jobs in the *Managerial and Management-Related Occupations* cluster (above).

Lawyers do most of their work in offices, law libraries, and courtrooms. Lawyers are included in the cluster titled *Lawyers, Social Scientists, Social Workers, and Religious Workers* (right).

These men are employed by the largest employer in the country—the military. Their positions in the United States Navy are incorporated under *Job Opportunities in the Armed Forces* (above)

Chemists search for and use new knowledge about chemicals. Like other scientists, they are grouped in the *Natural, Computer, and Mathematical Scientists* cluster (right).

This manufacturer's sales worker is giving information on prescription drugs to a hospital staff member. Sales jobs are included in *Marketing and Sales Occupations* (above).

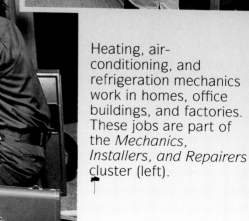

Heating, air-conditioning, and refrigeration mechanics work in homes, office buildings, and factories. These jobs are part of the *Mechanics, Installers, and Repairers* cluster (left).

This cannery worker is preparing food products. His job is included in *Production Occupations* (left).

This truck driver transports people's furniture and personal goods when they move. His job is included in the *Transportation and Material Moving Occupations* cluster (right).

A major part of a librarian's job is dealing with people. This job is included in the *Teachers, Librarians, and Counselors* cluster (right).

Physical therapists treat patients in several ways. They help to relieve pain, limit disabilities, and restore motor function. This is one of many jobs in the *Registered Nurses, Pharmacists, Dietitians, Therapists, and Physician Assistants* cluster (right).

This television correspondent is reporting "live" from a foreign country. Her job is in the cluster titled *Writers, Artists, and Entertainers* (above).

Child care workers' duties depend on the setting, but all of them must enjoy being around children. Their jobs are part of the *Service Occupations* cluster (above).

Computer programmers write the detailed instructions that a computer must follow in order to organize information or solve a problem. Their jobs are part of the *Technologists and Technicians, Except Health* cluster (left).

5

Jobs and the Workplace

When you have studied this chapter, you should be able to:

➡️ Summarize what employers take into account when they hire new employees to fill jobs

➡️ Explain how companies design jobs, why managers are necessary, and how career ladders work

➡️ Describe two options open to workers who do not want to take full-time jobs

Vocabulary Words

Delegate

Productivity

Profit

Manager

Career ladder

Freelancer

Entrepreneur

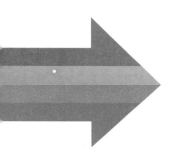

When you go into your local record shop to buy a new compact disc, a business transaction takes place. You hand over a certain amount of money and the shop owner gives you a compact disc. Both you and the shop owner benefit from the transaction, because each of you receives something you want from the other.

In much the same way, a job is a business transaction between an employer and an employee. The employer needs a worker who can help produce a product or a service, and the employee needs money in order to meet needs and wants. They agree to an exchange—the employer's wages for the employee's work—that benefits both parties.

In other words, a job links an employer and an employee. For that reason, every job can be evaluated from two different points of view. An employee has reasons for accepting that particular job, and an employer has reasons for hiring that particular person for the job that is available. In previous chapters, we focused on the people who make up the work force. In this chapter, we will focus on the workplace and the work itself.

The Two Sides of Employment

Mr. Wolfson, the president of Wolfson Construction Company, has just hired Gina to be the company's full-time bookkeeper. Last month Gina graduated from college with a degree in accounting, and she is looking forward to the challenges of her new job. Mr. Wolfson is glad Gina accepted the job. Up until now, he has used temporary bookkeepers and has supervised them himself. Both Gina and Mr. Wolfson expect to benefit from the employment

For every job there are two different points of view. There are the employer's viewpoint and the worker's viewpoint.

agreement they have reached. Because one is the employee and the other is the employer, they expect to gain different things from the employment transaction.

The Employee's Side

Gina decided to look for a job after she finished school because she needs a regular paycheck to meet her basic needs and supply some of her wants. Why did Gina choose to earn her money by working as a bookkeeper, and not as a machinist, a historian, or a forest ranger? Why, once she had received her degree in accounting, did she decide to accept this particular job instead of one with another company?

From the time she entered the first grade, Gina had displayed an aptitude for working with numbers. She confirmed this when she took an aptitude test in middle school. She also had a keen eye for business opportunities. When she was in high school, Gina employed five other classmates in her own business, which was a cleaning service for local businesses. Because of these experiences, and because she preferred an occupation that offered physical and financial security, Gina decided to attend college and major in accounting.

Toward the end of college, Gina learned about the job with Wolfson Construction Company. If she took the job, she would be trained to head the company's finance department. Gina enjoys working with other people and looks forward to being successful as a manager. In the other jobs Gina could have taken, she would

Each worker contributes to the overall success of a business.

not have been trained to manage a finance department. She also feels happy knowing the company she works for will help provide new homes for other people. From Gina's point of view, her new job suits her well because it meets her needs for financial security, social acceptance, and self-esteem, and because it matches her interests, aptitudes, and personality.

The Employer's Side

Why was Mr. Wolfson eager to hire Gina as his new bookkeeper? Because of Gina's education, previous business experience, and personality, Mr. Wolfson believed that Gina would be a productive employee. Gina's education has given her the general skills she needs, and she has shown that she has the aptitudes necessary for learning quickly and performing well on the job. Mr. Wolfson liked Gina's attitude—she was always courteous, enthusiastic, and on time. He was especially impressed with Gina's office-cleaning company. It showed not only that Gina has good work habits, but also that she has leadership qualities and an ability to get things done without supervision.

In general, Mr. Wolfson believes that Gina will be an asset to his company. He wants to avoid the expense of having an employee who is unable to do the job well and who does not get along with co-workers. If Gina is not successful in her new job, the company as a whole will suffer. Mr. Wolfson will have to spend money to advertise the job again, interview more applicants, and train another person.

That is why Mr. Wolfson hired temporary workers to help with the bookkeeping for a month until he found an applicant who was right for the position. Some companies hire temporary workers as full-time employees, after the workers have proven they can do the job well. By doing that, the companies reduce the risk of having to dismiss workers who were hired and then perform poorly. The goal of the employment agreement, from the point of view of both the employer and the employee, is a business transaction that is profitable and beneficial to both parties.

Review Questions

1 ▶ What are some things employees expect when they are hired?

2 ▶ Why does an employer want employees to be successful in their jobs?

3 ▶ How can temporary workers help companies reduce the risk of having to dismiss workers who do poorly?

Employers and the Jobs They Offer

To understand jobs properly, you need to look at the workplace from the viewpoint of employers. Asking the following questions can help. Why do jobs exist in the first place? How does an employer decide which duties should be combined to make up a particular job? Why are some people hired to give direction to others in the workplace? Once you have a job, how can you move up to better paying and more responsible positions?

The Reason for Jobs

We do not live in a society in which the majority of people grow their own food, build their own houses, and make their own clothes. Long ago, people discovered that everyone benefits if each worker focuses on producing one type of good or service. One person, for example, might choose to make only shoes and then offer those shoes for sale to anyone who needs them.

There are, however, very few goods or services that one person can produce quickly enough to make a reasonably good living. Imagine how many tennis shoes you could make in a month if you had to refine and mold the rubber, weave and cut the canvas cloth, assemble the shoes, and distribute them to shoe stores and department stores—all by yourself! To make production quicker and more efficient, people hire other workers to help them in the production of goods and services.

Jobs are created when a company needs workers to help produce things. The owners of the company cannot do all the work themselves, so they **delegate,** or assign part of the work to people they hire. The number of jobs available depends on the size of the company and the amount of work that needs to be done.

How Jobs Are Designed

Jobs do not create themselves, and they do not come into being just because someone decides to make a product. When the owners of a machine shop decide to manufacture aircraft parts, for example, they must decide how the manufacturing process should proceed.

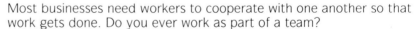

Most businesses need workers to cooperate with one another so that work gets done. Do you ever work as part of a team?

On many assembly lines, productivity increases when workers do one specialized task.

In some jobs workers must be qualified to do many specialized tasks.

Imagine that it takes 60 separate steps to manufacture an aircraft propeller. Should the owners of the business hire 60 workers, who will each complete one step, or should the owners combine some of the tasks so that 25 people could complete the process? How can they decide which way is better?

The goal that business owners have in designing jobs is to maximize **productivity,** or the amount of work a person can produce per hour. Because productivity is often the difference between making a **profit** and losing money, business owners must plan the production process and design the jobs carefully. Profits are the money left over after all bills are paid.

In many cases, productivity can be increased if each person does one very specialized task, but this is not always true. For example, if a cafeteria serves 2,000 sandwiches each day, it may be more efficient for one person to put parsley sprigs on each sandwich as a garnish after another person has assembled each sandwich. Sometimes, though, the increase in efficiency lowers the motivation of the workers. Would you be happy putting parsley on sandwiches for 40 hours each week? You probably would not! You would be more satisfied if you worked at a variety of tasks, including assembling sandwiches and serving customers, as well as putting on the garnish. Specialized jobs may appear more technically efficient, but workers usually are more motivated if they are involved in a larger part of the production process.

Another consideration when employers design jobs is what other companies are doing. If jobs are patterned after similar jobs

Even an experienced worker benefits from having a manager to direct an operation and solve problems if things go wrong.

in other companies, employers can find workers who already are trained for those tasks. As these patterns become fixed, schools and other training institutions can provide instruction in the skills necessary for these specific jobs.

The Reasons for Managers

Most companies hire at least two or three workers to help meet the goals established by the owners, and some companies may even hire as many as 30,000 workers. The success of any business, whether it is a corner newsstand or a huge assembly plant, depends on how efficiently the workers complete their assigned tasks and how well all the employees work together. For this reason, the owners also hire **managers** to coordinate the efforts of their employees and to ensure that everyone is working toward the same goals. Managers help the business to function smoothly and efficiently by giving directions to the employees.

Managers work with the owners of the business to plan the best way to meet the overall goals of the company. Then they organize and coordinate the personnel, materials, and other resources of the company to carry out their plan as efficiently as possible. In many cases, managers demonstrate to the workers how each task in the process should be performed. Managers also control the operation of the company. They examine results to make certain the goals of

(continued on page 92)

PRODUCTIVITY: THE KEY TO SUCCESS

I own a travel agency. The thing that brings clients to my agency is the quality of the service my employees offer. When service is excellent, business booms. That is why I insist that my employees be willing to go out of their way to satisfy a client's needs.

Donna is a perfect example of how valuable a dedicated employee is. She got her agent's license right after high school. The job in my agency was her first. It took her a while to learn the details of daily operations, but she was bright. Within a month she knew the routine and was doing as much work as the other agents.

One day a client came in looking for help. As soon as Donna saw her, Donna asked her to have a seat. The client introduced herself as Rosa and then told Donna about the problems she was having planning her trip. Rosa explained that she and her husband and six other couples wanted to go on vacation together to the coast. She said that she had spoken with agents at several other agencies. Each agent had consulted a computer and found what seemed to be the least expensive rate. Rosa felt that she deserved a better rate since she was traveling with such a large group. She decided to try one more agency. Fortunately, Rosa tried my agency.

When I left the office to go home that evening, Donna was making phone calls. She already had made dozens of calls. She told me that she was close to solving Rosa's problem. Donna said that she wanted to keep working until she solved it.

The next day Donna called Rosa. She told Rosa that she had found a small charter company that chartered planes for groups of people and flew them to the coast. The cost of this service was much more reasonable than for 14 people to fly on a commercial airline. Rosa was delighted. We got her business, and she recommended us to several other people. Now we have not only her traveling companions' business but also that of all their friends and family.

Donna has worked for me for almost three years. She is now the best and highest paid of all my travel agents. In addition to doing her assigned work, she consistently makes the extra effort to meet challenges and help all of her clients. She is the most productive employee I have ever had. ■

the business have been met, and they make changes whenever they are necessary.

If managers perform their tasks effectively, they can help workers become more productive. A good manager will make sure that workers know how to do their jobs, have plenty of materials with which to work, and understand the goals they are trying to reach. When this happens, the employees can work together to meet the business owner's goals.

Jobs and Career Ladders

Mario, a critical care nurse, has been working in the intensive care unit of a university hospital for about three years. Although he has enjoyed his work, he recently has decided to look at another hospital for a job involving more responsibility. He would like to become a supervisor of the intensive care unit where he works. If he is not hired for that position; however, he probably will look for a position in another hospital.

The university hospital directors would like to keep Mario on their staff, and they do need a new supervisor. Mario is an efficient

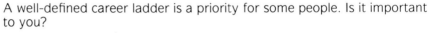

A well-defined career ladder is a priority for some people. Is it important to you?

and productive employee, and he knows the procedures of the hospital well. Training a new employee to be a supervisor would be expensive, and the hospital would lose the benefit of Mario's years of experience if he left to take a job at another hospital. For these reasons, the hospital directors decide to offer Mario the position as supervisor of intensive care.

Most businesses try to provide promotion opportunities for their employees, because promoting good employees to fill vacant positions usually is less costly than hiring and training new employees for positions. Many companies have well-defined **career ladders,** or standard paths employees can follow that will lead to positions of greater responsibility. One advantage of working for a large company or government organization is that the potential for advancement usually is greater than it is with a small company. However, small companies may offer the opportunity for more variety and responsibility on the job. Often, employees advance by becoming managers of people who do the particular tasks that those employees used to do. Because these managers understand the jobs they are supervising and know what problems can develop, the company benefits.

Review Questions

1 ▶ What leads to the creation of jobs?

2 ▶ What is an advantage and a disadvantage of designing highly specialized jobs?

3 ▶ What are some tasks performed by managers?

4 ▶ How can a career ladder help keep good employees?

Other Job Options

The jobs we have discussed so far have all been jobs designed by other people. A company, for example, may hire you to paint cars in its body shop in exchange for a certain wage. Once you are an employee, the company takes the responsibility of finding cars for you to paint. For most people, this employment arrangement gives them job security, because they rely on the employer to ensure that they will always have work to do. However, working for someone else is not the only option available. Some people like the freedom and rewards of working for themselves.

Temporary Employment

What do the owners of a retail department store do if they need 20 extra workers to handle the Christmas rush? What happens in an insurance company when three of the best data entry clerks have the flu for two weeks? How can a construction company meet the scheduled date of completion on a particularly large project? Where can a medical clinic find a physician who is available to work for two months while staff members are on vacation? When companies need specialized help for a short period of time, they often hire temporary workers.

Many companies rely on flexible, temporary staffing so they do not have to pay full-time employees they need only some of the time. That is why many different kinds of companies need temporary workers with many different skills, from construction laborers to engineers and managers. Because of the importance of computers, word processing, and data management in the workplace, workers with keyboarding and computer skills are in great demand as temporary workers. These temporary jobs can provide employment opportunities for workers who want the freedom to plan their own work schedules.

In many fields, temporary or staffing agencies help companies meet their need for qualified employees. In some ways, working for an agency is like having a regular job. You are paid by the agency, which rents your services to another company. One of the benefits of temporary work, however, is that you can work as much or as little as you like within certain guidelines. You can choose a work schedule that suits your particular needs. Most agencies require you to work full days, but you are free to choose which days you want to work.

For some occupations, such as journalist, writer, and photographer, there are very few temporary agencies. In these occupations, workers interested in short-term job assignments must find their own work for each job. These workers are called **freelancers.** Many freelancers start working independently after working full time in the same field. That way, they know contacts in particular companies who can give them work.

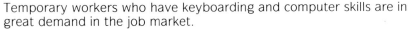
Temporary workers who have keyboarding and computer skills are in great demand in the job market.

When entrepreneurs first start their businesses, they often must do all the work themselves.

Entrepreneurship

If you want to be a successful entrepreneur, you need to have a positive attitude.

When Michael finished high school, he found a job working for a florist in a shopping center near his home. Michael enjoyed working with flowers, but he did not like working for someone else. If he had his own flower shop, he thought, he could make more money by selling other things, such as houseplants and vegetable plants. If he built a greenhouse to grow some of the plants from seed, he could increase his profits even more. Michael borrowed some money from his aunt and uncle to buy the things he needed to open his own business.

Michael is an **entrepreneur.** Entrepreneurs are people who start their own businesses. They do this for a number of reasons. Some people have had an idea for a new product or service, or for one that is better than anyone else's. Others want the freedom and independence of working for themselves. Still others like the idea of making money if their business succeeds.

Starting a new business, however, is a risky move. Eight out of ten new businesses fail within the first five years. Entrepreneurs must be willing to live on a relatively low income for at least a few years, since a new business can seldom pay the owner an adequate salary in the beginning. Entrepreneurs do not receive the vacation, pension benefits, insurance, and other fringe benefits that most employees receive from their employers. Making a new business profitable takes long hours of hard work, and even for dedicated entrepreneurs there is no guarantee of success.

Review Questions

1 ▶ What is the main reason that most people choose to work for someone else?

2 ▶ What are the advantages of temporary employment from an employer's point of view?

3 ▶ What type of person makes a good entrepreneur?

Perhaps you already have had some experience as an entrepreneur. Maybe you have enlisted several friends to help you mow lawns, walk dogs, look after people's houses while they were away, and run errands for busy parents. If you have done any of these jobs, then you know the benefits and risks of being an entrepreneur. You know that successful entrepreneurs have to work hard and have positive attitudes about their ability to succeed. Since they may need to hire employees or choose partners, entrepreneurs also must be able to make good judgments about people. Good employees can make the difference between success or failure for a new business.

You may decide, as most people do, that temporary work and entrepreneurship are not for you. However, if you want the freedom and flexibility to design your own career, the benefits of working for yourself may outweigh the risks. After all, every business that exists once was started by someone who had an idea and believed it could become profitable.

Summary

☐ You can look at an employment agreement from two different points of view—that of the employee and that of the employer.

☐ Jobs are created when there is work to be done, and they are designed to maximize productivity in doing the work.

☐ Managers help people work together in achieving the goals of a business.

☐ Career ladders and promotions can help employers keep good employees and reduce the cost of training new workers.

☐ Temporary employment and entrepreneurship are two options for people who choose not to seek full-time employment.

Vocabulary Exercise

delegate	manager	freelancer
productivity	career ladder	entrepreneur
profit		

Write a paragraph in which you use each of the vocabulary words in its correct context. You may have to write a sentence or two in the paragraph without any vocabulary words in it so that the paragraph flows smoothly.

Discussion Questions

1. Why is it helpful for employees to think about jobs and the workplace from the point of view of the employer?

2. What qualities do you think a good manager should have and why?

3. Can you think of any disadvantages of being a temporary worker? Why would you like or dislike being one?

4. Why do you think so many new businesses fail?

Thinking Further

1. (Speaking and Listening) Go to one of the small businesses near your home and ask if you can speak with the owner. Discuss some of the following questions with the owner. What makes a good employee? How do you decide which tasks make up an employee's job? How do the managers in your business do their jobs? Do your employees have an opportunity to advance in the company? Have you ever hired a temporary employee? Why did you decide to start your own business?

2. (Writing) Think about whether or not you would like to be an entrepreneur. Then write a paragraph about yourself, explaining why you would or would not be happy as an entrepreneur. What qualities do you have that would help you or hinder you? If you know someone who is an entrepreneur, you might want to compare his or her traits to yours.

3. (Math) Imagine that you are an entrepreneur who has just started a new business. At 8 a.m., you realize that you have scheduled too much to do that day. You have the following tasks to complete: 10 a.m. meeting with new clients (will last 2 hours), noon meeting with suppliers (will last 1½ hours), 3 p.m. meeting with real estate agent to see office sites (1 to 2 hours), 5 p.m. appointment with accountant (1 hour), business proposals to write (3 hours), computer work (2 hours), paperwork (3 hours). How would you arrange your day? Would you cancel or reschedule any meetings or appointments? Why or why not? Explain your decisions.

4. (Reading) Read the following feature to learn more about jobs.

WHO TREATS THE PATIENTS?

You probably know what a doctor is and what a doctor does, but there are many different kinds of doctors. See how many of these doctors you know.

Carmen is a partner in a medical practice set up to treat patients of all ages. As an obstetrician, Carmen treats women throughout their pregnancies and helps them deliver their babies. The babies then become the patients of Rodney, who is a pediatrician. When they reach adulthood, Joan, who is a general practitioner, takes over their care.

Carmen, Rodney, and Joan—like all physicians in private practice—perform medical exams, diagnose illnesses, and treat their patients' illnesses and injuries. All three are doctors of medicine, or M.D.'s. There also are other physicians who are doctors of osteopathy, or D.O.'s. M.D.'s and D.O.'s use the same techniques.

Carmen and her partners frequently refer patients to other physicians or specialists for specific kinds of problems. For example, patients with serious eye diseases or injuries are sent to ophthalmologists, who specialize in treating eyes.

Carmen, Rodney, and Joan work long, irregular hours. They have evening office hours twice a week. They visit patients in the local hospital before going to their offices most mornings. All of them—but especially

Carmen—frequently get calls at home from patients in the middle of the night.

Since Carmen and her partners run their own practice, they can be viewed as entrepreneurs. They risk their own money on office equipment and employees' salaries. To keep their practice profitable, they must manage their resources carefully.

Not all physicians are in business for themselves, however. Physicians who work in salaried jobs for corporations, hospitals, schools, prisons, and other institutions usually work the standard 40 hours per week. That is also true of physicians who work as researchers in laboratories.

Physicians have the highest average income of any occupation. Their incomes vary widely, however, depending on their specialties, where they practice, how long they have been in practice, and their professional reputations.

One reason for physicians' high incomes is the high cost of their training. A few years ago, the average physician just graduating from medical school owed more than $33,000 in loans taken out for college and medical school.

The educational requirements for M.D.'s and D.O.'s are slightly different, but both must spend about eight years in college and medical—or osteopathic—school. In college, they must concentrate on science courses, although medical schools prefer applicants who have rounded out their educations with courses in many other fields. After medical school, M.D.'s generally spend three or four years in graduate medical education programs, or residencies. D.O.'s generally serve one-year internships that include experience in a number of specialties. To be certified as specialists, physicians must spend three to six years in advanced residency training followed by another two years practicing in their specialties.

Competition for admission to medical schools is fierce. Medical schools select students on the basis of their college grades, admission test scores, after-school activities, and letters of recommendation. Even students with excellent grades often are unable to get into medical school.

Employment opportunities for physicians are expected to increase much faster than for other occupations through the year 2000. The demand for physicians is increasing due to population growth as well as insurance programs that enable more people to pay for medical care. However, the supply of physicians is expected to grow even faster than the demand. This may result in lower incomes for physicians. Big cities, especially, may have more physicians than they need. As a result, more physicians may set up practices in rural areas, where fewer people live.

In addition to physicians, careers in the Health Diagnosing and Treating Practitioners cluster of the *Occupational Outlook Handbook* include:

- ❏ chiropractors
- ❏ dentists
- ❏ optometrists
- ❏ podiatrists
- ❏ veterinarians

6

Looking at Jobs

After you have studied this chapter, you should be able to:

➤ List the major sources of job information

➤ Explain several ways of dividing the job market

➤ Describe the 20 cluster system

➤ Use the 20 cluster system to narrow your search for an occupation

Vocabulary Words

Cluster

Cooperative education

Employment trend

Employment agency

Transferable skill

Risa, a high school student, thinks a lot about which occupation she would like to pursue. She has considered her occupational interests and preferences. She has looked at the type of activities she enjoys and has spoken with her guidance counselor about her aptitudes. In fact, Risa recently took an aptitude test, which helped her narrow her range of options to two fields, including agricultural science and biological science. This is because she showed an aptitude in biology and chemistry.

Risa found plenty of information that helped her think about her personality, interests, aptitudes, and skills. Where can she find information on the different occupations that are available? Risa knows that there are many occupations just within the two categories she has selected—some of which she probably has never even heard! How can she choose an occupation unless she knows what all of her options are?

Like the rest of us, Risa needs reliable sources of detailed information about jobs that interest her. In this chapter, we will examine some of these sources and discuss how you can use them to identify occupational groupings that are right for you.

Job Information Sources

Locating information about occupations is like finding your seat in a football stadium—it is easy if you know where to go. The job market can be very confusing, especially since there are thousands of occupations from which to choose. Knowing where to look for information can simplify the process, and it can help you determine which occupations will suit you best.

In addition to locating the information itself, you will need to locate information about specific occupations, or groups of occupations. The way occupations are grouped differs from one resource to another, depending on the goals of the resource. Resources typically arrange the occupations they cover into **clusters**, or groups of occupations that are similar. People can use these resources to identify clusters that interest them.

People

The best way to learn about a particular occupation is to talk with a person who works in that occupation. Many of the people you encounter every day have jobs they enjoy, and some of them may know about other occupations. People who know you personally can be especially helpful, since they know your personality and interests. Your family and friends, for example, can tell you about their own experiences in the job market. They also might be able to help you select careers that interest you.

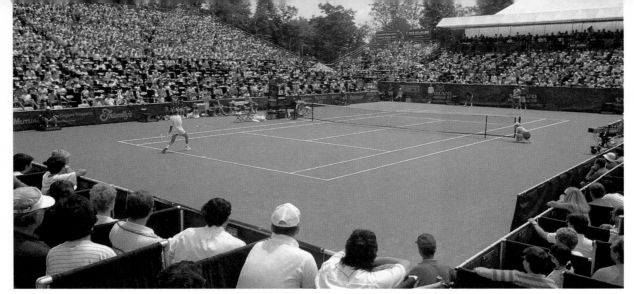
In this crowd there probably are more than 1,000 jobs represented.

Many other people can help you find the information for which you are looking. Some of the teachers in your school, especially those placing students in jobs through **cooperative education**, can tell you more about some of the jobs that match up aptitudes and skills. Cooperative education teachers use needs assessment instruments to help students match their abilities to jobs that are currently available. Students who are involved in cooperative education typically spend part of the day at school and part of the day training in a job to gain work experience.

School guidance counselors are an excellent source of information. They are trained to provide you with descriptions of many occupations and help you evaluate the possibilities. They usually keep a library of printed materials on occupations, which includes information on the most recent **employment trends**. Employment trends tell which jobs are becoming more in demand and which jobs are declining in employment opportunities. When you are older, your guidance counselor might direct you to an **employment agency** in your area. Employment agencies help people find suitable jobs, so they are a good source of information on many occupational opportunities.

The two main types of employment agencies are public employment agencies and private employment agencies. Public employment agencies are free and are operated by state governments. Each state has an agency, with offices in major cities. Private employment agencies charge a fee for their services. They may charge the people for whom they find jobs or the companies that ask the agency to help fill jobs.

If you have a particular occupational field in mind, such as hotel/motel management, you could talk to the personnel managers at local hotels. They could tell you about occupations within hotel management, the training you would need, and where you could learn more about the hotel industry.

You also should talk with the reference librarians at your school and public libraries. They can help you find printed reference sources, as well as local listings of agencies and professional associations you could contact. If you are interested in a military career, you should make an appointment to see a military recruiter when you start high school.

Printed Government Sources

The United States Department of Labor has three publications that will provide you with thorough descriptions of most occupations that are available today. These should be available in your guidance office, school library, or public library.

The *Occupational Outlook Handbook*, or *OOH*, describes more than 200 occupations in detail and offers brief descriptions of 200 other occupations. For each occupation, it describes the nature of the tasks performed by the workers, typical working conditions, the number of people employed, training requirements, job outlook in the future, and potential earnings. The *OOH* also contains job interview tips, a section on "tomorrow's jobs," and a listing of places to go for further information.

The *OOH* groups occupations according to the type of task performed. For example, a musical instrument tuner and a computer

You can learn a lot about the working world from people who work.

The *GOE* asks you to look at your interests in order to identify occupational clusters to explore.

service technician both fit into the Mechanics, Installers, and Repairers cluster, even though a grand piano is very different from a laser printer. We will look more closely at this method of classifying occupations in the next section of this chapter. It is referred to as the 20 cluster system.

The *Guide for Occupational Exploration*, or *GOE*, has been designed to help you match your interests and skills to occupations. It describes 348 groups of jobs by answering questions about each group, such as what kind of work would you do? What skills and abilities would you need for these occupations? How would you know if you would like or could learn to do this kind of work? How can you prepare for and enter these occupations? The *GOE* helps people identify occupational clusters that may interest them by first evaluating their own interests and skills. The *GOE* divides interests into 12 broad areas. They are artistic, scientific, plants and animals, protective, mechanical, industrial, business detail, selling, accommodating, humanitarian, leading-influencing, and physical performing. For example, if Dave has an interest in fulfilling the needs and wishes of other people, then he may want to work in one of the accommodating occupations. He might enjoy taking people on tours of model homes, or working as a chauffeur for a company, or as an automobile rental clerk, a cosmetologist, or ski-tow operator at a ski resort. The emphasis in the *GOE* is not on the job function. It is on the interests of the person who is doing the job.

After describing each group, *GOE* lists job titles for people in that occupational area. For example, the physical sciences group is

(continued on page 106)

USING A COMPUTER TO LEARN

Today was my first day of careers class. My teacher helped me realize that I need to spend some time thinking about a career. He said it is never too soon to begin planning for the future. Then he gave the class an assignment, saying it would start us on the path of career exploration. When I saw that the assignment came with a computer disk, I decided to check it out right away. After class I ran to the computer lab and reserved a computer for the next afternoon.

I never thought I would have fun doing homework. The *Discover* program was great! It started by explaining it would help me learn about planning my future, discover what my interests and abilities are, learn about occupations, and select my high school courses.

The program was divided into four parts. The first one helped me learn an easy way to organize jobs using a special map. There were four directions on the map representing four work tasks.

In the next activity, I played a game that helped me learn how to organize jobs. The game involved helping a mouse get out of a maze by placing job activities on a map.

The last section of Part 1 was about my interests. The program told me that first step in career planning is finding out what I like to do, so *Discover* helped me do this by asking me to select work tasks I might like.

I went on to Part 2 of the program—Exploring Occupations. First, I rated some of my abilities including reading, numbers, and more. Then I had to fill in my grades in English, math, art, science, and industrial arts classes.

I went on to make combinations of the four work tasks to learn about occupations. Those occupations were divided into six groups or clusters. After I told the computer about my expected educational plans, it showed me how the abilities and grades I had entered before could be applied to an occupation. Then it showed me some sample jobs in that cluster and descriptions of them.

Before I knew it, my time on the computer was up. I signed off and hurried to the sign-up sheet to put my name down again. I cannot wait to come back tomorrow so I can explore more clusters and jobs, and plan my high school courses. ∎

made up of 28 different jobs, one of which is physical metallurgist. To find out exactly what a physical metallurgist does, you can turn to the *Dictionary of Occupational Titles*, or *DOT*, which lists more than 20,000 different occupations. For each occupation, *DOT* defines the job and explains the tasks that are performed by the workers. Physical metallurgists, according to *DOT*, use microscopes, X-rays, and spectroscopes to determine the physical characteristics of metals and alloys. They then develop melting, hot-working, cold-working, and heat-treating processes to change the characteristics of the metals. Like *OOH*, *DOT* groups occupations by using the 20 cluster system.

Other Sources

The United States Department of Labor publications are not the only printed sources of job information that are available to you. *The Encyclopedia of Careers and Vocational Guidance* is made up of three separate volumes: *Reviewing Career Fields, Selecting a Career*, and *Selecting a Technician's Career*. Most libraries and career centers also contain files of job pamphlets, such as those published by Chronicle Publications. All of these resources describe the job itself, education and training requirements, how to get the job, advancement possibilities, employment outlook, and earnings and fringe benefits.

Some career information is available through computer databases, such as *Discover* from American College Testing and *SIGI Plus* from the Educational Testing Service. Both of these resources assess the interests and aptitudes of the user before selecting a number of occupations that may be suitable.

SIGI Plus classifies occupations within a particular field by the amount of education they require. *SIGI Plus* first asks you to indicate the level of education you have achieved or the level of education you wish to achieve. It then selects occupations that are appropriate to your educational level.

In addition, many large public libraries have computerized listings of jobs that are available in the local area. Consult the librarian to find out about these listings.

Review Questions

1 ▶ When talking with people about jobs, how can you get help from family and friends?

2 ▶ How does the approach of *GOE* differ from that of *OOH*?

3 ▶ Where can you look to find occupations organized by the level of education they require?

The Twenty Cluster System

You may think that 20 different job clusters are a lot to think about, but remember that it is easier than thinking about 20,000 occupations! The point of the cluster system, after all, is to make it easier for you to identify the groups of occupations that interest you. In the 20 cluster system, a cluster is made up of a group of occupations that require many of the same types of **transferable skills.** These are skills that can be used in, or transferred to, different jobs.

This college student is gaining skills that she can apply in any job in any cluster. Do you know why?

If you have the skills to be successful at one occupation in a cluster, you can probably move to another occupation in the same cluster without needing to learn a whole new set of skills. For example, although religious workers and social workers receive different training, both require skill in working closely with people, often in difficult situations. As we briefly look at each of the 20 clusters, think about which ones interest you most. The next section will discuss how you can use the clusters when you are thinking about your future occupation.

People-Serving Clusters

The *Service Occupations* cluster will probably be the fastest growing occupational group for at least the next 10 years. It includes workers who are involved in protective service, cleaning and building service, food service, health service assistance, and personal service. These workers, for example, serve others by investigating crimes, maintaining schools, cooking food, driving ambulances, and taking care of children.

Health Diagnosing and Treating Practitioners have a strong desire to help other people. Their job is to diagnose and treat illness. The doctors, dentists, and veterinarians in this cluster need the help of workers in the *Registered Nurses, Pharmacists, Dieticians, Therapists, and Physician Assistants* cluster. Many of these health

Pharmacists work in many different settings, including hospitals, clinics, drugstores, and community pharmacies.

professionals have completed four or more years of training after high school. For example, speech pathologists and audiologists, who treat speech and hearing problems, often need master's degrees. *Health Technologists and Technicians* include licensed practical nurses, medical laboratory workers, and surgical technicians. Workers in this cluster support the efforts of those who diagnose and treat injuries and illness.

Human Interaction Clusters

You may be interested in occupations that involve a high level of interaction with people. The *Lawyers, Social Scientists, Social Workers, and Religious Workers* cluster includes a wide variety of occupations. Some study the political and economic behavior of various people, while others help them with their legal problems, provide religious or psychological counseling, or help families and teens troubled by alcoholism or drug abuse. *Teachers, Librarians, and Counselors* help people learn new information and gain new insight into themselves and the world around them.

The occupations in the *Writers, Artists, and Entertainers* cluster require a great deal of creativity and hard work. They include actors, television newscasters, musicians, photographers, and designers. These people use words, sounds, and images to express some aspect of the human experience.

These government inspectors are checking food. Their jobs are included in the *Managerial and Management Related Occupations* cluster

Business-Related Clusters

Are you fascinated by the challenge of making a sale, managing a profitable business, or working in an efficient office? If you enjoy convincing people to buy a product, then you should investigate occupations in the *Marketing and Sales Occupations* cluster. Advertising workers, insurance agents, models, and travel agents all look for new ways to make products more attractive.

The *Managerial and Management-Related Occupations* manage and oversee the daily operations of many different types of organizations. In fact, almost every occupational cluster includes some type of manager. This cluster also contains the accountants who examine finances, inspectors who check to see that regulations are kept, and hotel managers who make certain travelers have a comfortable place to stay.

Workers in the *Administrative Support Occupations, Including Clerical* cluster help keep offices running smoothly and efficiently. They might be receptionists, typists, bank tellers, airline ticket agents, or mail carriers. They manage the communications between people, direct the endless flow of paper and documents, and operate the computers on which most businesses depend.

Industrial and Construction Clusters

Workers in these six clusters construct, manufacture, assemble, transport, and repair a wide variety of products, from houses and office buildings to cars, televisions, books, and furniture. The *Production Occupations* cluster is made up of the workers who build boilers, bind books, operate power plants and factory machines, and assemble products by hand. When the finished products are ready for shipment to the store and the consumer, workers in the *Transportation and Material Moving Occupations* take over. Workers in this cluster also carry passengers from one place to another on buses, trains, ships, and airplanes.

Do you have a problem with your car, photocopy machine, television set, or elevator? If you do, just call on one of the *Mechanics, Installers, and Repairers*, who are trained to diagnose the problem and make the necessary repairs.

The *Engineers, Surveyors, and Architects* cluster includes the engineers who design roads and bridges, electrical equipment, heating systems, aircraft, and chemical products. Surveyors map out land boundaries and construction sites, while architects design the layout and structure of buildings. Workers in the *Construction Trades and Extractive Occupations* are trained in the skills required to build and maintain houses, office buildings, and other structures. They pour concrete foundations, erect steel beams,

This captain works for the merchant marine. His job is included in the Transportation and Material Moving Occupations.

install electrical and plumbing systems, and nail the paneling and trim into place. Miners and oil field workers, who extract coal, oil, and other minerals from the ground, also are included in this cluster. Finally, all these industries depend on *Handlers, Equipment Cleaners, Helpers, and Laborers* to assist in the construction, manufacturing, and production process.

Other Clusters

Technologists and Technicians, Except Health support the work of professionals in a wide variety of fields. Occupations in this cluster include air traffic controllers, radio and television broadcast technicians, legal assistants, and library technicians. In most cases, these workers use specialized equipment, such as computers, television cameras, robots, and radar equipment.

People who choose occupations in the *Natural, Computer, and Mathematical Scientists* cluster search for answers to how things work. They may study a recently discovered star, investigate the cause of disease in plants, analyze statistics or dates, or develop systems for computerizing tasks. *Agriculture, Forestry, Fishing, and Related Occupations* are involved with the earth as well, but in a different way. They till the soil, plant crops, manage logging and replanting operations, and harvest trees.

The armed forces of the United States employ more people than any other employer in the nation. Many workers in the cluster titled *Job Opportunities in the Armed Forces* perform the same tasks as civilian workers, but with a different goal—the defense of our country. This cluster also includes occupations such as paratrooper, infantryperson, and gun crew member.

Review Questions

1 ▶ What is the difference between the job clusters that involve serving people and the human interaction clusters?

2 ▶ What is unique about the *Managerial and Management-Related Occupations* cluster?

3 ▶ What is the goal of the occupations in the *Natural, Computer, and Mathematical Scientists* cluster?

Using Clusters to Make Choices

The 20 cluster system is designed so that it collects all the occupations that require related skills into a single cluster. For example, the skills needed by pharmacists and physician assistants are similar, so those occupations are in the same cluster. The cluster system is a useful tool even though some of the 20,000 occupations do not fit neatly into any one of the 20 clusters. By studying occupations in skill clusters, you can decide more easily which clusters contain the type of occupations that interest you.

Selecting Key Clusters

Skill clusters are like the signs in supermarket aisles, because those signs help you decide which sections of the store you need to visit. If you do not own any pets, then you probably skip the pet food aisle. In the same way, you probably can rule out 8 or 10 of the clusters without much thought. People who do not like working indoors in offices, for example, can automatically rule out administrative support occupations.

Would you like to know how you can narrow your options even further? Using the information on the previous pages and in the two-page features on clusters located in each chapter, make a list of all the clusters containing occupations that interest you. Next, go to your library or guidance office and take out one or more of the printed resources discussed in this chapter, such as *OOH* or *DOT*. Browse through the sections that discuss the occupations in the clusters on your list, comparing the characteristics of each cluster with your own interests and preferences. If you do not have an interest in the occupations in that cluster or an aptitude for the required skills, cross that cluster off your list. Try to shorten the list until it contains only two or three clusters.

There are many preferences to take into consideration when you review the details of a job. One important preference is whether you would rather work indoors or outdoors.

Selecting Certain Occupations

You can easily see, however, that two or three clusters contain a great number of occupations. Even if you narrow your search to one cluster and decide that you want to pursue an occupation as a technologist or technician, you must still consider a wide range of potential jobs within that cluster. You could be a library assistant, air traffic controller, or legal assistant. The list of jobs is long and varied. The next step in the process of selecting a suitable occupation is to consider the details of some of the occupations that appeal to you. The next chapter will discuss how you can accomplish that goal and narrow your search further.

Review Questions ___

1 ▶ How should you make use of the 20 cluster system?

2 ▶ Why should you shorten your list to two or three clusters that interest you?

Summary

❑ You can find detailed information about various occupations by talking to your family, friends, teachers, and guidance counselors.

❑ You can obtain printed information on occupations in government publications, careers encyclopedias, and computer database programs.

❑ The job market can be divided and organized by area of interest, type of job, or educational level.

❑ The 20 cluster system divides the job market into clusters of jobs that require similar skills.

❑ Within the 20 cluster system, there are people-serving clusters, human interaction clusters, business-related clusters, industrial and construction clusters, and other clusters.

❑ By comparing your interests and aptitudes with the characteristics of the occupations in each cluster, you can identify the clusters you should examine more closely.

Vocabulary Exercise

cluster	employment trend	transferable skill
cooperative education	employment agency	

Complete the sentences below with the best word from the list above.

1. Different resources use different systems to put jobs into _____.

2. Teachers of _____ can have useful information on occupations.

3. If you want to find a suitable job, you might visit a(n) _____.

4. A(n) _____ can be used in more than one job.

5. When a job is becoming popular, a(n) _____ might predict the future demand for it.

Discussion Questions

1. Why do you think it is important for you to begin now to identify the occupations that interest you?

2. What are the goals of your search for an occupation?

3. Choose an occupation that interests you. Where do you think you would find the most useful information on that job and why?

4. Which way of dividing the job market do you think is the best, and why?

Thinking Further

1. (Reading) Using the 20 cluster system, identify which cluster contains each of the following occupations. If necessary, look up the occupations in a dictionary or careers encyclopedia.

underwriter   actuary   ophthalmologist
cosmetologist   millwright   glazier

2. (Writing) In order to keep your personal file of career resources up to date, you should add the materials discussed in this chapter to your file. List the name of each book, encyclopedia, pamphlet series, and database on a separate index card. Then go to your guidance office, career center, or library and find each of the resources. Ask for assistance if you are unable to find all the items. Fill out each index card, listing the contents of the resource and where you found it.

3. (Speaking) Choose a cluster that interests you. Then when the teacher calls on you, describe aloud the personality, interests, aptitudes, and skills that a person might want to have for occupations in that cluster.

4. (Reading) Read the following features to learn more about jobs.

WHO PERFORMS MEDICAL TESTS?

Have you ever visited a hospital? If you have, then you probably know that many doctors and nurses work there. What you may not realize is that the diagnosis and treatment of patients at hospitals depends not only on doctors and nurses but also on a wide range of technicians.

Alan, for example, is a laboratory technician at Metropolitan Hospital. Working in the lab in shifts around the clock, Alan and his co-workers run tests on body tissues and fluids to help physicians monitor patients' health. Alan, who has an associate degree from a junior college, is responsible for preparing specimens and operating automatic analyzing equipment. He also performs other tasks that require him to follow highly detailed instructions.

Alan's supervisor, Carla, is a medical technologist. Like many other medical technologists, Carla has a bachelor's degree in science. In addition to supervising the technicians, she helps to develop the laboratory's testing techniques. She also performs complex tests on samples of patients' tissues and fluids to detect the presence of bacteria, fungi, and diseases.

Not all technologists and technicians deal with tissues and fluids or work in laboratories. Ray, for example, operates an electro-

encephalograph, which measures the electrical activities of patients' brains. This instrument produces electroencephalograms (EEGs), which are maps of brain activity that help physicians diagnose and treat neurological disorders.

When Ray takes a patient's EEG, he generally starts by obtaining a short medical history from the patient and encouraging the patient to relax. Then he attaches electrodes to the patient's head and body. The electrodes are wired to the electroencephalograph. Ray must use the right combination

of controls so that the electroencephalograph will produce the kind of information the patient's physician needs.

Ray and the other EEG technologists generally work during the day, five days a week, but one of them always must be on call for emergencies. They may take EEGs in patients' rooms, in operating rooms, or in the hospital's emergency room.

Some of the other EEG technologists have only high school diplomas, but Ray has an associate degree. His degree may help to qualify him for a supervisory position and eventually for a job as a chief EEG technologist. He expects to advance quickly in his career because jobs for EEG technologists are increasing at a very fast rate. Changing technology is the main reason for the increasing number of jobs, and Ray plans to continue attending classes to keep up with developments in his field.

Luis, who takes patients' electrocardiograms (EKGs), has a job similar to Ray's. He operates an instrument that monitors the activities of patients' hearts. EKGs help physicians treat heart disease and monitor the effects of drugs and other treatments. Luis also takes EKGs of patients who are scheduled for surgery, so their doctors can decide whether their hearts are strong enough for the surgery to be safe.

EKG technicians generally receive on-the-job training, but they need high school diplomas. The average income for an EKG technician is a little less than for an EEG technologist, and employment opportunities are not increasing as rapidly.

Metropolitan and other hospitals employ other kinds of technologists and technicians as well. Metropolitan Hospital depends on medical record technicians, for example, to organize and maintain the files that contain all of the patients' medical records. Metropolitan also needs radiologic technicians to operate the X-ray machines and related technical equipment. Surgeons depend on surgical technicians to help set up operating rooms for surgery and to pass the surgeons the instruments and supplies they need as they operate on patients.

These jobs are listed in the Health Technologists and Technicians cluster in the *Occupational Outlook Handbook*. Other occupations in this cluster include:

- ☐ dental hygienists
- ☐ dispensing opticians
- ☐ emergency medical technicians
- ☐ licensed practical nurses
- ☐ nuclear medicine technologists

WHO DEFENDS THE COUNTRY?

Who is the largest employer in the United States? If you answered the United States armed forces, you are right. Altogether, more than two million men and women have jobs in the Army, Air Force, Navy, Marine Corps, and Coast Guard. These employees spend their time preparing to defend the United States in the event of war.

When you think of jobs in the military, you may picture soldiers driving tanks, firing artillery, or parachuting out of airplanes. While jobs related to combat and military transportation make up about 40 percent of the jobs in the armed forces, many other kinds of jobs are available.

The military has many of the same occupational groups found in civilian life. For example, there are health care occupations, human service occupations, and construction trades. You will find doctors, secretaries, carpenters, and truck drivers in the armed forces. All these jobs help the armed forces function smoothly.

As in civilian life, the type of job a person has in the armed forces depends on abilities, interests, training, and experience. Because they have more training and experience, officers serve in supervisory or highly skilled positions. For example, in the administrative occupational group, officers work as personnel managers and hospital administrators. Enlisted members, on the other hand, work as payroll clerks and typists.

Enlisted personnel such as Mary Jo and Wayne volunteer to be in the armed forces for a certain length of time. They may enlist for two to six years. On completing their tour of duty, they may sign up again. Some enlisted personnel make a career out of being in the armed forces.

Enlisted members enter the armed forces with no previous military training. Many young people enter the armed forces to learn job skills they can later use in civilian life. Mary Jo, for example, enlisted in the Air Force so she could learn how to operate flight control equipment. Wayne enlisted in the army to learn to be an electrician. They

are getting an education while being paid to serve their country.

To be accepted into the armed forces, Mary Jo and Wayne had to pass a physical examination. They also had to pass a written examination that determines which training programs would be appropriate for them. Enlistees must be between the ages of 17 and 35. Most armed forces training programs require a high school diploma.

After enlistment, Wayne and Mary Jo participated in basic training. In addition to rigorous physical exercises, they took courses in military procedures, first aid, and health. Then Mary Jo and Wayne began classroom training to prepare them for their occupational specialties.

Russell and Nina entered the armed forces as officers. Russell, a second lieutenant in the Air Force, is in flight training, and Nina, a second lieutenant in the Army, is a computer systems manager.

To become officers, Russell and Nina participated in armed forces training while earning college degrees. Russell attended the United States Air Force Academy, one of the government's federal service academies. Nina received military instruction through the Reserve Officer Training Corps (ROTC) on her college campus.

After graduation, students who partici-pated in officer training and received financial benefits from the government must serve as officers for a certain number of years. Russell, for example, must be on active duty for more than five years.

Officer training also is provided through the Officer Candidate School (OCS), the National Guard, and other programs. Upon entering the military, certain people qualified to perform special duties, such as doctors, automatically become officers.

When serving as enlisted members or officers, armed forces personnel must be able to handle discipline and regimentation. They must be able to take orders. In addition, they must be willing to conform to strict requirements regarding their appearance and behavior.

Some additional Job Opportunities in the Armed Forces that are listed in the *Occupational Outlook Handbook* include:

❑ armored vehicle operator

❑ artillery crew

❑ combat engineer

❑ demolition expert

❑ rocket specialist

❑ weapons specialist

Investigating the Details

After you have studied this chapter, you should be able to:

➡ List key aspects of different jobs that could influence your final decision on choosing a job

➡ Determine how you can apply this detailed job information to your selection process

Vocabulary Words

Overtime

Salary

Commission

Bonus

Fringe benefit

Pension

Networking

Job shadowing

Because Stephen is such an outgoing and friendly person, no one is surprised that he has decided to pursue a career in marketing and sales. It certainly will match his personality, and besides, he always seems to be selling something—if not chocolates to benefit the school orchestra, then magazines to help the Little League buy uniforms. Stephen has considered a number of other occupational clusters, but none suits his interests and aptitudes as well as marketing and sales.

Stephen knows that he still has to choose from among hundreds of different occupations in the marketing and sales field. He has read some job descriptions in the *Dictionary of Occupational Titles*. The *SIGI Plus* database lists several sales occupations that might match his particular interests. Even with all this general information, Stephen knows he needs more details before he can choose one specific job.

He is not sure, based on the information he has, whether he would rather sell medical equipment to hospitals or men's suits in a clothing store. Maybe he would prefer selling large computers to banks and insurance companies. Stephen decides to investigate the details of some of the sales and marketing occupations he has identified. Stephen recognizes the tasks he would perform at work as only part of the job picture. He knows he must consider all the different aspects of a job in order to choose one that will be satisfying and fulfilling.

Specific Facts to Know

Stephen has narrowed his search for a suitable job by focusing on his interests and aptitudes. Since most sales occupations would match his interests and aptitudes, he needs to examine the details of various sales jobs. By doing that, he can decide which particular job will suit him best. If he takes a job selling men's clothing, for example, he might receive a smaller salary than if he sells medical equipment to doctors, clinics, and hospitals. What is the long-term picture? If Stephen decides he wants to work for himself, he probably will find it easier to open a small clothing store than to begin manufacturing medical equipment. Thinking about the occupation as a whole is the best way to choose among the many occupations that are grouped within a single cluster. Stephen needs to consider salary, benefits, prospects for promotion, work environment, and the future of the field.

Salary and Benefits

The first question some people ask about a job is, "How much money will I be paid?" Stephen is no exception. If two sales jobs are similar in other ways, he naturally will prefer one that pays

You need to look at all aspects of a job before you choose to pursue that job.

$20,000 per year to one that pays $15,000 per year. As he investigates the question of salary and benefits further, however, Stephen discovers an important fact. He learns that pay also can come in many different forms.

Some employees are paid an hourly wage and receive a paycheck every week. These workers may be paid **overtime,** or a higher hourly wage if they work more than their regular hours per week. Other employees receive a **salary,** or a fixed amount of money each time they are paid no matter how many hours they work. Salaried workers are usually paid once a month or twice a month. Salespeople, Stephen found, often receive part of their salary in the form of a **commission,** or a set percentage of the sales they make. Some employers also give their employees a **bonus,** or extra money at the end of a profitable year or at the end of a successful project. In some manufacturing jobs, particularly assembly line jobs, workers are paid according to the number of products they produce or assemble.

As he looks more closely at salary estimates for salespeople, Stephen realizes that the figures vary widely depending on the part of the country and the type of industry. He also notices that some companies provide more **fringe benefits** for their workers than others. Fringe benefits are forms of payment for work other than money. Most companies, for example, give their employees paid holidays, paid sick days, medical insurance, and some form of **pension,** or provision for an income after retirement. Others may pay for life insurance and child care, provide a company car, assist with tuition payments, pay moving expenses for new employees, or sponsor employee sports teams. Every benefit a company provides is one less item an employee needs to buy.

Because more and more households contain two wage earners, flexible benefit packages are becoming more popular. If a woman is covered by her husband's medical insurance, her employer may increase her child care allowance instead of paying for her medical insurance. For some people, salary and benefits—the financial side of employment—are the most important aspects of a job. Stephen also has another question in mind. How quickly can he advance in the jobs he is considering?

Promotion Prospects

Stephen has given a lot of thought to working as a sales representative for a large computer and business machines manufacturer. The company, like many large companies, provides extensive train-

Many companies provide fringe benefits, such as medical insurance, to their employees.

In some companies, if you get a promotion, you may have to move to another part of the country.

ing and continuing education programs for its employees. Stephen knows he will have plenty of opportunity for advancement with such a large company. He also recognizes the advantages of working for a smaller company. There, he probably will be given more responsibility within a shorter period of time, and his job will include a wider variety of tasks.

Stephen's guidance counselor suggests a good strategy for evaluating the prospects for promotion within a company. "Talk to people who have been with the company three to five years," his counselor says. "Find out what they started out doing and what they are doing now. Ask them the following questions: How long do employees generally remain in the positions for which they are hired? Do they advance quickly? If they wish, are employees able to move into other departments within the company?" Stephen is particularly interested in this last point. He wants to work in various areas of sales and marketing. That would help him prepare to start his own company.

The counselor also suggests that Stephen ask how the company decides whom to promote. Do they promote everyone who has a certain amount of experience? Do they require employees to get more education or an increased level of skill? Will the company pay for the additional education and provide the training, or are these the employee's responsibility?

Like Stephen, you must think about all these aspects of your own career plan. Do you want the advantages of working for a small company or a large company? Are opportunities for advancement important to you? Remember to keep in mind that people who accept a promotion usually must accept more responsibility as well. Look carefully at some companies in the occupational cluster you have selected to see how the careers of their employees develop. Is that what you think you want for your future? Answering these questions will help you decide whether a particular type of company suits you.

Work Environment

At first, Stephen is much more concerned about salary and promotion than about the type of environment in which he will work. As he learns more about various sales occupations, however, he begins to realize how much work environments can vary. Some jobs will require him to travel a lot, either during the day or for several days at a time. In others, he will spend most of his time in a small office talking to potential customers on the telephone or perhaps on the showroom floor of a large retail store. If he sells construction equipment, Stephen will spend some of his time out at construction sites. He recognizes that selecting an occupation

(continued on page 124)

WHO DO YOU KNOW?

Have you ever heard the old saying, "It is not what you know, it is who you know"? Nowhere is that more true than in my line of work. I am a reporter for the local newspaper, and networking is an important part of my profession.

I even got my job through networking. I was a journalism student and a reporter on the school newspaper. Once, after having interviewed a city politician, I talked to her assistant and mentioned how much I wanted to work on the local newspaper. The assistant took my name and number. About a week later he called me. He put me in touch with a woman he knew at the newspaper's city desk, and she tipped me off to a summer job as a rookie reporter. Then, when I graduated from college, I became a full-time reporter covering the city beat.

I always get my best stories through networking. Over the years, I have met a lot of people and made a lot of contacts. I have contacts at City Hall, the mayor's office, the police department, the buildings department, and every other city agency. I make it my business to go into all the neighborhoods to keep up on community activities. If anything newsworthy is happening in the city, I will know about it. If I need information or contacts, there is always someone I know who can help me out.

Of course, networking is a two-way street. People I know will help me because they trust me. I write stories fairly and help my contacts when they need to be put in touch with someone I know. If you are honest and respect the people you network with, there is almost no limit to the benefits a good network can provide.

One thing you have to remember when networking is that you cannot be too shy. You need to speak up. Talk to people who are interested in the things you are interested in and who are doing the things you want to do. You do not have to know the mayor to be networking. Sewing circles are networks, unions and trade associations are networks, and schools and clubs are networks.

I could not do my job without networking. No matter what you do or want to do, a network of good contacts will help you do it. It is just people helping people. ■

The conditions in manufacturing plants vary depending on the kind of products that are produced there.

with a work environment that is acceptable to him is a key part of his decision.

As you read about various jobs, you should think about where people perform the tasks involved. If you decide to pursue an indoor occupation, your work environment can vary from an individual office to the assembly floor of a large factory. People who choose occupations that involve working outdoors, such as construction workers and police officers, may have to work even in extreme weather conditions.

Where you work also will affect the level of noise surrounding you. If you have an office to yourself, you can close the door and work alone in peace and quiet. Some people, however, would feel isolated in that situation. They might prefer to work in a large office with many other people.

You should think about safety in your work environment as well. If you work around heavy construction equipment, aircraft, or factory machinery, you may be required to wear devices to protect your hearing from damage. In addition to loud noises, some workers must deal with bright lights, dangerous machinery, and poisonous chemicals and gases. Deep sea divers and oil rig workers may face other dangers at sea. Office workers also must be careful that their eyes are not damaged by looking at a computer terminal all day for many years.

Do you prefer to sit down or stand while you work? If Stephen sells furniture in a retail store, he will be on his feet all day. If, on the other hand, he sells financial services on the telephone, he probably will sit at a desk. Do you prefer to stay in one place, or would you rather travel as part of your occupation? Some workers spend all their time in one place on an assembly line, while others travel to many countries. Finding a work environment that suits you is an important part of choosing an occupation. The best way to find out about different types of work places, of course, is to visit them. You could call and ask if anyone could give you a tour of the premises, or let you observe the work environment for a short time. Also, you might try to find part-time or summer jobs in the types of workplaces that interest you.

The Future of the Field

Peering into a crystal ball will not help you find a job, but thinking about the future of the occupation you plan to enter can help you keep your job. For several reasons, workers in some occupations are no longer needed by employers. Increasing technology and advances in production methods have eliminated some jobs. For example, railroad companies once employed many signal workers to convey messages from train dispatchers to train crews. Today, these messages are transmitted electronically. In modern automobile assembly plants, robot welders have replaced many of the workers who were once employed to weld together the frames and body panels of new cars.

Other jobs have been lost because of foreign competition. The steel, textile, shoe, and electronics industries all have faced stiff competition from foreign companies. As a result, many companies have closed plants and laid off workers.

While employment has declined in some areas, it has increased rapidly in others. For example, job openings in the service industries should continue to grow rapidly for the next 10 years. Looking at trends in the occupational clusters you have selected will help you decide how to plan your career. If you take the cluster approach to the job market, you can switch to another occupation within the cluster if demand for your occupation declines. That is why it is important to develop flexible skills.

Review Questions

1 ▶ How can your benefit package affect your income?

2 ▶ What aspects of your future work environment do you need to take into consideration?

3 ▶ Why is it important to develop flexible skills?

Finding Out the Facts

Stephen did not realize there are so many details to consider when choosing an occupation. He did not stop to think, for example, about how much he wanted to travel. He has learned that some people who work in sales spend most of their time on the road, while others rarely travel at all. Stephen needs to know the facts about each sales occupation. He has learned how to develop an accurate picture of the details of individual sales occupations. He

Today many people adapt to changing employment trends by changing careers. Sometimes their training involves going back to school.

needs to use the careers resource information available to him, talk to other people, visit different workplaces, and perhaps work part-time in his area of interest.

Library Work

Stephen knows the sources he uses to narrow down his list of clusters are a good place to begin looking for facts. The *Occupational Outlook Handbook* and *SIGI Plus* contain specific facts about salaries, advancement possibilities, working conditions, and industry outlook. Stephen remembers his guidance counselor told him always to check the date of publication before using a reference resource, to make certain that the salaries and outlook it describes are up to date. Even if the publication is recent, the salary figures may be three or four years old.

Because these resources cover so many different occupations, the information they provide is very general, covering all industries across the country. Stephen goes to see his guidance counselor and librarian to ask where he can find more detailed information. With their help, he checks the most recent editions of the major printed resources and computerized data bases. His guidance counselor and librarian also tell him about several other resources he should check. The public library in a city near his home maintains a computerized listing of job openings in the region. This listing provides

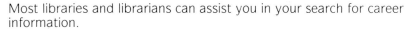

Most libraries and librarians can assist you in your search for career information.

For some projects, architects have to build models based on their building plans.

him with current salary and benefit figures, as well as accurate descriptions of specific jobs at different companies. Stephen also makes note of the employers' addresses and telephone numbers, so he can contact those employers directly for more information.

While he is at the library, Stephen finds out about *Occupational Outlook Quarterly* (*OOQ*), a publication issued four times a year by the Bureau of Labor Statistics. *OOQ* describes recent trends in the job market and highlights changes in certain occupational fields. Although Stephen's local library does not have *OOQ*, the librarian will be able to get it for him from another library through the interlibrary loan system.

At the library, Stephen also discovers that quite a few magazines include current information about jobs and careers. Some of those magazines are *Changing Times, Forbes, Inc., Working Woman*, and *Black Enterprise*.

The key to using the resources of the library effectively is to ask the librarians for assistance. They have been trained to help you find information. They have directories that list careers publications and show where they are available. They can direct you to other sources of detailed information, such as a large library in a nearby city, an employment agency that specializes in area job listings, a data base that lists regional job offerings, or a trade association in your field of interest. Follow Stephen's example and take advantage of the reference resources in your school career center and local libraries.

Networking

Stephen, however, does not limit his search for information to books and data bases. He also asks his family and friends if they know any people who actually work in sales occupations. This process of exchanging job-related information with a group of people is called **networking.** Stephen's strategy is simple but effective. If the people in his network know a salesperson, Stephen will contact that person by letter or telephone, asking for more information about the person's job.

Stephen's strategy pays off. His best friend, for example, does not know anything about sales occupations, but he has an uncle who is the sales manager of an auto dealership. Stephen's friend calls his uncle, and one afternoon Stephen spends an hour talking with the sales manager in his office.

Nothing can substitute the perspective you will receive from people who have experience in an occupation. When you contact such a person, be polite and ask if the person has time to talk with you. Most people will gladly talk with someone who has a genuine interest in their occupation.

You can obtain a lot of information about jobs by networking.

Before you meet with anyone, you should prepare some questions. That way you will not waste the time you spend together. "Tell me what you do," is a poor way to begin. Instead, you might ask, "What skills do you need to do your job well?" Listen to the answer carefully and attentively. Every bit of information will help you develop a feel for what the job is like. Rather than asking "How much money do you make?", you could ask what salary level you could expect upon starting the job and after five years of experience. Also, ask if most people employed in that occupation receive benefits, and what those benefits are. You might want to ask questions about promotion prospects, the work environment, and the future of the field as well.

When you finish talking, thank the person for the information and follow up with a short thank-you note. Keep people you have talked to informed about your decisions—let them know if they have helped you choose to work in their field. Do not expect them to help you find a job. If you have impressed them with your personality and attitude, however, they may be willing to write a letter of recommendation for you. Or they may be able to put you in touch with other employers. You will find those networks are an important aspect of the working world.

Firsthand Information

Speaking to people is a good way to learn about an occupation. Visiting a workplace is even better. When you do that, you can experience the work environment, check the level of noise, evalu-

Not all firsthand information comes through a network. Some companies allow you to visit their offices, where you can learn specific details about jobs.

You can learn a lot about an occupation by working part-time in the field.

ate any dangers involved, and see what tasks the workers actually perform. There are several productive ways to acquire this kind of firsthand information.

Some large employers give public tours of their facilities. At the Ford Motor Company assembly plant near Detroit, for instance, you can watch workers performing many different jobs. At Fermilab, a high energy physics research laboratory near Chicago, you can discover the type of environment in which research physicists and technicians work, and you can observe how they deal with possible safety hazards. On tours of these facilities, people who are familiar with the work are generally available to answer questions that visitors may have.

Smaller companies may allow you to visit as well. Guidance counselors often can arrange for you to visit a company that employs workers in the occupations that interest you. They also may be able to arrange for you to do a **job shadowing**, or spend time with a worker in a particular occupation. You also could try getting a position at the company through your school's cooperative education program. When you are in these situations, remember, you are a prospective employee and as such you should use every opportunity to make a good impression. Show interest and enthusiasm by asking informed questions. You may, after all, be applying to these companies for a part-time job next summer or for a full-time job at some time in the future.

Working Part-Time

It is unlikely that you will find a part-time job working in the actual area that interests you. For example, you cannot work part-time as a dentist while in high school, nor can you drive a long-distance freight truck. You can, however, assist in a dentist's office or work on the loading dock of a freight terminal. In these work environments, you will have an opportunity to meet and watch dentists and truck drivers.

In this way, you can learn about the structure of an occupation and the possibilities for promotion and advancement. You also can talk with people who have just entered the field. How did they choose their occupation? How did they qualify for the particular job they have now? Does their occupation meet their expectations? Is there any aspect of the job they do not enjoy? Are they satisfied with their salary and benefits? Would they recommend this occupation to people like you?

Stephen eventually got a part-time job selling stereos. That job has helped him decide that he is on the right occupational path. He particularly enjoys the technical aspects of the equipment he sells—an important consideration in light of his long-term career goal. Stephen realizes that he still needs a plan and a strategy if he wants to reach his goal of owning his own business.

Review Questions

1 ▶ What should you check before using a reference resource?

2 ▶ What is the best way to learn about an occupation?

3 ▶ How can part-time work help you discover the details about the job in which you are interested?

Summary

❑ When you consider any occupation, you should investigate specific facts.

❑ Important details to consider include salary, fringe benefits, promotion prospects, work environment, and the future of the field.

❑ Libraries and librarians are excellent sources of facts.

❑ You can learn about occupations from people through networking.

❑ One of the best ways to learn details about jobs is through tours, job shadowing, cooperative education, or part-time employment.

Vocabulary Exercise

overtime   bonus   networking

salary   fringe benefit   job shadowing

commission   pension

Identify which six of these words are related, and explain their relationship. Give a short definition for each word.

Discussion Questions

1. Which working conditions described in the text do you think you would prefer? Are they similar to the type of occupation that interests you?

2. Why is it important to go beyond general careers resources when looking for information? How can this additional research improve your chances when you are interviewed for a job?

3. Which source of facts do you think would be most helpful to you? Why?

Thinking Further

1. (Math) Find out the low end and high end of the pay scale for workers in three occupations that interest you. Based on those figures, compute the average salary paid to all workers in those occupations. For each occupation, calculate the percentage difference in salary between the low end and the high end of the pay scale.

2. (Listening) It is common and acceptable for people to change careers. Ask an older relative or friend to explain why he or she has or has not ever changed careers. If he or she did change, what skills were transferable?

3. (Writing) Imagine you have just made an appointment to meet a manager to discuss the field that interests you. Make a list of five thought-provoking questions you would like to ask the manager.

4. (Reading) Read the following feature to learn more about jobs.

WHO HELPS PEOPLE WITH PROBLEMS?

You may know someone who has a serious problem. Perhaps an acquaintance is abusing alcohol or some other drug. Maybe a relative is unemployed and is unable to pay the bills. Social workers are trained professionals who can help people when troubles such as these occur.

Social work is one of the major helping professions. Social workers deal with problems of every description, but they mainly help the children, the elderly, and those who are poor. Cindy, for example, works with the county's child protective service. She investigates reported cases of child abuse. If necessary, she starts legal action to remove a child from a home with abusive parents and arranges to place the child in an emergency shelter or foster home.

Cindy's friend Kurt is a social worker for a community agency. Kurt counsels low-income and unemployed men and women. He helps clients apply for food stamps, public housing, Medicaid, and any other welfare programs for which they are eligible.

Lynn is another social worker who works for a government agency. She helps families who are caring for an elderly relative at home. Lynn tells them about programs for the elderly. When the elderly person becomes too frail or ill to remain at home, Lynn helps the family with nursing home placement. She also leads support groups for adult children who take care of their aging parents.

To become social workers, Cindy, Kurt, and Lynn earned bachelor's degrees in social work. Lynn also is working on her master's degree in social work. She wants to become a supervisor.

Another helping profession is psychology. Psychologists help people who are mentally or emotionally disturbed. They interview patients and give them diagnostic tests. Once they understand more about the patient's problems, they design and carry

out a program of therapy. Psychologists work in schools, hospitals, and clinics.

Greg is a psychologist at a mental health clinic. He specializes in helping teenagers with chemical dependency problems and eating disorders. Greg often includes the young person's family in the counseling sessions that he organizes. To earn a doctoral degree in psychology, Greg completed four years of graduate work.

Religious workers also are trained professionals who can help people with their problems and special needs. Rabbi Mark Shapiro, Pastor Patricia Brown, and Father Larry McNeal are on call 24 hours a day to help people with emergencies such as a death in the family or sudden illness. In addition to leading worship services, Pastor Brown visits parishioners who are in hospitals or nursing homes. Rabbi Shapiro counsels couples who are having marital problems. Father McNeal manages a food shelf and used clothing store for the needy. After earning a college degree, rabbis, pastors, and priests must complete three to five years of religious training.

Lawyers, or attorneys, help people in two main ways. Trial lawyers, such as Grace, defend people who have been accused of crimes or who are being sued by other citizens. Her husband, Max, is a lawyer who gives clients advice on matters such as taxes, wills, and contracts.

To be licensed as lawyers, Grace and Max had to attend law school for three years and pass a difficult bar exam. In addition to their regular practices, Grace and Max donate several hours of free legal advice each month to people who cannot afford an attorney.

Social workers, psychologists, religious workers, and lawyers must have a strong desire to help others. Since counseling is a major part of their jobs, they also must be able to communicate effectively. People in the helping professions must have good listening skills. They must be able to inspire trust so clients or patients will feel comfortable talking about their problems.

If you like helping other people, you might consider a career in one of these fields. Here are more opportunities in the Lawyers, Social Scientists, Social Workers, and Religious Workers cluster of the *Occupational Outlook Handbook*:

❑ counselor

❑ human services worker

❑ judge

❑ recreation worker

❑ urban planner

UNIT 3

PLANNING A STRATEGY

▼

▲

WILLIAM'S SEARCH FOR A JOB

William finds a few jobs in the newspaper that sound interesting, so he makes notes that include the following important information: the name and address of the company, the phone number, who to contact, and the job qualifications (below).

William has decided he wants to get a part-time job. His goal is to acquire experience and to earn money. As a first step, he looks through the help-wanted section of the newspaper to see if there are any jobs available that interest him (above).

When William finishes making notes, he calls each company. He speaks clearly and listens carefully because he knows how important first impressions are, even over the phone. William takes more notes as he talks to each employer, and he sets up an appointment to meet with one employer (left).

That evening William tells his father about his plans. His father is very impressed with William's initiative (left).

William asks his father to help him practice interviewing. William knows that will help him to be better prepared. His father assumes the role of the interviewer as they go through each step of the interview (right).

It is the day of the interview, and William is dressed and ready to go. He takes one last look at himself in the mirror to make sure he looks neat and well-groomed. He is satisfied and confident (above).

Part of William's preparation includes picking out the right clothes. He remembers that appearance is another important part of making a good impression (left).

After William completes the form, the store manager calls him into her office. They go over the form and she asks William a few questions (right).

William leaves early enough so that he arrives at his interview a few minutes before his appointment. When he checks in at the main desk, he is given an application form to complete while he waits (above).

After they finish talking, the manager explains that she is taking William on a tour of the store. She shows him where all the merchandise is located and which department he will work in if he is hired (right).

The manager gives William a brief demonstration of how to operate the cash register. She explains that all new employees are trained in all of the store's basic operations (left).

William asks the manager a few more questions, and then the interview ends. William and the manager shake hands, and she tells him that she will call him with her decision within a week (right).

When William gets home, he writes the manager a brief note in which he thanks her for her time. He also includes a few sentences about his continued interest in the job (right).

A few days later the manager calls and asks for William. He can hardly wait to hear what her decision is (below).

When the manager congratulates William on getting the job, he feels excited and proud. Now he can begin to work toward his first goal (below)!

Planning, Goal Setting, and Evaluating Options

When you have studied this chapter, you should be able to:

▶▶ Summarize the basic steps in the career-planning process

▶▶ Give examples of short-term and long-term career goals

▶▶ Research various ways to achieve your career goals

▶▶ Demonstrate the ability to adjust your strategy based on new information

▶▶ Develop a schedule for meeting your career goals

▶▶ Show how to implement and evaluate your career plan

Vocabulary Words

Alternative	Deadline
Apprenticeship	Evaluate
	Implement

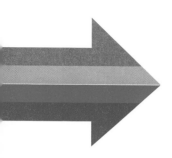

When we left Stephen at the end of the last chapter, he had found a lot of detailed information on marketing and sales jobs. He spent hours in the library, talked with family and friends, visited several different companies, and spoke to a variety of salespeople. He also found an evening job selling stereos in a local electronics store. By gathering all that information, Stephen had gained a thorough knowledge of many different sales occupations.

Stephen's next step is to take his knowledge about sales occupations and shape it into a plan of action. He dreams about being the regional sales manager of a national computer and business machines company. Since he is 17 years old, he is a long way from a corner office in regional headquarters. Stephen knows, of course, that his interests and plan of action may change in the future. For that reason, he wants to develop a plan that will not only advance him toward his career, but also keep open many other options.

In this chapter, we will examine how you can use information about yourself and jobs that interest you to chart a course from where you are today to a successful and satisfying career.

Planning

When Lori and her father plan their yearly vacation, they start months in advance. First, her father reads articles and brochures to find out where they can afford to go. Next, he and Lori discuss the choices to see which place interests them most. Lastly, they make the specific plans—when they will go, how they will get there, and where they will stay. Lori and her father know it is worth spending time to plan their trip, because then they will be more likely to enjoy it.

Although choosing a career is a more serious consideration, the same planning holds true. The more time you spend, the more you can plan a career that suits you. Since a career is much more important and complex than a vacation, it is helpful if you start planning years in advance. You will need to have plenty of time to consider your interests, to investigate options, and to work hard to develop your plan.

An Overview of the Process

This chapter will discuss each step of the planning process in detail. The process itself is made up of several stages. An outline of the stages follows.

A. Planning—In which direction should I go?
   1. Determining goals
   2. Researching possibilities
   3. Narrowing options

The planning process described in this chapter is very similar to the techniques used by successful organizations. It is a basic skill that can be used further in life.

B. Goals and Means—Where and how will I go?
    1. Setting goals
    2. Researching means
C. Strategies and Schedules—Which path should I follow? How long should I take?
    1. Thinking about a strategy
    2. Creating a schedule
D. Action and Evaluation—How am I doing?
    1. Acting on your plan
    2. Mid-course corrections
    3. The importance of evaluation

Steps Already Taken

Planning your career may seem like a difficult and complex task. With the work you have done in the second unit of this book, however, you already have completed the first stage of the process. By studying your own personality, interests, and aptitudes, you have determined some career goals. By looking at various printed and computerized careers resources and viewing career videos, you have increased your knowledge of possible jobs. Finally, you focused on specific details of those jobs and narrowed your options to two or three occupational clusters.

    Let us think about planning a career in another way. If Beth has to write a history paper, she would plan her paper in much the

Review Questions _____

1 ▶ How can you make the complex process of planning your career more manageable? (cont.)

2 ▸ Why is finding out about yourself an important stage in the career planning process?

same way she would plan her career. She knows her goal is to write a good paper on some topic of American history. Her teacher has given the class a list of 20 topics from which to choose. As with the job clusters, Beth can eliminate some topics without further research because they do not interest her. If she wants to narrow her options further, she needs to gather more information. Beth looks in several history books and encyclopedias to research the remaining topics. After she has this information, she is ready to choose a topic for her paper.

Goals and Means

We can continue to compare the two processes in the following way. Just as information about a topic does not make a completed paper, information about occupations does not make a career. Beth has plenty of work to do between now and the day the paper is due. She has selected her topic. Now she needs to develop her thoughts about it into a definite plan of action. To build this plan, she needs a clear understanding of her goals and a carefully pre-pared description of how she will achieve those goals. That plan of action will answer the second question—Where and how will I achieve what matters to me?

Setting Goals

Beth's goal is to write a paper on Thomas Jefferson. That is her long-term goal. If she hopes to reach it, she also needs to establish short-term goals. Those include finding resources in the library, completing the readings, making an outline, writing a rough draft, making revisions, and writing the finished paper.

A long-term goal usually can be broken down into short-term goals, or a series of goals that are easier to achieve. Eventually, if you reach each of your short-term goals, you also will reach your long-term goal. If Ellen's long-term career goal is to become a min-ing engineer, two of her short-term goals may be to pass her math course and to get a part-time job as an assistant to the township engineer. Jay's long-term goal is to become a residential counselor. His short-term goals might include taking a sociology course next year and working as a volunteer at a nursing home in his community.

In both of these cases, the short-term goals lead naturally toward the long-term career goal. You might wonder how to decide which short-term goals you should set in order to reach your career goal. What are the ways in which you can reach your long-term career goal?

For this team, the long-term goal is to win the football game. Every play is a short-term goal to help them achieve their long-term goal.

Researching Means

When Beth is working on her history paper, how can she decide on her short-term goals? She can do so by looking at her teacher's requirements for the paper. It must be based on at least two different sources, and it must be carefully researched and organized, well written, and neat. Once Beth knows the requirements she has to meet to reach her long-term goal, she can set herself some short-term goals.

The same principle holds true in setting short-term career goals. You need to find out what it takes to be successful in the occupation you want to pursue. You already have been introduced to many sources of job information. Those sources can provide you with the education and training requirements for various jobs. You can use the requirements for your occupation to set some of your short-term career goals. In addition, you can talk to people with experience in the field, and you can read books, and current newspaper and magazine articles. This will help you discover how different kinds of people became successful in that particular occupation.

To be a dental hygienist, for example, Sandra must meet some job requirements. They include completing an approved training program, that includes both classroom study and practical experience, and passing an exam to receive certification. When Sandra sees these requirements, she decides to speak with her own dental hygienist to find out which high school courses will best prepare her for the training program. Her hygienist recommends she take science courses, particularly in anatomy and human physiology. The hygienist also says her English and math skills have been helpful, since she has her own business in association with several dentists. The hygienist recommends that Sandra also take a course in psychology. This will help her understand and control the fears that some people have about going to the dentist.

Sandra uses these job requirements and the advice she was given to set specific short-term goals. By beginning to prepare for her future occupation while still in high school, Sandra is better prepared for the next stage of her training. She also can advance more rapidly toward her long-term career goal. In establishing her short-term goals, Sandra is able to begin planning a strategy and setting a timetable for becoming a dental hygienist.

Review Questions

1 ▶ How are short-term goals related to long-term goals?

2 ▶ How can you learn what your short-term career goals should be?

Strategies and Schedules

Once you have set a series of short-term goals, you need to develop a strategy for reaching those goals. There are several things you need to keep in mind. They include making alternate plans in case you cannot reach some of your short-term goals, setting a reasonable schedule for reaching those goals, and considering how you will meet the financial costs of reaching your goal. Carefully planning a strategy and schedule will help you organize your time and resources as efficiently as possible.

By asking other people how they established themselves in a career, you might get ideas for your own life.

For students who plan to go to college, visiting campuses may be part of their overall strategy.

Thinking About Strategy

How can Beth plan her strategy for reaching the short-term goals she has set for writing her history paper? To find the required resources for the paper, for example, she can go directly to the largest library in her area. There, she probably will find all the resources she needs. If not, Beth has another plan ready. She will contact a college library or arrange to borrow books through inter-library loan. The other plan can be referred to as an **alternative**. An alternative is another possible choice.

Sometimes a strategy must be adjusted to include a change in either short-term or long-term goals. If Beth discovered that she could not find enough resources to write the paper on the topic she chose, she would have to switch to another topic. She also may find, as she writes the rough draft, she needs to go back and make some changes in the outline. The key to an effective strategy is to pursue the goals with determination while remaining flexible enough to change the tactics and schedule if necessary.

Remember that one of Sandra's short-term goals was to take a course in human anatomy while in high school. When she discovered that her high school was no longer offering this course, she simply adjusted her strategy. Instead, she will take a summer

(continued on page 150)

FLEXIBILITY: MAKE IT PART OF YOUR LIFE

Now that I think back on how I felt a year ago, I realize how silly I was being. I remember thinking, how can my mother do this to me? I cannot believe she is being transferred. Now we have to move. I have to leave my friends. I have to leave Rusty and our farm.

I tried not to complain, but I was really unhappy. I dreaded moving to the city and living in an apartment. I felt sick every time I thought about leaving my horse, Rusty, behind. I had lived on the farm ever since I was born. Rusty had been given to me as a gift when I was 10. I took care of him completely—from grooming to exercising. I grew to love horses so much that I planned to breed racehorses when I was older.

Now that I have lived in the city for almost a year, I can say it is not so bad. After we moved and I started at my new school, it did not take me long to make a few friends. Adam has become my closest friend. His father is a veterinarian. It was not long before I was helping Adam and his father at the animal hospital. Adam's dad said that I am a natural with animals.

It has worked out great. A few months ago Adam's father hired me part time to help out at the animal hospital. I love the work. I have decided I want to go to school to be a veterinarian. I cannot believe that I thought my career working with animals was over when I left the farm. Now I know that change can work out for the best. ■

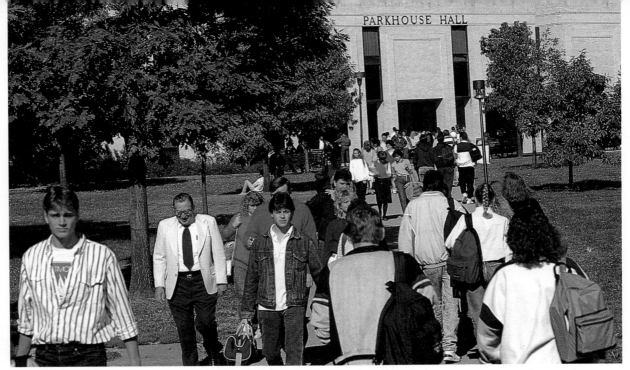

Every student has a different strategy for reaching his or her goals. However, determination and flexibility should always be part of that strategy.

course in anatomy at a local community college. The course is offered at a very low cost, and Sandra will receive credit for it when she begins her training as a dental hygienist.

You probably will have to adjust your career strategy several times before you reach your long-term goal. You may find one of the necessary job skills difficult to develop, or you may discover another occupation that interests you more. You may not be admitted to the vocational-technical school you want to attend, or you may not be able to find a suitable **apprenticeship** in your area. An apprenticeship is a formal system of on-the-job training for teaching people technical or manual skills. As long as your strategy remains flexible, you will be able to make the necessary adjustments along the way.

Creating a Schedule

Most students, unfortunately, have experienced the difficulty of trying to write a paper the weekend before it is due. They may have developed an impressive list of goals and devised a clever strategy when the paper was assigned two months ago, but they neglected to set a schedule for themselves. Every good plan includes **deadlines** for reaching each of the short-term goals. A deadline is a date when a task must be completed. The deadlines might be one week to do research, two weeks for reading and making notes on the material, one week to develop an outline, two weeks to write the rough draft, one week for revisions, and a week to rewrite the final paper. All of these deadlines allow extra time to make adjustments in your goals and strategy. By following this schedule, you will complete your paper on time, even if you have unexpected problems.

A paper may take weeks to write, but a career usually takes years to develop. Even so, it is important to set deadlines for reaching the short-term goals you set for yourself. A schedule will encourage you to begin working toward achieving your goals, even though some of them may take years to accomplish. Creating a schedule also will help you progress as quickly as possible. For example, if you do not take all the courses you need in high school to qualify for a training program, you may not be admitted to the program after graduating.

Of course, your schedule must fit in with your overall strategy, and you may have to change your schedule if your plans change. Once again, it is important to be flexible.

Review Questions

1 ▶ What is the key to an effective strategy?

2 ▶ Why is it important to set a schedule for your career plan?

Action and Evaluation

Even after you set your career plan in motion, you must continually **evaluate** your progress and adjust your strategies if necessary. Evaluating means judging the worth of something. At times your evaluation may result in changing your basic career objectives or even your long-term goal.

Schedules are important in most businesses, because they help people plan so they can meet deadlines.

If you plan to be an entrepreneur, you must take certain steps to set your plans in motion. This entrepreneur is starting by getting his flier printed.

Acting on Your Plan

A journey of a thousand miles begins with the first step. In the same way, even the most ambitious career plan is useless until you set it in motion. That motion may involve completing your algebra homework or looking for a part-time job in your area of interest. You may hesitate to **implement**, or carry out your plan because you are not completely satisfied with it. If you wait to act until you have the perfect plan, however, you may never begin. You should not be afraid to act because you might make a mistake. You can make changes to your plan at any stage if you are unhappy with the progress you are making.

Elise has narrowed her occupational interests to jobs in two clusters. They are mechanics and repairers, and construction and extractive occupations. More specifically, she is interested in becoming either a carpenter or an automotive mechanic. Elise's career strategy includes finding a summer job, but she is not sure whether to look for work in a service station or with a construction company. Because she is unable to make up her mind, Elise is tempted to wait until next summer to find a job.

Instead of waiting, Elise decides to implement her plan by looking for a job in either area. In the end, she takes a job in a small service station where she works alongside an automotive mechanic. She does so after discovering if she takes a job with a construction crew, she will gain little experience in carpentry. Elise knows that taking this part-time job does not mean she has to become an automotive mechanic. If she chooses to become a carpenter in the future, her summer work still will have met her short-term goal of gaining work experience.

Mid-Course Corrections

Elise has the opportunity to find out now whether automotive mechanics is an occupation that suits her. If it does not suit her for some reason, she has plenty of time to explore other options.

Some people have to make major changes in their career plan when they are trying to reach their long-term goals. For instance, people may lose their jobs because of circumstances beyond their control. Foreign competition, changes in technology, or a turn in the economy may cause businesses to close or let workers go. In other cases, people alter the direction of their career path because of changes in their principles or objectives. A customer service representative may leave a company because he does not think it is treating its customers fairly. An operating technician in a power station may discover that the company she works for is not following safety rules carefully enough. Each of these people will need to develop a new career plan.

Even though you may face changes like these, some things will remain the same. They include your personality, your aptitudes, most of your needs and interests, and many of your skills. Whether

Plans will not always work out the way you want, but you usually can make adjustments that will eventually give you the same results.

you are just beginning to plan your career or have worked in an occupation for 20 years, you can use these characteristics as the foundation for a new career plan. You should, however, think through your new plan as carefully as you did your original plan. If you hope to find satisfaction and happiness in your job, every career plan you make needs to be flexible enough to accommodate changes in your life.

The Importance of Evaluation

Every career plan is made up of several elements. Those are a long-term goal, a series of short-term goals, and a strategy and schedule for meeting them. In order to implement your plan successfully, you also should check your progress at frequent intervals. Each time you reach a short-term goal, ask yourself the following questions. Does my long-term career goal still fit my occupational objectives? Will my short-term goals still help me reach my career goal? Have I learned new information that can improve my strategy? Is my schedule for reaching my short-term goals and long-term goal still realistic?

In many situations that require planning, this type of evaluation happens almost automatically. As Beth writes her history paper, for example, she constantly adjusts her strategy and schedule as she learns more about her subject. Of course, in a career plan, the short-term goals do not follow each other in such rapid succession. Even so, they can remind you to stop and evaluate your progress.

Review Questions

1 ▶ What remains constant throughout the changes you make in your career plan?

2 ▶ What should you do each time you reach a short-term goal?

Summary

❑ A career plan is made up of many different stages, some of which you already have taken.

❑ Every career plan should include both short-term and long-term goals.

❑ To set short-term goals, you need to find out what the requirements are in the occupation you want to pursue.

❑ A career strategy can help you achieve your goals within a set time period.

- ❑ After you put your plan into action, you may need to make mid-course corrections.

- ❑ You should check your progress at frequent intervals and make changes when necessary.

- ❑ An effective career strategy needs to be flexible.

Vocabulary Exercise

Use each of the following words in a sentence.

alternative   deadline   implement

apprenticeship   evaluate

Discussion Questions

1. Discuss how you can act on your career plan, even if you have not set long-term goals.

2. What do you think will be the most difficult part of the planning process? How can you make it easier for yourself?

3. What is the most important step in a career plan? Why?

Thinking Further

1. (Reading) One way to research requirements for an occupation is to read books and current newspaper and magazine articles. Find one or two sources of information on an occupation that interests you. While you read, look for specific requirements on which you could base short-term goals.

2. (Writing) Use the information you found in the previous exercise to write a list of short-term goals you might set for your career plan.

3. (Math) Use the list of short-term goals and make a timetable for achieving each one. The deadlines you set should be realistic. Keep in mind the amount of time it will take you to reach your long-term goal.

4. (Reading) Read the following feature to learn more about jobs.

WHO MANAGES WORK AND WORKERS?

Think about the last time you went shopping in a department store. Did you notice what was going on? Chances are, customers were buying items from cashiers, clerks were straightening merchandise, and people were dressing mannequins.

Margaret is the person who manages all these activities at the Westview Mall branch of Chapman's Department Store. This is a busy job and an important one. It is Margaret's responsibility to make sure the Westview store makes a profit. This will show Chapman's executives that Margaret is managing the store well.

Margaret is responsible for the store's success. Its success depends on many factors that Margaret controls. Those factors include advertising, having merchandise the public wants to buy, and displaying the merchandise attractively. Whatever happens at the store will reflect on Margaret. As that branch store's top executive, she directs the work of all the other managerial employees who are responsible for different aspects of the store's operation. There are many employees managing those operations.

Sheila is in charge of the advertising department. She creates all of the ads that appear in the local newspapers.

Jake, Brett, and Sari each manage their own departments. They take care of the

inventory in their departments, manage the employees in their departments, and make sure the amount of money in the cash register matches the amount of merchandise sold. Each of them worked in department stores as a salesperson while they went to college.

Clara, Dwayne, and Franceen work behind the scenes. Clara is the accounting manager. She oversees all the people who handle the financial records for Chapman's. She analyzes these financial records to see if Chapman's is making a profit.

Dwayne manages the employee cafeteria. He is responsible for selecting and pricing the food offered to the employees. He must oversee the cafeteria workers and

ensure that all the food is prepared properly and efficiently.

Franceen is the store's security manager. She and the people who report to her work to prevent theft and vandalism. Franceen also protects the customers, employees, records, merchandise, and equipment.

All of these people report to Margaret. She makes sure that each one does a good job. Margaret does this in many ways. She walks around the store each day to stay in touch with its day-to-day operations. Each Monday morning, she meets with Sheila, Jake, Brett, Sari, Clara, Dwayne, and Franceen. The members of this team discuss their plans for the week ahead as well as any problems they have had.

Margaret also requests that each manager submit a monthly report to her. For example, Jake, Brett, and Sari report on how the current month's sales figures compare with last month's, how much of the department's salary budget is used, and many other details. Franceen reports on any equipment she would like to buy and other details about managing the security force. By reading these reports, Margaret can see whether the store is running smoothly and which employees are performing well.

Margaret's background has prepared her to handle all the responsibilities of her job.

She worked as a salesperson in Chapman's shoe department while she was going to college. She combined this on-the-job experience with a college degree in business administration. After college she was an assistant manager and then a manager in one of Chapman's departments. Her personality suits her position well, too. She is self-confident and flexible, and she communicates well. Because of these traits, her experience, and the responsibility she has, Margaret earns a high salary.

The jobs of store managers, department managers, advertising managers, and security managers are described in the Managerial and Management-Related Occupations cluster in the *Occupational Outlook Handbook*. Other careers in this cluster include:

- ❏ employment interviewers
- ❏ financial managers
- ❏ health services managers
- ❏ hotel managers and assistants
- ❏ labor relations specialists
- ❏ purchasing agents and managers
- ❏ wholesale and retail buyers

Building Job Qualifications

When you have studied this chapter, you should be able to:

➨ Name the basic skills in which you are strong

➨ Suggest how you could improve basic skills in which you are weak

➨ Identify specific skills you would need for jobs or careers that interest you

➨ Explain some ways to acquire qualifications for jobs or careers

Vocabulary Words

Qualification

Work-study

Postsecondary education

Bachelor's degree

Major

Postgraduate degree

As you are finding out, the variety of jobs is almost endless. However, for whatever job you want, you need to have the right **qualifications**. The word *qualification* means any characteristic, skill, or knowledge that enables you to do a job. For example, being able to sew will help you if you want to be a furniture upholsterer or a fashion designer. Sewing is a qualification for those jobs.

Qualification also means any award, degree, or activity that shows you have the appropriate skills or knowledge for a job. Chris wanted to work in a local service station. She told the station manager about her high school courses in auto shop and about her summer job assembling bicycles at a local toy store. These qualifications helped her get the job at the service station, because they showed the station manager that Chris already had skills and knowledge that would be useful for the job.

Improving Your Basic Skills

You may remember from Chapter 4 the basic skills that are essential for most jobs. They are math, written language skills, and spoken language skills. Recently, employers in many fields have complained that their new trainees lack these basic skills. This often happens because students fail to understand how important these skills are. They think they will be able to work without applying what they learn in school when they get a job.

All students can succeed in school. If you have difficulties with basic skills or any particular classes, get help from your teachers and school counselors. You can help yourself, too, by allowing time for schoolwork, by trying hard, and by learning and using study skills. If you need help, though, get it.

Math Skills

As you read in Chapter 4, there are very few jobs that do not involve math skills. This is true of part-time as well as full-time jobs. For example, Jim found his math skills came in handy when he was babysitting. He explained long division to Suzie so she could do her math homework, and he also checked that her parents gave him the right amount when they paid him.

Anyone can improve his or her math skills by practicing them frequently. If you purchase four or five items at your local drugstore or supermarket, add up the prices in your head before you reach the checkout counter. You will know if your calculations were right when the clerk totals the prices of the items. Watch how salesclerks count out your change, and silently count along with them. If you ever take a job that involves ringing up sales, you may have to count out change in the same way.

Math skills are used in many interesting occupations.

Is there any math that goes with your favorite activities? Keep your own baseball statistics, for yourself or for your whole team. Build a bookcase, a clubhouse, or a ramp that requires measuring. If you like to cook, practice halving or doubling your favorite recipes. As with anything you learn, you will find the more you practice math skills, the easier they become.

Basic Written Language Skills

Reading and writing are two other basic skills you will need for any job. Reading is perhaps the most basic skill of all. Yet many adults are unable to read even at an elementary school level. The National Literacy Council estimates that 26 million American adults—one out of seven—cannot read.

Nearly every job involves reading. You may have to read work orders, memos, and instructions from managers or supervisors. People who operate equipment or computers have to read directions. If you work in a department store, you must read price tags on merchandise and sales fliers. In a factory or warehouse, you must read equipment manuals and work orders.

People who are not able to read usually find it hard to advance in their jobs or earn much money. They also miss one of life's great pleasures, the joy of reading a good book, or of learning about things from magazines and newspapers.

One way to improve your reading skills is to look up in the dictionary all of the words that you find unfamiliar. Keep a list of the words that you look up along with their meanings. By the end of a month or a year, you will be surprised at how many new words you have added to your vocabulary.

Anita felt she had a reading problem, because she could not keep up with her required reading in school. She talked to her parents and her English teacher about her concerns. She learned that there are many programs to help people improve their reading skills. The federal government funds Adult Basic Education programs for adults and teenagers. The National Literacy Council and other organizations also have reading programs. In these programs Anita can choose to study privately with a tutor, or she can attend classes with other students.

Anita enrolled in a local reading program. She also made an effort to read books and magazines about sewing, one of her favorite hobbies. When she needed to know the meaning of a word, she looked it up in a dictionary. Then she kept a list of those words. Not only did Anita learn about sewing techniques she wanted to use, but she also greatly improved her reading skills. That, in turn, helped her to improve her prospects for a good job.

Writing is part of many jobs. You may have to write messages, reports, or records. For example, Carlos's boss had introduced new machines to the production line. She wanted her workers to study

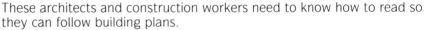

These architects and construction workers need to know how to read so they can follow building plans.

In this photo, every person in the room is using language skills. Do you know why?

the instructions and give her a written report on any difficulties. Because his report and other written communications were so good, Carlos was quickly promoted.

To develop your writing skills, you could begin by writing more often in your free time. Do you leave notes for other family members when you go out, or do you write notes when you take phone messages? If so, be sure they are clear and complete.

Another good way to practice writing is to write letters to distant friends and relatives. You might want to start a journal in which you write your personal feelings about events or experiences. You also could join the school newspaper or literary magazine. When you write, make sure you have a good dictionary handy to check the spelling of words.

In particular occupations, employers want to hire people who have very steady and precise hand movements.

Basic Spoken Language Skills

No matter where you work, you will have to listen and speak to your boss or supervisor. You probably also will have to listen and speak to customers or other employees. That is why spoken language skills are essential skills to have.

You can tell if your listening skills are good if you hear and understand what other people tell you. This test of skills was useful for Ahmed, who often needed to ask others to repeat what they said. He found that instead of listening to people, he was always thinking about what to say next in the conversation, or he was dreaming about something totally different.

If you are like Ahmed, you may want to try to improve your listening skills by following these few steps. When people are talking to you, be sure you understand what they are saying (and take notes, if appropriate). Try not to interrupt them. When they finish talking, wait to answer. Review with them what they said. If part of what they said was unclear, ask them to explain that part over again. At first, you may have a hard time doing these steps. If you practice focusing on the thoughts of others, instead of your own, you will become a better listener.

A good way to develop your speaking skills is to contribute more to conversations with your friends or parents. Ching's adopted family liked to talk about current events and family matters at the dinner table. She began to join in more often with her own opinions and comments. She also began to ask more questions in class, and she made an effort to give complete answers when her teacher called on her. She soon felt more confident about speaking at home and in school.

Review Questions

1 ▶ Describe two ways to practice basic math skills on your own.

2 ▶ What basic communications and language skills should all job applicants master?

3 ▶ Describe four ways you could practice these skills outside the classroom.

Identifying Specific Skills

The three basic skills are essential in almost every job. What about skills that are needed in particular jobs, or in particular groups of jobs? Many of these skills also can be developed during your high school years. Some, such as foreign language skills or science skills, can be learned directly in the classroom. Other skills can be learned through part-time job experiences.

Special Skills for Special Jobs

Do you want to be an appliance repairer, a commercial artist, or an airline pilot? Each job requires a different set of qualifications. Repairers must have a thorough knowledge of appliances, great skill with their hands, and good problem-solving skills. Commercial artists need imagination and artistic ability. They usually must have a two- or four-year degree from an art school or college. Pilots must have several qualifications to get a pilot's license. Just to get a beginner's license to fly, they must be 17 years old, must take a physical exam, and pass both a written test and a performance test.

If a job appeals to you, you already may have some qualifications for it. Kimberly, for example, became interested in being a pediatrician (a doctor who specializes in taking care of children) when she volunteered at her local hospital. She realized that as a volunteer she was learning some of the skills pediatricians need. Of course, she also knew there still was a lot to learn.

You often can learn about job qualifications by reading the appropriate help-wanted advertisements.

Review Questions

1 ▶ Name some specific skills that would be required of an appliance repairer.

2 ▶ Name some specific qualifications that would be required of a person if he/she wishes to begin learning to fly an airplane.

3 ▶ What are three types of sources you could consult to identify specific qualifications needed for other jobs?

What Qualifications Will You Need?

How can you find out what skills and knowledge to acquire for jobs that interest you? Start by checking vocational and career books in your local library. You learned about these in Chapter 6. Books like the *Occupational Outlook Handbook* describe the educational qualifications you need for any particular job. Some of these books also list professional associations you can write to for more information about particular careers.

Another way to research the qualifications you will need is to consult catalogs of junior colleges, technical schools, and vocational schools. These list the specific courses they offer that apply to different jobs and occupations. Catalogs also can tell you how much such training costs and how long it takes. You also could contact major companies in your area or your state government to find out about qualifications for particular jobs.

Your guidance counselor can suggest other sources where you can find out about skills and qualifications that are needed for particular occupations. He or she can also give you an aptitude test to see if you have the personal characteristics you need for certain occupations. For example, if you are detail oriented and a good problem solver, you have two abilities needed by successful research scientists and labor relations specialists.

(continued on page 166)

LEARNING BY WORKING

Dear Kayla,

Hi! How are you? I miss you a whole bunch. How is your new school? Do you like it there? You are not going to believe the new program they started at Pennswood High. I have been involved in it for over two months, and I love it. You will wish you never had to move to the Midwest.

The program is called a work-study program. I go to school for half of each weekday and then I go to work for the other half. My guidance counselor suggested I do this because she thought the experience would be good for me, especially since I do not plan to go to school after high school.

The first thing my counselor did was ask me what interests I have. I told her I liked chemistry, but that I also was interested in the health care field. She had a great idea! She thought I might enjoy working at a lab in a hospital. That way I would be combining both of my interests. She told me that at the beginning I would be doing the filing and cleaning up, but I figured it would be a start. She gave me some numbers to call about getting work and told me to check back with her the next week to tell her which position I wanted to take.

You will never believe it! I only had to call two hospitals before I was able to create a work-study position. As it turns out, every day I go to school from 8 to 11, and then I go to work from 12 to 3. The lab technician who is my boss said that if I want to I can stay later than 3 any day of the week. She said that I will learn a lot by watching what other people in the lab do. She also said that there are good opportunities for jobs in hospital laboratories for high school graduates.

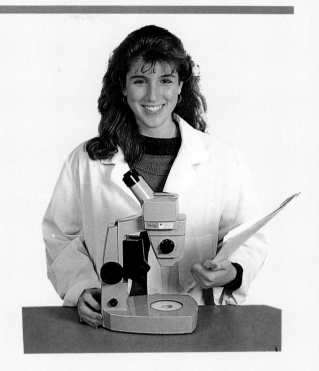

I really like working in the lab. I clean up after the technicians do their lab work. I schedule appointments for people to come in for tests. I do a lot of filing, too. Sometimes when my boss is not too busy, she lets me watch her work, and she explains everything she does. I am really glad my guidance counselor suggested I look for work in a lab.

Kayla, I wish you could be here so we could work at the lab together. Does your new school have a program like Pennswood's? If it does, and if you work in a lab, too, then maybe we can work together after we finish high school!

Write soon, and let me know how you like your new school and your new home.

Your friend,
Dina

Ways to Acquire Particular Qualifications

There are many ways to acquire qualifications for your first full-time job. You could learn some of the skills at part-time jobs or through volunteer work. Many of the qualifications you need, however, will come from your education and training. If you choose your junior high school and high school courses wisely, every course you take and do well in can be an important step in preparing for a particular job. Every level of education you complete—junior high school, high school, college—can provide you with better qualifications. Therefore, staying in school can enable you to choose from a wider range of jobs and careers.

High School Courses

As you have read, courses in English and math are good ways to prepare for any career. You will use these skills no matter what career you choose. Other courses also are useful in many jobs. Typing and word processing are a part of many jobs in today's world. Secretaries, technicians, and corporate executives often spend part of their days working at computer keyboards.

Other courses teach skills for specific careers or career clusters. Tanya wanted a job in medicine, but was unsure what she wanted to do. She took many courses in science and math—good qualifications for nurses, paramedics, and doctors. Jerome, who wanted to be a corporate executive, took many business courses. These

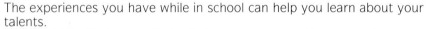
The experiences you have while in school can help you learn about your talents.

This landscape architect is preparing a drawing of a buiding site. Drawing is a major part of his occupation.

included typing, business English, bookkeeping, business math, business machines, and computer courses.

High school is a good place to begin developing your talents and aptitudes into skills. Do you think you have good mechanical abilities? If you do, then take auto shop, mechanical drawing, or metal shop courses. Do you think you have a talent for the performing or fine arts? If so, then take any art courses your high school offers. Try out for a talent show or design scenery for the class play. Keep in mind that even though such activities are fun, they can help you learn valuable skills and learn about what you like to do. You can develop new skills even while you enjoy yourself.

Keep in mind that high school classes cannot teach you everything you need to know to qualify for most jobs. Some employers also look for accomplishments in school and extracurricular activities that show them your aptitudes. Do you often run the film projector in school? Then you can surely operate a photocopier or facsimile machine. Are you strong in math? You could certainly take work orders and make out customers' bills at a warehouse. If you are the editor of the school newspaper, then you could help with the company newsletter. Being a member of a sports team shows that you work well with a group and can follow directions—two skills employers look for in employees.

Work-Study Programs

Many school districts offer **work-study,** or cooperative education opportunities. Their purpose is to help individuals apply classroom learning in an actual job setting. Students attend school for only part of each weekday. The rest of the time they work for local businesses. The schools match the students' skills and interests to the businesses that employ them. Paddy was interested in working in retail sales, so he was given a part-time job to train as a salesclerk in a pet store. Carol Ann was interested in electronics, so she trained in a television repair shop. Both Paddy and Carol Ann found that their employers and co-workers helped them learn skills they needed for their jobs.

Employers like to hire applicants with work-study experience, because they know they are getting employees who already have worked in a job. Work-study programs also let students investigate a particular job and decide if it is right for them.

Postsecondary Education

Many jobs require education and training beyond high school, or **postsecondary education**. After graduating from high school, you could take fashion design or heating and air-conditioning courses

You can gain specific qualifications by taking postsecondary courses.

at a private vocational school. You might enroll in a technical school that teaches people how to operate heavy equipment, such as cranes and bulldozers. Business and secretarial schools offer training in clerical skills. A number of schools offer special training in computer operations and repairs.

These postsecondary vocational schools are designed to prepare you for specific careers. Some also will work hard to get you a job after you finish the program. In fact, some employers prefer to hire graduates of these programs, because they know such graduates have received proper training. In order to find out if a vocational school can provide students with the job opportunities it promises, it always is a good idea to check out its track record for job placement of graduates before you register there.

Postsecondary education can cost several thousand dollars. You may need a loan to finance your training. Many schools will allow you to pay in monthly installments or on a semester basis. Many schools hold evening or weekend classes so students can work during the day to pay for the courses.

Typical two-year postsecondary education opportunities are found at vocational-technical schools and at community colleges or junior colleges. They provide specific skill training for particular occupations, or academic transfer courses that often are accepted for credit at four-year higher education institutions.

Four-Year Higher Education

Four-year colleges and universities provide many people with a **bachelor's degree,** which is a four-year program ending with a bachelor of arts (B.A.), or a bachelor of science (B.S.). Many jobs and professions require this qualification. You must have a bachelor's degree to become a political scientist, for example, or an elementary school teacher, or a dietitian.

Ryan started his bachelor's degree at a two-year college. He took a number of general courses, including English, history, math, and a foreign language. His friend Karl went to a four-year college immediately after high school and took similar courses the first two years. After two years of general courses, Ryan transferred to the four-year college. He and Karl were able to choose a **major** at the four-year college to study in their final two years. A major is a course of study in a particular field, such as chemistry or English.

Bachelor's degrees may lead to specific jobs, or they may be used as qualifications for general occupational fields. If you want to be a teacher, you can major in education. Your degree would qualify you to teach in a junior high school or high school. Other majors allow you to work in a variety of fields. People with psychology majors, for example, may become corporate personnel officers, parole officers, or government administrators.

A college degree not only tells employers the type of information you have learned, but also that you probably can master complex information in related fields.

A bachelor's degree also is needed by those who wish to earn **postgraduate degrees**. Students who do this go to graduate school. There they may earn a master's degree or a doctorate degree. Postgraduate degrees also include professional degrees such as Doctor of Medicine and Bachelor of Law.

Studies show that, over their working lives, college graduates usually earn many hundreds of thousands of dollars more than nongraduates. College graduates also are likely to receive faster promotions than nongraduates. However, a college education usually is very expensive. If you choose to go to college, you will have to plan carefully to save money. There also are other options, such as loans, scholarships, and financial aid plans.

Explore opportunities for scholarships and financial aid with your guidance counselor. Many colleges offer scholarships to students with good grades. Most counselors have books on how to apply for scholarships and loans. Many guidance departments have computer programs that list the scholarships available and the necessary qualifications. There also are referral agencies that will help you find out about scholarships and loans for a fee.

Work Experience

Another source of qualifications is part-time employment. Evening and weekend jobs not only help you earn money, they also help you acquire skills. These skills can be an important qualification when you apply for your first full-time job. You will learn more about applying for jobs in the following chapter.

Review Questions

1 ▶ Name three different levels of education that can provide useful qualifications for jobs.

2 ▶ What is the purpose of work-study programs?

3 ▶ What are two types of programs that may be offered at community colleges?

Summary

- [ ] Qualifications include the skills that enable people to do their jobs, and degrees and certifications related to these skills.

- [ ] The basic skills—math, written language, and spoken language—are essential for almost every job.

- [ ] People can improve their basic skills by finding ways to practice them more.

- [ ] Most jobs require people to have some specific skills.

- [ ] Job-specific skills can be identified in several ways, such as by studying career reference works, contacting major companies or your state government, and consulting guidance counselors.

- [ ] People can gain many career skills by choosing appropriate courses at high school, including work-study courses.

- [ ] Postsecondary and college courses also can provide valuable qualifications for getting jobs.

- [ ] Temporary jobs and summer jobs are another way to gain useful qualifications.

Vocabulary Exercise

True or False?

1. An example of a job qualification is the need for money.

2. Work-study and cooperative education both mean students are applying coursework in related jobs.

3. Postgraduate education usually describes vocational programs you take after high school.

4. A major is part of a bachelor's level program.

5. The B.A. and the B.S. are both two-year programs.

6. You can study general courses for a bachelor's degree in a community college or in a four-year college.

Discussion Questions

1. What additional ways can you think of that would enable you to practice math skills during your everyday life? Think of activities you like, such as entertainment and travel.

2. Can you think of any job where reading would *not* be needed at some point during your workweek? Make a list of suggestions, and then think through each job and see if you can find tasks where some reading might play a part.

3. What qualities does a good speaker have? Think about people you have admired for the way they present ideas in conversation. Write down the different qualities you come up with and discuss how people could develop these qualities.

4. How many jobs can you think of that might require foreign language skills? Try to think of at least one from each cluster of jobs discussed in Chapter 6.

5. Think of a career that appeals to you. What kind of beginner's job might make a good work-study experience for a student participating in a cooperative education class?

Thinking Further

1. (Math) A. You have decided to take the advice in this chapter, and you are mentally adding up the purchases you make at a drugstore in a neighboring state. The items you buy include mouthwash at $3.60, a toothbrush at $2.43, dental floss at $1.99, toothpaste at $1.99, and soap at $1.99. What is the total for the purchases you have made?
B. The cashier asks you to pay $12.72. For extra practice you decide to work out the state's rate of sales tax without looking at the bill. What rate does the state charge?

2. (Listening) The next time you have your career course, take notes on what your teacher says. Take rough notes during the class, and write them up afterward while you still remember the additional information discussed. How much do you think you missed? Now get together with some classmates and compare their versions with your own. Were your notes more complete than theirs? If your teacher requests it, combine your notes and those of your classmates and show the finished product to your teacher.

3. (Writing) Base this project on the job you have selected for your own career, a job from a cluster that appeals to you, or any job that seems interesting. Following the advice in this chapter, identify some of the qualifications the job calls for, and write up a plan for developing the qualifications you have identified. Name some high school courses you will have to take, and indicate what types of postsecondary, college, or postgraduate qualifications you will need. Also include any type of work experience you think would be helpful.

4. (Reading) Read the following feature to learn more about jobs.

WHO SELLS PRODUCTS AND SERVICES?

When you think of buying and selling, you probably think of stores. However, there are many other settings in which products and services are sold. Let us look at a few.

Paulina, Lenny, and Frances sell office supplies. Their jobs are very different, however, even though Lenny and Frances work for the same company.

Lenny and Frances work for a wholesaler called Sunshine Office Products. A wholesaler is a company that buys huge quantities of goods from manufacturers and resells them to retail stores as well as to schools, hospitals, and other institutions. Lenny's and Frances's customers are store managers and institutional purchasing agents who may order 500 boxes of pencils or 300 rolls of tape at one time.

Paulina, on the other hand, works as a salesperson at Sharp's Stationery, a retail store. A typical customer at Sharp's buys a pen or a small quantity of some other item. Sharp's purchases much of its stock from Sunshine Office Products and, in fact, is one of Lenny's customers.

Lenny is a field representative for Sunshine. Like the other field representatives, he does not have an office. He spends his time visiting stationery stores and other big buyers of office supplies. His hours are flexible,

but he does most of his work between the hours of nine and five because that is when his customers are available.

During these visits, Lenny uses catalogs, brochures, and samples to promote the goods he is selling. He tells customers about special deals Sunshine is offering, and he gives them pointers on how to set up displays that sell more merchandise. Sometimes Lenny demonstrates a new gadget or he gives potential buyers samples of items.

Frances, an inside sales worker for Sunshine, works nine to five in an office and never meets customers face-to-face. She takes their orders over the telephone. She also places calls to try to get business from

potential customers and from old customers who have not placed any orders lately. In addition to selling, Frances's duties include processing customers' orders and keeping track of products that need to be reordered from manufacturers. If she succeeds as an inside sales worker, Frances may advance to a job in the field like Lenny's.

All successful sales workers—whether they are wholesale, retail, in an office, or on the road—need enthusiastic, persuasive personalities to interest people in the goods they are selling. They do not need education beyond high school, although salespeople with college degrees are more likely to advance into management positions.

Retail sales workers often start their careers as teenagers, working after school or in cooperative education programs. They generally get their training on the job, from store managers or co-workers. Small retail stores offer little opportunity for advancement. At Sharp's, for example, the owner manages the store himself and employs only two other salesclerks, so there is no job to which Paulina can be promoted. In big department stores, people who do well in retail sales can become managers. Increasingly, however, department stores are hiring college graduates as management trainees instead of promoting people.

Stores are open on weekends, so people in retail sales often work Saturdays or Sundays, and have off one or two weekdays. They also may work evening hours.

Most retail sales workers earn very low wages at first. Their incomes vary widely according to how much experience they have and what they are selling. Retail sales workers who sell clothing are among the lowest paid. Those who sell cars and boats are among the highest paid. Sales workers often earn a combination of commissions and wages or salaries.

In the *Occupational Outlook Handbook*, sales workers' jobs are described in the Marketing and Sales Occupations cluster. Other jobs in this cluster include:

- ❑ cashiers
- ❑ counter and rental clerks
- ❑ insurance sales workers
- ❑ manufacturers' sales workers
- ❑ real estate agents and brokers
- ❑ securities and financial services sales representatives
- ❑ travel agents

10

How to Get Jobs and Work Experience

When you have studied this chapter, you should be able to:

➡️ Discuss child labor laws

➡️ Explain what a work permit is and what kinds of jobs you can find with and without a work permit

➡️ List several techniques for finding jobs

➡️ Discuss how a private or volunteer job can become a business

Vocabulary Words

Work permit

Private job

Junior volunteer

Help-wanted advertisement

Situation-wanted advertisement

Placement service

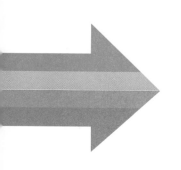

Working while you are a teenager is valuable for several reasons. You can gain important information about the work world from such jobs. You also can build useful basic or occupational skills or qualifications that you will need as an adult. Future employers will admire your motivation and dependability.

Sheila, for example, was interested in becoming an architect. This career requires a college degree, so Sheila was working hard in school to earn high grades in order to get a college scholarship. In addition, she had free time after school each day so she decided to look for part-time positions that might help her prepare for this career. She wanted to work on a construction site, but this was not permitted until she was 18. As a 15-year-old, however, she *was* allowed to do odd jobs for an architect's office. She took the job in order to learn more about what architects do and to gain experience.

Jobs for Teenagers

Like Sheila, you will find that your options for getting part-time work are limited by federal and state laws. However, there still are many opportunities for work. All you have to do is look for them. In fact, seeking work as a teenager can teach you many techniques that will be useful to you when you are an adult. You can even start your own business in your teens, though the type of work you can do is, once again, limited by law.

Child Labor Laws and Work Permits

The laws that limit people's employment options are called child labor laws. They include some federal laws and some state laws. This means that the details of the laws will differ according to where you live. The purpose of the child labor laws, however, is similar in all states across the United States.

At the start of this century, some factories, farms, and other businesses gave children as young as seven years old difficult and even dangerous jobs. These children often worked long hours for low pay. Besides the health hazards, such work kept the children from attending school. This often barred them from getting better jobs when they were older. Lawmakers began to pass laws to protect children from these abuses. A federal law, the Fair Labor Standards Act, passed in 1938, prevents businesses from employing anyone under 14 years of age (though families and the agricultural industry still can hire younger children). This federal law states that when you are 14 or 15, you can only have certain safe jobs, and only for a few hours each day.

State laws generally require that workers over 14 years of age get a **work permit**, or employment certificate, to have business

If you seek work when you are a teenager, you will learn many useful techniques to apply later in life.

jobs. This certificate may be needed until you are 16, or 18, depending on the state in which you live. Before looking for a job, learn about your state's child labor laws by calling your state's labor department. To find out where to obtain a work permit, check with your school's guidance counselors. In most states, they can give you the application forms you will need.

With a work permit, you may be able to work in a variety of places, from gas stations and grocery stores to hospitals or farms. The United States Department of Labor estimates that 5 million people between the ages of 14 and 18 hold jobs at some time each year. More children work on farms than anywhere else.

Of course, your parents or guardians also may have rules about what kinds of work you can do, how many hours a week you may work, and what time you must be home from work. They know whether or not you can handle a job in addition to your school-work and extracurricular activities. Always discuss your plans with your parents or guardians before you look for a job.

Working in Private Jobs

If you are too young to get a work permit, it is still legal for you to work at **private jobs**. In a private job, you generally work for an individual or a family rather than for an organization. Your own neighborhood may offer many opportunities for private jobs, such as babysitting, raking lawns, and washing cars. Your neighbors also may hire you to walk and feed their pets when they are away, or to collect their mail and water their plants. Perhaps you can help your neighbors with housework, or with chores, such as painting, gardening, or serving food at parties.

You also can do volunteer work. Volunteer work does not pay money but it can give you valuable experience for later employment. You could be a **junior volunteer**, helping patients in a hospital or nursing home. Many religious or nonprofit civic organizations need volunteer workers, too. You could sort cans and bottles at a city or county recycling center, read to a blind person, distribute food and clothing to needy people, help out at an animal shelter, or run errands for someone who is ill.

There are many jobs you can get in your own neighborhood.

There are many different kinds of volunteer work that teenagers can do. These teenagers are collecting clothing for the needy.

Before accepting a private job or volunteer work, make sure you understand what is expected of you. If the job requires equipment or supplies, such as a lawn mower or paint brushes, find out if you should bring your own or if you will be using your employer's. Even if you are not being paid, you may need to wear a uniform or to follow a strict schedule so that others can depend on you. Before you agree to take any job, find out about the rules of the job as well as the kind of work you will be doing.

All of the job-related activities you participate in will provide valuable experience you can use when beginning to apply for full-time jobs in the future. Job-related activities can give you ideas for starting your own business someday, too.

Entrepreneurship

Instead of working for one person or business at a time, you may decide that you wish to start a small business of your own. You can do this even if you are only allowed to do private jobs such as washing cars or doing yardwork. Running a business carries more responsibility than finding jobs one at a time, and it is more complicated. It also can be more rewarding.

A person who starts a business is called an entrepreneur. Many entrepreneurs base their businesses on work they did in individual private jobs or as volunteers. What is the difference between working at private jobs or as a volunteer and running a business? Let the story of Carl's Cookie Company tell you.

Carl's Cookie Company is an example of volunteer work that turned into a small business. Carl baked some oatmeal cookies to help a neighborhood charity organization raise money at a street fair. The cookies sold out quickly. After that, Carl realized that he could earn money for himself by baking cookies if he could find grocery stores that would be willing to sell them.

After making a list of small grocery stores in his town, Carl baked another batch of cookies. Then he took them to the stores. He gave each store owner a sample and a sales pitch. Some of them agreed to buy Carl's cookies to sell in their stores.

If you want to be a successful entrepreneur, you should be good at organizing resources.

At first, Carl did all the baking on weekends and took the cookies to the stores on his bicycle each Monday after school. Since he did all the work himself, he got to keep all the money he earned. Then he started receiving more orders, so he began baking and selling different kinds of cookies—peanut butter, chocolate chip, and oatmeal. Soon, Carl discovered that he could no longer do all the work alone. He needed to hire help.

Carl decided to ask some friends to join him in his cookie business. Sandra and her brother Jack began working for Carl, baking the chocolate chip cookies at their home—using Carl's recipe, of course. Gene soon was hired to help, and he bakes the peanut butter cookies, while Carl continues to bake the oatmeal cookies. Carl now makes deliveries on Thursdays as well as Mondays. Out of the money Carl receives from the grocery store owners, he pays his helpers and purchases ingredients for more cookies. The money that is left over after Carl pays these expenses is his profit. In order to find still more buyers for his cookies, Carl now plans to spend some of his profit on advertising.

Carl is on his way to becoming a successful entrepreneur. He and other successful entrepreneurs have three qualities in common. First, they have the ability to think of a product or service they can sell at a profit. Second, entrepreneurs are willing to take risks. Carl risked time and money to bake the samples he gave to the store owners. Now he may risk some of his profits to pay for advertising. The third quality of a successful entrepreneur is the ability to organize resources. Carl's resources include his recipes, the ingredients for the cookies, the people who help him do the work, and the bicycle he uses to take the cookies to stores.

Carl enjoys the challenges of running a business, and he earns more money than he could by selling oatmeal cookies at only two or three grocery stores. However, being an entrepreneur is not for everyone. Jack often says he could not stand the pace, and he is glad to be just a paid helper. Each person must decide what suits him or her the best when considering employment options.

Review Questions

1 ▶ What limits does the federal Fair Labor Standards Act of 1938 set on work by teenagers?

2 ▶ How long will you need a work permit?

3 ▶ What kinds of jobs can you do without a work permit?

4 ▶ Name three qualities that successful entrepreneurs have in common.

Finding Jobs

Whether you want to get a job, or be an entrepreneur, finding work takes determination and effort. Many people may be competing for the kinds of job opportunities you want. You may have to inquire about many jobs before you are offered one that is suitable. As an entrepreneur, you may be turned down by many companies before you find any that will accept your product for the price you want. Therefore, to give yourself the best chance of success, you must find as many opportunities as possible.

(continued on page 182)

WHERE THERE IS A WILL THERE IS A WAY

This year I met and became friends with some people at school who really care about the environment. The first big thing I did with them was to get the cafeteria staff to stop using plastic foam containers, cups, and plates. Thanks to our work, the lunchroom will use only paper products next year.

During the year, I learned a lot about garbage. I learned that plastic trash is bad because it takes a long time to break down in landfills. I also found out that America has too much trash, and most of it is paper.

I asked my mother if the publishing company she works for recycles used paper. She told me she had tried to start them recycling paper, but her small company did not produce enough waste paper to interest the paper recycling company.

I devised a plan to collect used paper from many small companies to have enough to sell to the paper recycling company. Then at the beginning of summer vacation, I put my plan into action. I contacted dozens of companies. Most of them were eager to help by recycling office paper, but they were too small to do it on their own.

Then I called the recycling company. They told me the minimum weight of paper they would accept and how much they would pay. I realized I could make money and help the environment.

In June a friend and I borrowed my brother's pickup truck and started our business. We scheduled weekly paper collections at the companies that wanted our services.

They did not have to pay us; all they had to do was stack their paper together. We collected until the truck was full. Then we drove to the recyclers who weighed the paper and paid us for it.

We used some of our money to get fliers printed. We distributed them to all the offices and businesses in our area. In one week our business doubled. By the end of the summer we had two more friends helping us. We were using two pickup trucks to collect paper from over 100 companies.

We did so well that we plan to keep working even after school starts. We will work part-time to keep our recycling business going. When I graduate from high school at the end of the year, I think I will make recycling my full-time business. ■

You should tell your friends when you are looking for a job. They might know about job openings of which you are not aware.

Help from Friends and Relatives

Claire's first step in finding a summer job was to let her friends, relatives, and neighbors know she was looking for one. She did not have a specific job in mind, but she wanted to get work experience. The idea of earning money seemed attractive, too. She found out that her aunt, who ran a small grocery store, needed help. A neighbor offered to hire her to do housework. Her cousin told her about a job notice he had seen on a bulletin board. She discovered that people she already knew were very good sources of information about jobs that were available.

She told as many people as possible that she wanted to find a job. This is an excellent idea. Even people who are unable to offer you work might know others who can. A recommendation from a friend or relative may help persuade an employer to hire you—though you also must have the necessary skills.

Claire was careful not to put pressure on other people to help her find work. She just let them know about her search and asked them to let her know if they heard of any jobs. Of course, she remembered to thank everyone whether they could help her or not. She also recognized that even if they could not help her find a job now, they might be able to later.

Your School's Guidance Office

Claire also talked to the counselors in the guidance department at her school to let them know she was looking for a job. School guidance departments often are approached by local employers who

Common Classified Ad Abbreviations

AA	affirmative action	NS	nonsmoker
Adm. asst.	administrative assistant	O/T	overtime
Appt.	appointment	Perm.	permanent
B.A., B.S.	Bachelor of Arts, Bachelor of Science	Pos.	position
Co.	company	PR	public relations
Emp. agy.	employment agency	P/T	part time
EOE	equal opportunity employer	R & D	research and development
Exc. opty.	excellent opportunity	Refs.	references
Exp'd.	experienced	Resp. incl.	responsibilities include
Exp. nec.	experience necessary	Sal. reqs.	salary requirements
Exp. pref.	experience preferred	Temp.	temporary
Exp. req.	experience required	To $300	to $300 per week
Fee pd. (F/P)	fee paid by employer for job placement	W/P	word processing
F/T	full time	wpm/50+ wpm	words per minute, 50 or more words per minute
H.S. grad.	high school graduate	$5/hr.	$5 per hour
LPN	licensed practical nurse	$950/mo.	$950 per month
M/F/H/V	male, female, handicapped, veteran	$15K–$20K	$15,000 to $20,000 per year
Mgr.	manager		

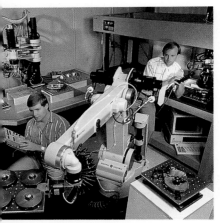

The job outlook for people, like these programmable controllers, who work on computers is very favorable.

have part-time jobs suitable for teenagers. On occasion, guidance counselors also actively search for jobs for teenagers with local businesses. Be aware, though, that guidance counselors are likely to tell several students about a particular job opening. This means you may find yourself competing with friends from your own class for jobs. Try not to let that discourage you, though. Competition is a normal part of many friendships.

Bulletin Boards and Store Windows

Jobs that teenagers are qualified to do are frequently advertised in store windows and on bulletin boards. Many store merchants and fast-food chains place help-wanted signs in their windows. People who need help in their homes or businesses often put job notices on bulletin boards in their community. You will find these bulletin boards in community centers, supermarkets, drugstores, and other locations near your home and school.

In addition to scanning bulletin boards for notices about work she could do, Claire also put up her own notice to advertise her services. Be sure to check with a parent or guardian before doing this. A bulletin board notice should say what kind of work you want to do (Claire said she would do all domestic tasks) and how an employer can get in touch with you. You also may want to list your qualifications on your notice. Only include essential information so it will be neat and easy to read.

Newspaper Advertisements

Employers also advertise jobs in newspapers. Claire scanned the listings under the help-wanted heading in the classified advertising section of her local newspaper. Most of the **help-wanted advertisements** were for full-time jobs or work that required adult skills. Some, however, were for jobs that teenagers over the age of 16 could do. Sunday newspapers usually have more job ads than weekday newspapers. To avoid wasting your time and an employer's time on inquiries about jobs you are unable to do or do not want, read each listing carefully before you respond to it.

Newspapers' classified advertising sections also list **situation-wanted advertisements**. These are placed by people looking for jobs. Like bulletin board notices, they should include all the essential information but should be brief. Newspapers charge money to print situation-wanted ads. Before you decide to place one, find out what it will cost. Claire decided against it because she had not decided exactly what type of job she wanted.

WAITER/WAITRESS

Neil's Cafe, Rt. 80. P/T nights/wkends.
Exp. pref. but not necessary.
Pleasant evrnmnt. Must have
own transportation.
Apply in person or call:

Neil Brown 555-3912.

Review Questions ____

1 Why is it important to tell friends, relatives, and neighbors when you are looking for a job?

2 If your school's guidance office tells you about a job opening, can you count on getting that job? Why? Why not?

3 Name four other places from which you can learn about available jobs.

Placement Services

Some communities have placement services that help teenagers find after-school, weekend, or summer jobs. Those services often are run by civic or religious organizations. A **placement service** gathers information about available jobs, as well as about people who want to work. The placement service tries to match job-seekers with employers who need their skills.

To find a job through a placement service you must register with the service. As a rule, these services are free to teenagers, but always ask if you must pay a fee to register. Claire's community placement service not only asked for a fee, but also required information about her skills, her grades, the kinds of job she wanted, and when she could work. Claire also had to get written permission from her parents in order to register.

Some communities provide jobs for teenagers in other ways. Many city governments work with local businesses to offer summer jobs to teens. If you live near a city, you might want to call the mayor's office to see if programs like that exist.

Making the Extra Effort

The more actively you seek a job, or seek customers for the service you offer, the more work you are likely to find. Claire's wide search gave her several opportunities for work. It is no different if you wish to start your own business. Suppose you want to earn money painting homes. You may get a customer or two just by telling your

Researching jobs takes many forms. An older brother or sister may be able to give you leads on jobs.

closest neighbors. However, to turn this service into a business of your own, that is, to be an entrepreneur, you will do best if you expand your search for work and conduct it in a well-organized way. You are also likely to get more work in your business by doing a good job for the customers you already have.

Distributing a Flier

One way to get the word out that you are looking for work is to create a flier, photocopy it, and distribute it to friends' families and neighbors who you know well. A flier is inexpensive to make, and it can be a very effective way to advertise your services. Once again, it is important to discuss your plans for seeking work with your parents or guardians before you begin.

Eileen enjoyed creating a flier for her dog-walking service. To make sure all of the important information was clearly presented, she sketched a stylish picture of three dogs on a leash. She also used large letters and numbers to give the main details of her service, including her name, the work she was offering, her telephone number, and the rates she was charging. Then she found a store in her neighborhood to photocopy her flier for her.

Do not clutter a flier with too much information. Make it as neat and attractive as possible. You can deliver the flier to your friends' and neighbors' homes. Perhaps if you are working with other people, you can make a plan for distributing the flier. The more people who see the flier and read it, the better your chances of getting work. That is why it is important to distribute the flier to as many friends and neighbors as possible.

Before you distribute a flier anywhere in your community, discuss your plans with your parents or guardians.

The impressions people present after they are hired are very important.

Door-to-Door Advertising

Calling on your friends and neighbors door-to-door to tell them about the service you offer is another effective way to get customers. In addition to letting people know about your services, it gives them an opportunity to meet you and decide whether they would feel confident about hiring you. Unlike some other means of advertising your services, making door-to-door calls will not cost you any money, but it does require a lot of time and energy.

Also, before you begin going door-to-door, you should discuss your plan with your parents or guardians to be sure you have their permission. Some neighborhoods are more appropriate than others for door-to-door calls. Your parents may not approve of your plans, especially if you live in, or will be visiting, neighborhoods with higher crime rates. Depending on the neighborhood, they may permit you to go door-to-door with a friend but not by yourself. If you do obtain your parent's permission to go door-to-door, be careful. Do not go into people's homes or accept food or drink from them unless you know them very well.

If possible, do some research before you begin going door-to-door. Eileen, for example, who was looking for dog-walking jobs, already knew which of her neighbors had dogs. In fact, she knew every dog within six blocks of her home. When she followed up on her flier with personal calls, she knew which houses to visit. This enabled her to spend her time efficiently, calling on only those people most likely to want her services.

If you are making door-to-door visits, you also can ask neighbors you know to refer you to people in the neighborhood who you do not know. Similarly, if someone you call on is not in need of your services, ask him or her to refer you to someone who might be. Most strangers will be more willing to listen to you if you mention that someone they already know suggested you call on them.

Making a Good Impression

To win customers you must not only convince them that they need the service you are offering, but also that you can perform the service well. You must give customers the impression that you are capable, trustworthy, and dependable.

When you meet people who might have jobs to offer you, try to look, speak, and act like the kind of person you or your parents might hire for that job. Would you want a messy-looking person to clean your house or wash your car? Most people would prefer someone whose appearance demonstrates neatness and cleanliness, even if the jobs themselves are messy. On the other hand, they probably would feel just as uncertain about you if you showed up in a business suit to do work around their home.

Look at the two people in the picture. Which one do you think will make the best impression on others and why?

Review Questions _____

1 ▶ What are the most important points to include in a flier?

2 ▶ What kind of impression should you try to create when meeting someone who has a job to offer?

Choice of clothes is important because it helps make a good first impression. Similarly, if you are phoning about a job, you should think about the impression your manner on the phone is making. Unless you are looking for a job in a band, or as a disc jockey, it is best to speak pleasantly but conservatively. Speak as you would address your parents' friends, not your own friends.

The way you present yourself also will affect the impression you make. People will be more apt to hire you if you are friendly, enthusiastic, and positive about your abilities. The next chapter will give you a few additional pointers on how to make a good impression—a very important aspect of getting a job.

Summary

☐ Your job experience as a teenager can help prepare you for work as an adult.

☐ State and federal child labor laws limit the kinds of work school-age children may do.

☐ If you are under 18, or 16, depending on your state, you need a work permit to accept a job with a business. You can, however, accept private jobs, such as babysitting, without a permit. You also can do volunteer work or work on a farm.

☐ You can find one private job, or you can start a business by offering your service.

☐ The first step in finding a job is to tell people you know that you are looking for one. Other sources of information about jobs are your school's guidance office, bulletin boards and signs in store windows, classified advertisements in newspapers, community placement services, and city governments.

☐ The more effort you put into finding work, the more jobs you are likely to find. You can look for work by distributing fliers or by calling door-to-door on neighbors if your parents or guardians approve.

☐ You must convince potential employers or customers that they will benefit from hiring you. Your appearance and manner will influence them at least as much as what you say.

Vocabulary Exercise

True or False?

1. A junior volunteer works in a store.

2. A work permit is a certificate that allows you to hold private jobs.

Match the definitions on the left with the terms on the right:

3. An organization that matches jobs with people looking for work

4. A listing placed in a newspaper by a person looking for a job

5. Employment with an individual rather than with organizations

6. A listing placed in a newspaper by an employer

a. placement service

b. situation-wanted ad

c. private job

d. help-wanted ad

Discussion Questions

1. How much should Carl pay the people who help him in his cookie business? Should he split his earnings with them evenly? Is he entitled to make more money than they do? Why or why not?

2. What qualities would you look for in someone you hired to take care of your pets and water your plants while you were out of town? How would you recognize those qualities in someone you were meeting for the first time?

3. Do you think children younger than 14 should be permitted to work in businesses? Why? What do you see as the advantages of child labor laws?

4. Would you rather hold a job or run your own business? What are some advantages and disadvantages of being an entrepreneur?

5. How do you think Carl should decide what price to charge for his cookies?

Thinking Further

1. (Math) Suppose you are the owner of Carl's Cookie Company. Find a recipe for oatmeal cookies. Figure out the amount of each ingredient that you need for six dozen of the cookies. Then visit a grocery store and figure out the cost of the ingredients. How much profit would you make if you sold the cookies to store owners at 25¢ apiece, assuming that you have no expenses other than the ingredients?

2. (Reading) Study the help-wanted advertisements in the classified section of your local newspaper. How many of them seem to be for jobs you could do? How many would you be permitted to do? Circle the ads you could apply for and bring the classified pages to class.

3. (Speaking) Suppose you are Eileen (or her brother who is helping her). Work out what you will say on the telephone to offer people your dog-walking service. Practice with a friend. Then, do a performance for the class.

4. (Reading) Read the following features to learn more about jobs.

WHO FIXES WHATEVER IS BROKEN?

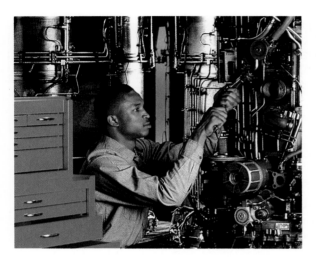

Our society is filled with machines—cars, stereos, computers, and dishwashers. At one time or another, most of these machines will break down. Thanks to mechanics and repairers, they usually can be fixed.

Vince takes pride in fixing a dented car so that it looks as if it had just left the showroom. On the other hand, he knows very little about engines or other mechanical parts. When customers' cars have mechanical problems as well as damaged bodies, he refers them to the garage where Bonnie works as a mechanic.

Bonnie has to figure out what is wrong with cars before she can fix them. For instance, a car's owner may know it makes a strange sound when he steps on the gas pedal. Bonnie, however, must determine what parts of the car are making the sound and whether they should be replaced, repaired, or merely adjusted.

On the cars Vince fixes, some problems are obvious—fenders or other parts are dented or smashed. However, Vince also must look for hidden problems, such as cracked frames and bent axles. Like Bonnie, he must decide which parts can be repaired and which must be replaced. He must give the cars' owners reliable estimates of how much the repairs will cost.

In addition to customers whose cars need repairs, Bonnie's garage also has regular customers who bring cars in for routine service to keep the cars running well. Bonnie and the garage's other mechanic change the oil, rotate the tires, and perform other maintenance tasks at regular intervals.

Bonnie and her co-worker perform all kinds of mechanical repairs, but many mechanics specialize, especially those who work for automobile dealers and large repair shops. Some may work only on cars' air conditioners or radiators.

Vince's and Bonnie's jobs are similar in a lot of ways. Both jobs are dirty and strenuous, and they require people who pay close attention to detail. Vince and Bonnie both

work mainly with their hands, using a variety of tools and equipment.

Both jobs pay well, but Vince earns more money than Bonnie. This is because, like many auto body repairers, he owns his own business. Body repairers who work for other people generally earn about the same as mechanics. Their incomes often include commissions as well as wages or salaries.

Bonnie first began acquiring her job skills in high school, where she took a course in automotive mechanics. After graduation, she took a six-month training course at a vocational school, which qualified her for the job at the garage. Even though Bonnie works with her hands, she finds that her reading skills are important. She must read technical manuals to learn about new cars and new technical procedures for repairing them.

Vince's career began in high school when he took a summer job as a helper in a body shop. At first he helped his boss remove damaged parts and install repaired parts. Later that summer, his boss taught him how to make simple repairs, such as removing small dents. After graduation, Vince found a full-time job in another body shop. For several years he worked in that job, acquiring a full range of skills using different materials and equipment to make all kinds of body repairs. Then he began making plans to open his own business.

Job opportunities for mechanics and auto body repairers are expected to increase more slowly than for most occupations over the next decade or so. The number of cars on the road—and in accidents—is increasing; however, manufacturers are building cars with parts that are less prone to rust and are easier to repair or replace. Formally trained and experienced mechanics like Bonnie should not have much difficulty finding jobs, but untrained workers can expect heavy competition for entry-level jobs.

Automotive mechanics' and body repairers' jobs are described in the Mechanics, Installers, and Repairers cluster in the *Occupational Outlook Handbook*. Other jobs in this cluster include those of:

- ❑ aircraft mechanics
- ❑ computer service technicians
- ❑ farm equipment mechanics
- ❑ heating and refrigeration mechanics
- ❑ home appliance repairers
- ❑ musical instrument tuners
- ❑ telephone installers
- ❑ vending machine servicers

WHO DISCOVERS NEW THINGS?

You probably will live most of your life during the 21st century. Does that sound strange to you? You may wonder what life on earth will be like then. Will people travel to distant planets? What will houses, cars, and everyday products be like? Will there be a cure for cancer or solutions to problems such as pollution and world hunger?

Natural and mathematical scientists search for answers to these and many other questions. In their search, they investigate plants, animals, rocks, chemical substances, stars, and hundreds of other things. Their discoveries help to determine what life will be like in the years ahead.

Some natural and mathematical scientists do basic research. They enjoy studying the natural world or mathematics simply for the sake of expanding knowledge. Other natural and mathematical scientists do applied research. They want to find practical uses for their discoveries.

Truman is a mathematics professor at a major university. In addition to his teaching duties, he does basic research in mathematics. He creates new mathematical theories and tries to show the relationship between existing principles. Truman usually does his research in his office or in his classroom.

Donna also does basic research. She is an

astronomer who uses radiation detecting equipment to study the sun, moon, planets, and stars. She wants to find out more about the universe. Donna analyzes the data she collects and writes scientific papers.

Many other people use some of the findings of basic research done by people like Donna and Truman. Some applied research is done to create new products or improve existing ones. Jeremy, a chemist, works in the laboratory of a major chemical manufacturing firm. He is studying the characteristics of atoms and molecules to discover better sources of energy. Other chemists in the laboratory may develop improved adhesives or synthetic fibers.

Lillian is an agronomist, or agricultural

scientist, with the federal government. She studies how field crops such as corn, wheat, and cotton grow. Her research will lead to improved quality and greater quantity. Lillian spends a lot of time on farms or at agricultural research stations.

Other natural and mathematical scientists do applied research to save people's lives or improve people's health. Barbara is a biologist who works in the new field of biotechnology. She experiments with the genetic material of animals and plants. Barbara hopes to apply her findings to the development of medicines that can be used in the treatment of cancer and other diseases.

As you can tell, natural and mathematical scientists need a great deal of education. Some applied research positions are available for scientists with bachelor's or master's degrees. To teach at a college or university or to do basic research, they need to have an advanced degree. Scientists must have a doctoral degree to supervise applied research in most laboratories.

Natural and mathematical scientists narrow down their field of study. For example, Ken is a scientist. Within that broad field he is a life scientist. Within the category of life scientist he is a zoologist, or someone who studies animals. Ken only studies birds. That makes him an ornithologist.

Natural and mathematical scientists share certain characteristics and abilities. One of the most important is an undying curiosity. These scientists are driven by a desire to find out how things work or why things are a certain way. They must be able to work on their own. Their work must be carefully done and they must follow exact procedures. They also must be extremely patient. Sometimes it takes years before scientists see any results from their research.

The United States has a great need for talented scientists. Here are just a few more careers in the Natural, Computer, and Mathematical Scientists cluster in the *Occupational Outlook Handbook*:

- ❑ actuary
- ❑ botanist
- ❑ computer systems analyst
- ❑ conservation scientist
- ❑ geologist
- ❑ operations research analyst
- ❑ physicist
- ❑ statistician

Getting the Job You Want

When you have studied this chapter, you should be able to:

➥ Explain the advantages of learning about particular jobs and employers that interest you

➥ Tell how to gather information about a job or an employer

➥ List ways in which you can make a good impression even before you appear for a job interview

➥ Evaluate different ways of preparing for a job interview

➥ Discuss what is likely to happen during an interview

Vocabulary Words

Prospective	Personnel department
Applicant	Stress interview
Reference	Body language
Application form	

When you look for a job of any kind, you need to have a plan. The first part of the plan is to find people or businesses who need the service you are offering. The previous chapter gave advice on how to do that. The second part of the plan is to convince employers you can do the job. As you learned earlier, that often takes place in a job interview, when a job seeker and an employer meet. This chapter explains how to gather information about jobs and employers, approach employers, prepare for interviews, and act during and after an interview.

Suppose you want to earn money by doing yard work for people in your neighborhood. You may know of some neighbors who are away on business so much they don't have time to mow their lawn or weed their garden. You can be pretty sure they need the service you are offering. How can you convince them they will get their money's worth if they hire you? You need to provide evidence that you know how to care for a lawn and garden. You also need to prove that you are reliable and honest.

Understanding Prospective Employers

Whether you are looking for work as an entrepreneur or for a job with a company or business, you can view any **prospective** employer as a customer. Prospective means they are likely to need your product. The product you want to sell is your work. You must learn how to sell it. Good salespeople understand their prospective customers, because the salespeople find out what their customers' general wants and specific needs are.

Gathering Information About Employers

Find out as much as possible about prospective employers and their wants before you talk to them about jobs. By understanding their overall goals, you become better able to sell them on the benefits of hiring you. You can address an employer's needs directly, without wasting time on services the employer cannot use. Showing you understand what services an employer needs builds confidence that you can provide those services.

You can gather information about a prospective employer's needs in several ways. For local work, you can learn a lot from the friends or neighbors who gave you the job lead. They probably can tell you something about the employer they suggested, such as why he or she needs help. If you want to work for a business in your area, a visit to the library or the local Chamber of Commerce can provide you with plenty of useful information.

Before Liz applied for a job as a maintenance worker with the Zip-Zap Electronics Corporation, she checked her library's *Read-*

It takes planning and work to get the job you want.

er's Guide to Periodical Literature. She found a magazine article about the company, which discussed how Zip-Zap manufactured some of its products. They used a specially designed, dustproof "clean room" to avoid contamination. During her job interview, Liz asked if there were special maintenance requirements for the clean room. This showed the interviewer that Liz was interested in the company and wanted to do the job well. Because Liz was qualified and informed, she was the person they hired.

At the library, you also may find newspaper articles about a business. Reference guides such as *Moody's Industry Review* lists financial facts and other information about companies. The librarian may be able to guide you to other sources as well.

A telephone call to a prospective employer can help you get specific information about a job. Don wanted to work as a messenger for a travel agency in his neighborhood. He called the agency and asked which of the big companies in town were among its clients. He then looked at a map and figured out the quickest routes from the agency to each of these companies. During his job interview, Don mentioned the research he had done and discussed the routes he would take as a messenger. The interviewer saw that Don understood the importance of making pickups and deliveries quickly. He also was impressed by Don's resourcefulness.

Learning What the Job Requires

As you know from Chapter 9, every job requires specific qualifications—the skills, aptitudes, education, or other knowledge that the person hired for the job must have. Before you apply for a job,

Apparel workers are involved in the production and care of fabrics as they are made into consumer goods. This work is part of Production Occupations.

If you can get to *see* the kind of work that a job entails, it will be easier for you to decide if it is right for you and what qualifications you might need for it.

Review Questions

1 ▶ Why is it important to learn as much as possible about a potential employer before you apply for a job?

2 ▶ Where can you find information about people who may be able to offer you private jobs? Where can you find out about businesses?

3 ▶ How can you find out what qualifications a job requires before you apply for the job?

find out as much as you can about these requirements, then decide whether you are qualified. If you feel you have most of the right qualifications, then go ahead and apply for the job. Begin thinking about how to let an employer know about your skills and abilities. If you feel that you do not have the necessary qualifications, you can make a plan to acquire them, or you can look for another job that more closely matches your qualifications.

Employers who advertise jobs usually post them on bulletin boards, place them in the help-wanted section of the classified advertisements in newspapers, or list them with placement services. These places may spell out some of the job's requirements. A job listing may specify that an **applicant**, or someone who applies for the job, needs a certain kind of work experience or training. Perhaps applicants must be available to work weekends, flexible hours, or long hours. Read any job notice carefully, or pay close attention when a placement service worker tells you about a job. To avoid wasting your time and an employer's time, apply only for jobs that you feel qualified to do.

Sometimes just thinking about a job and what it is likely to involve will help you decide if you are qualified. Aaron wanted to work as a counselor at a children's camp or as a helper in a child care center. He determined that both jobs would involve helping children and working with arts and crafts. In a camp job, Aaron thought, he also might be teaching children to swim. He had worked as a babysitter for several neighbors, and he enjoyed working with small children. In addition, he did well in art classes, and he had taken a lifesaving course at a local pool. Without any research, Aaron saw that his qualifications would suit either of these jobs. It is possible, however, that there are additional requirements of which he is not aware. The only way he will know about the whole picture is if he contacts the prospective employer.

Approaching an Employer

Your first approach to a prospective employer often is the most important because it creates the employer's initial impression of you. If you give the impression that you can do the job competently, you stand a good chance of being hired. On the other hand, a poor first impression is hard to change.

You can approach employers about jobs in several ways: by applying in person, on the phone, or in writing. Regardless of the approach you take, your goal is to get a chance to meet with the person who is doing the hiring so you can convince him or her that you are the right person for the job.

Applying in Person

Charlie saw a sign in the window of Foghorn's Chicken & Ribs that said "Part-time Kitchen Help Wanted." The sign carried no further information such as an address or telephone number—the employer obviously expected people to walk right in rather than write or call. An employer who posts such a sign is likely to offer the job to the first applicant who seems qualified.

Charlie went in the restaurant, but the manager asked him to come back for an interview at 8 P.M., when the dinner rush was over. Charlie immediately asked what hours the job required. He learned that the job would entail working after school hours three evenings a week. Since they were after school hours, he knew that would be all right, so he agreed to return.

When Charlie returned at 7:55 P.M., he had taken special care to look neat and clean. The manager interviewed him at the scheduled time and gave Charlie the job.

In addition to Charlie's good grooming, the manager was impressed by three things. First, he appreciated Charlie's question about work hours, because coming back later to apply for a job he could not do would have wasted time for both of them. Second, Charlie left almost immediately when the manager asked him to return later. Continuing to ask questions when the manager was busy probably would have spoiled Charlie's chances of getting the job. Third, Charlie arrived promptly for his interview. If Charlie had arrived late for his 8 P.M. appointment, the manager might have assumed he would be late for work, too.

Calling on the Telephone

You also could begin to apply for a job by calling on the telephone. Perhaps you want to find out when and where to apply, or you may want to make an interview appointment. You might hope to learn about the job before deciding whether to apply.

(continued on page 202)

The telephone is an excellent resource. You can call your local library to find out if they have materials on occupations or jobs that interest you. You also can use the phone to call companies and ask some basic questions.

MY JOB INTERVIEW

I woke up before the alarm was set to go off. I had slept badly. My stomach was in knots. Rehearsals for my upcoming job interview kept going around in my head. When I got in the shower, I began to feel more positive about my chances. I reminded myself that I had the right qualifications and that I was eager to learn. Surely the interviewer would not be as mean as I had sometimes imagined. I dressed carefully and as I looked in the mirror I told myself, "You will get the job."

When I got to the hotel, I waited in the service manager's plush outer office. I tried to read a magazine, but I was not able to concentrate. Instead, I reviewed all the reasons why I was the right person for the job of service trainee. In the middle of my mental review, Mr. Hurley, the manager, came out to greet me. He was friendly but businesslike, qualities I realized are essential for dealing with hotel guests and for organizing hotel service. As we shook hands and walked into his office, I felt confident that I could show him I have those same qualities.

Mr. Hurley put me at ease right away by saying how impressed he was with my school record and summer jobs. He asked me to tell him what I liked best about the jobs. I described how much I enjoyed meeting and serving people from the front desk at the resort, and even from behind the delicatessen counter. He listened to my answers and asked me interesting questions. We really seemed to be communicating well.

I had prepared myself for the next and, I felt, the toughest question. "Do you have

anything you would like to ask me?" he said. I thought for a moment and then I questioned him about the job's duties and the possibilities for promotion. I could tell he was pleased that I was interested in hotel management as a career. When the interview ended, he shook my hand and said my application looked promising. Then he said I could expect to hear from him within a week.

I left the hotel feeling relieved and happy at the same time. Interviews are not as bad as people say they are. Fortunately, though, I probably will not be having any more interviews for quite awhile, since Mr. Hurley just called and offered me the job at the hotel. ■

The impression you make on the phone can influence your chances of being hired. Listen carefully when you are told how to apply for a job. If the employer asks you questions, answer clearly, honestly, and briefly. Do not ask questions if the person you are talking to cannot answer them. If the employer likes the way you handle yourself on the phone and you have the right qualifications, you may be asked to come in for an interview.

Writing a Letter

Another common way of approaching an employer is by sending a letter. Some help-wanted ads, especially for professional jobs, specify that applicants should send a letter and a resume. A resume is a one- or two-page document listing schools you have attended,

511 Columbia Way
Pine Heights, NC 04493
June 14, 1991

Ms. Carmen Durell
Odds 'n Ends Gift Shop
92 Valley Road
Hillside, NC 04667

Dear Ms. Durell:

In response to June 14, <u>Gazette</u> advertisement for a cashier, I am enclosing my resume.

During the past two summers, I have greatly enhanced my interpersonal skills by working in service-related positions. I am a top student in math. I feel that my experience with the public, coupled with my computation ability, makes me an excellent candidate for the opening at Odds 'n Ends.

I would be very pleased to meet with you for an interview, and I look forward to hearing from you at your convenience. My telephone number is 555-2212.

Sincerely,

Marie Kelley

Marie Kelley

Enc.

jobs you have held, and other information about your qualifications. See the example below.

You should prepare a letter—and your resume—to persuade an employer to interview you for a job. In the letter you should tell which job you want, highlight skills you have that pertain to that job, and ask for an interview appointment. If the advertisement asks you to send a resume, do so, and refer to it in your letter. The letter and resume should be brief and to the point. You only need to include the most important information.

Letters and resumes also provide employers with information about your basic skills. A letter or resume that has grammatical errors, misspellings, or words that are used incorrectly will create a poor first impression of your basic skills. Be sure to check your

---

Marie Kelley
511 Columbia Way
Pine Heights, NC 04493
(600)-555-2212

JOB OBJECTIVE	Summer business position involving interaction with the public, leading to career opportunities in sales.
EDUCATION	Rhode and Horton High School, Pine Heights, NC Honors student. GPA: 3.5.
EXPERIENCE	PUBLIC RELATIONS ASSISTANT, WXXN 98.3 Public Radio, Dobbsville, NC, summer 1990. Sold subscriptions to station's magazine/program guide "WXXNews," took orders for WXXN gifts during fund-raisers. Kept donation records.
	CASHIER, Wild Whirley's Amusement Park, Lamonet, NC, summer 1989. Handled cash and distributed prizes in carnival games. Was promoted to games supervisor in August and managed inventory. In this position, I gained experience working with the public, and developed a strong facility with numbers.
HONORS AND ACTIVITIES	Won a trip to California for the Rhode and Horton High School Band by selling the most candy in one month, 1991. Rhode and Horton High School Debating Team Vice President, 1991. Rhode and Horton Band Majorette, 1988–1991.

---

letter and resume carefully for mistakes. Always type the letter and resume on plain white or off-white stationery. Never use brightly colored ink or paper that has lines or pictures on it.

Other Approaches

While walk-in inquiries, telephone calls, and letters are the most common ways to approach an employer for the first time, other approaches also are possible.

In some trades, such as construction and shiploading, employers choose work crews each morning at hiring halls. To work on one of these crews, a person must show up at the hiring hall in time for the selection each morning.

Another technique is to get to know people in an occupation that interests you before you start looking for a job. This technique is called networking, because you develop a network of people who can give you information about job openings when you need it. You can start networking by becoming a volunteer in a field that interests you, or by participating in related organizations. For example, if you are interested in working with computers, join a computer users' group and attend its meetings. You are never too young to build contacts in fields that interest you. Those people might be able to help you find work when you are older.

Review Questions

1 ▶ What is important about your first approach to a potential employer?

2 ▶ List the three most common ways of approaching an employer about a job.

3 ▶ What is the purpose of a letter or resume that you send to an employer as your first approach about a job?

Preparing for an Interview

For the kinds of employment available to teenagers, job interviews often are casual. When Charlie applied for the job at Foghorn's Chicken & Ribs, for example, the manager spent just 10 minutes interviewing him. The manager asked Charlie questions to get a feeling for whether he would be cooperative and reliable. For professional jobs, and for a few jobs you may seek while you are still in school, interviews are more formal. You can do your best in any interview if you prepare ahead of time.

Review Your Information

To begin preparing for an interview, you should review what you already know. Go over what you have learned about the employer and about the job that is available. Think about your qualifications, too, and about what you can say to convince an interviewer that you are capable of doing the job well. Think about the kinds of questions the interviewer is likely to ask, and decide how you will

If you practice going through the motions of a job interview with a friend, you will be more confident when you actually go to an interview.

answer them in advance. As a rule, you will answer questions more smoothly if you are well prepared.

If possible, practice the interview with a friend, who will play the employer's role. Practicing can enable you to go into the real interview more relaxed. The less anxious you seem to the interviewer, the better the impression you will make.

Establish References

An employer often asks job applicants to provide the names of **references**, or people who can tell the employer about an applicant's character and quality of work. People for whom you have worked are often the best references. Even if you are seeking a job that is different from any you have held, you still can use a former employer as a reference. Someone whose lawn you cut, for example, can tell a manager if you are punctual and loyal.

Teachers or coaches also can be used as references. They can provide an employer with information about your character, your skills, and even your grades, if the employer should make that request. Scout leaders or adults who supervise other youth groups to which you belong also can be used as references. These people know you well enough to comment on your skills or knowledge, whether you are willing to work hard, how well you follow instructions, and how well you get along with other people.

Before you give a person's name as a reference, ask his or her permission. People may not want to discuss your abilities if they

Application for Employment

Print Clearly in Ink

Stokemar
OFFICE PRODUCTS, INC.

Eagle View Corporate Park
Building 1, Suite 4
Pale, OR 55435

Personal

Name (First, Last, Middle initial) Juan Perez A.	Today's Date May 19, 1991

Current Address 42 Candlewick Avenue Pale, OR Zip 55211 Phone (200)-555-2828

Permanent Address 9198 Oceanside Blvd. Balboa, CA Zip 00970 Phone (300)-555-9641

Referred to Stokemar by Mr. David Saks Address 2 University Plaza Pale, OR 55413

Have you ever applied to Stokemar before? NO Date

Education

Institution	Location—City, State Street Address	Major Area of Study	Graduate Y/N
High School Pacific County Central	Balboa, CA 2222 Avenida del Mar	Business Curriculum	Y
College/University Westmount College	Pale, OR 3000 Tilman's Road	Economics, Accounting	Degree, Year B.S., 1991
Technical, Other			Degree, Year

Please check all applicable skills	☑ Type **65** wpm ☑ WP ☐ Steno ☐ DEX PC 500 ☐ Zeron WP 80 ☑ Other _Techmate 212_

Employment History—List in order, giving last employer first.

Dates of Employment From Mo/Yr	To Mo/Yr	Employer Name, Address	Position Held	Immediate Supervisor	Salary	Reason for Leaving
5/90	12/90	Freeman and Sons 320 Teller Pavillion Pale, OR 55482	Junior Accountant	Bill Wall	6.00/hr.	temporary internship
5/89	8/89	The Bach Group Eagle View Corporate PK. Bldg. 2 Pale, OR 55435	Office Assistant	Andrew Holloway	5.00/hr	summer job
5/88	8/88	Westmount Bursar's Office 3 University Plaza Pale, OR 55413	Office Assistant	Nancy O'Brien	5.00/hr	summer job
5/87	8/87	Campus Copy Corner 11 Cherry Walk Pale, OR 55412	Cashier	Joshua Morgan	4.50/hr	summer job
6/86	9/86	Herrera's Grocery 2400 Santa Rosa St. Balboa, CA 00972	Clerk	Lucille Garcia	4.00/hr	summer job

May we contact your most recent employer? (✓) Yes ( ) No

have mixed feelings about your work. Finding this out can prevent awkward situations when employers call them and can help assure that you will get only the best recommendations.

Make Notes

Before you go for an interview, you need to make some notes. Your notes should include the names, addresses, and telephone numbers of your references. You also should make notes so that you will be prepared, if asked, to fill out an **application form**. An application form asks for details about jobs you have held, schools you have attended, your skills, and other qualifications. An application form organizes information in a standard way, helping the employer compare your qualifications with those of other applicants. The notes you need to make include:

❑ your social security number

❑ the names and addresses of all schools you have attended, along with the years you attended them

❑ the names, addresses, and telephone numbers of any former employers and the dates you worked for them

❑ medical information, such as the name and address of your physician or the dates of any surgical operations you have undergone

Be sure you take your notes to the interview, and refer to them if necessary when you are filling out the application.

Dressing for an Interview

Regardless of whether an interview is casual or formal, what you wear and how well you are groomed will make a strong impression on the interviewer. Avoid extreme clothing, extreme hairstyles, and too much makeup. If you wear nail polish, use a conventional color—not black or purple or a different color for each nail. The safest way to dress for an interview is in clothing that does not call attention to itself. It should give an impression of dependability, and it should allow the interviewer to concentrate on your skills, qualifications and aptitudes instead of on your looks.

Being well-groomed starts with being clean. This means taking a bath or shower every day, and making sure that your hair, nails, shoes, and clothes are neat and tidy. Clothing also should be washed, pressed, and in good condition. Do not wear clothes if they have stains on them or if they are ripped.

Review Questions

1 ▶ Describe two ways in which a practice interview can help you prepare for a real interview.

2 ▶ Who might you list as a reference if you have not held a job before?

3 ▶ What purpose does an application form serve for an employer?

4 ▶ What kinds of notes should you take to a job interview?

5 ▶ How should you dress for a job interview?

Being prepared can help lessen the stress that some people feel in job interviews.

Going to the Interview

Though many interviews are as informal as Charlie's interview at Foghorn's restaurant, other interviews are more complex and difficult. You may be interviewed by several people at once, or you may be asked to take intelligence or aptitude tests.

Types of Interviews

For some jobs, you may be interviewed by several people before the employer decides whether to hire you. Large organizations often have a **personnel department**, which interviews all applicants and decides which ones are good prospects. The personnel department then sends the most qualified candidates to interview with the person who is doing the hiring. If a personnel department selects you to interview with the person who will make the employment decision, that interview may even occur on a different day.

Some adults who are applying for jobs may have half-a-dozen interviews as the prospective employer narrows the field of candidates for the position. Sometimes an applicant is interviewed by several people at once. An employer also may put an adult applicant through a **stress interview**, where the employer purposely creates stress to see how the applicant behaves. The interviewer may ask the applicant difficult questions in an unfriendly tone. Applicants' responses are supposed to indicate how well they will handle stress on the job. Fortunately, the stress interview is not generally used on interviews for jobs that teenagers seek.

Displaying Your Qualifications

No matter what kind of interview you have, your goal is to convince the employer you can do the job. Even if you already have listed your qualifications on an application form or in a resume, an interview gives you a chance to say more about your abilities.

The interviewer's questions may be quite specific, or they may be more general, such as, "Why do you think you can do this job?" Talk about your qualifications honestly—do not downplay them, but do not exaggerate them, either. If you believe you can do the job because you have done volunteer work in that field, for example, then say so. Just be sure that you do not claim qualifications you do not have. Employers often check with schools, former employers, and personal references, and they are likely to discover the truth. Some employers do not check qualifications, but if you misrepresent yourself, they might expect you to complete tasks you do not even know how to begin.

The attitude you present to prospective employers also is important. Try to be enthusiastic and self-confident but not boastful. Show you are willing to learn from people with more experience—independence is important, but so is courtesy and sensitivity to others who are trying to help you.

The interviewer will judge your attitude not just from what you say, but also from how you say it. Your **body language**, or the messages you send through your mannerisms, helps convey your attitude. If you slouch in your chair and avoid looking at the interviewer, you may seem uninterested, inattentive, or just plain lazy. If you sit up straight and look the interviewer in the eye, you are more likely to appear enthusiastic and interested in what he or she is saying. Fidgeting will make you seem nervous or distracted. Keeping your hands and feet still will send the message that you are attentive, relaxed, and self-confident.

How can you tell whether the interviewee is interested in what the interviewer is saying? Do you think that body language has anything to do with it?

Filling Out Forms and Taking Tests

An employer may ask an applicant to fill out an application form or take a test before or after an interview. Fill out the application form as completely and as neatly as possible. It is part of the impression you will make to the employer. Before you begin writing, read the application to see what information it requires and where the information goes. This will save you from having to erase or cross out information that you have written in the wrong place. You will find it easier to fill out the application form if you have made notes ahead of time. If you do not understand something, ask your interviewer about it. It is much better to ask a question than to fill out something incorrectly.

24 Athens Drive
Charlotte Lake, NY 79920
June 4, 1991

Ms. Ronda Martiquette
Human Resources Director
Hollywood East Video Stores
570 Indian Coast Parkway
Charlotte Lake, NY 79923

Dear Ms. Martiquette:

I enjoyed speaking with you yesterday about the opening for a display manager at Hollywood East's Charlotte Lake store. Your taking the time to outline the details of the position was very much appreciated. Thank you for showing me all the creative designs that have been used for your Silver Screen Oldies theme this season. I am extremely interested in contributing my art skills to the project.

I look forward to hearing from you at your earliest convenience, and hope that I may work with your company soon.

Sincerely,

Gregory King

Gregory King

It is a good idea to arrive a little early for an interview. It creates a positive impression, and it gives you time to fill out any necessary forms.

You also may be given a test of your intelligence or your aptitudes. These tests resemble ones you may have taken in school to measure your abilities and aptitudes. You cannot study or prepare for these tests, so do not be alarmed if you are given one.

Some employers give tests of specific skills needed on the job. For example, if you are applying for an office job, the employer may test you by giving you a stack of cards to file or a letter to type. For a job that requires experience with specific equipment, the employer may test your skill at using the equipment. When applying for a job on a production line, you may be given a test of your ability to work with your hands.

Learning from the Interview

A job interview works two ways. It gives the employer a chance to evaluate you, but it also gives you the opportunity to find out if you are interested in the job. Before you accept a job, you probably will want to know how much it pays. If the interviewer does not give you this information, you should feel free to ask about money and other benefits. However, during the interview, do not make those your first questions or your only questions.

Ask questions about the job's specific responsibilities. By doing that, you can learn whether the job is right for you. If you are applying for a job as a babysitter, you may want to know if you will be responsible for cooking or cleaning. For a job stocking shelves in a neighborhood store, you might ask how often new merchandise is delivered to the store. Interviewers expect prospective employees to ask these kinds of questions. Asking questions also can help convey your enthusiasm about the job to the interviewer.

After the Interview

After the interview, as soon as you get home, write a thank-you letter to each person who interviewed you. The purpose of this letter is to thank the interviewer for his or her time and attention and to express your continued interest in the job. The letter should be very brief—only two or three sentences. It also should be neat, well written, and typed on plain stationery.

Even if you are no longer interested in the job—or if you did not get hired for the job—it still is a good idea to send a thank-you letter. You always should try to stay on good terms with potential employers. After all, employers may know of other jobs that are available in their companies or businesses, or they may remember you in the future when they have other job openings.

Review Questions

1 ▶ What kinds of tests might an employer ask you to take before or after an interview?

2 ▶ What kinds of questions should you ask during a job interview?

Summary

- [ ] Employers must be sold on two ideas: that they need your services and that you can perform those services well.

- [ ] You will have a better chance of selling your services if you understand an employer's needs before you apply for a job.

- [ ] In most situations, your initial approach to an employer will be an unscheduled visit, a telephone call, or a letter.

- [ ] To prepare for an interview, review what you know about the job and your qualifications, and practice interviewing if possible. Obtain permission to list several people as references. Make notes of facts the employer may request.

- [ ] You may need to fill out an application form, supplying details about jobs you have held, schools you have attended, and other information about yourself.

- [ ] During an interview, you must seem enthusiastic, confident, willing to learn, and polite.

- [ ] A job interview is an opportunity for you to learn more about the job as well as a chance for the employer to evaluate you.

- [ ] After an interview, you should send a thank-you letter to each person who interviewed you.

Vocabulary Exercise

applicant   reference

body language

Complete the sentences below with the best word from the list above.

1. _____ are people who tell an employer about your qualities.

2. The messages you convey with your mannerisms are called _____.

3. A person applying for a job is called a(n) _____.

Match the definitions on the left with the terms on the right:

4. This helps employers compare applicants' qualifications by organizing them in a standard way.

    a. prospective

    b. personnel department

    c. application form

5. This is means that an event is likely to come about.

    d. stress interview

6. An employer may use this technique to see how applicants will react to pressure.

7. In large companies, this department interviews all applicants to narrow down the field of candidates.

Discussion Questions

1. If you do not have much self-confidence, is it wrong to give an employer the impression that you do? What can you do if you lack self-confidence but still need a job?

2. Suppose you find out a potential employer is polluting a local river, and you feel this is wrong. Should you apply for a job with this employer anyway? If so, should you express your opinion during an interview?

3. Name two people you could ask to be your references, and explain why you would choose them.

Thinking Further

1. (Reading) Cut out three ads for part-time employment from the classified pages of a newspaper. List the qualifications for each job, including those in the ad and those that you discover in research at the library.

2. (Writing) Find an ad for part-time work in a local newspaper and write a brief letter and resume for yourself designed to get you an interview.

3. (Speaking) Think of a job you are qualified to do and would like to have. It could be a private job or a job with an organization. Give a three-minute talk in which you describe your qualifications and explain why you want the job.

4. (Reading) Read the following feature to learn more about jobs.

WHO MAKES THE PRODUCTS YOU USE?

Have you ever cut pieces of wood on a machine and then nailed them together to make a footstool? Perhaps you have used a sewing machine to make a garment for yourself. If you have worked on projects such as these, you have some idea of what it is like to be a production worker.

Production workers make the thousands of products that people use every day. Some production workers make consumer goods such as televisions, cars, and furniture. Apparel workers, for example, manufacture the clothes you wear. Other production workers make products for business and industry. Still other production workers monitor systems in power and water-treatment plants. Every time you take a shower or flip on a light switch you use the products created by these workers.

Production workers may be skilled or unskilled. Unskilled workers usually work in large factories where products are mass produced. Mass production, or producing many products at one time, makes manufactured goods less costly. Rather than working on one product from start to finish, a worker only works on a certain part of each product. Alicia, for example, works in a factory where blue jeans, shirts, and other items of clothing are manufactured. Her only respon-

sibility is to sew shoulder seams into men's shirts. Other workers are responsible for other parts of the process, such as sewing on the cuffs and collars, making buttonholes, and cutting loose threads.

Workers like Alicia are sometimes known as assemblers. Assemblers do not need to go to school to learn their jobs. Most employers, however, prefer to hire high school graduates. Assemblers learn through on-the-job training. If Alicia stays at this job, she may be trained to do more skilled work, or she may be trained to work on other parts of the assembly process. She might become an inspector or a supervisor.

Skilled production workers usually work in a small shop or in a laboratory. They must be able to perform all or most of the tasks

required to produce the product. These tasks often are complicated and detailed.

Hal, a machinist, is a skilled production worker. He makes precision metal parts for industrial machinery, airplanes, and cars. To make sure he knows what the customer wants, Hal studies the written specifications. Next he plans how to cut the parts out of metal. Then he operates the machining equipment to make the right cuts. Finally, Hal finishes and assembles the parts.

Skilled workers like Hal can learn production work on the job. Most often, however, they must complete a training course at a vocational or technical school before being hired. Many skilled workers learn their jobs by serving a formal apprenticeship. Hal, for example, learned the machinist trade as an apprentice when he worked with a skilled machinist for four years.

All production workers share certain abilities. To work with tools and materials, they must have good eye-hand coordination and manual dexterity. They must be able to concentrate on their work for long periods of time and work neatly and accurately. Production workers must have physical stamina because they are on their feet much of the time. Workers who operate power equipment must be constantly alert and safety conscious. Because they must meet quotas, deadlines, and company standards, production workers also must be able to work effectively even under pressure.

The outlook for production occupations in the United States is uncertain. This is especially true for unskilled workers. The United States is importing more products from other countries. More products are being made by foreign workers. Advances in robotics also threaten to reduce the number of assembly line positions.

Many types of production jobs exist. Here are just a few more careers in the Production Occupations cluster found in the *Occupation Outlook Handbook*:

☐ bindery worker

☐ butcher

☐ jeweler

☐ painting and coating machine operator

☐ printing press operator

☐ typesetter

☐ upholsterer

☐ woodworker

WHEN YOU ARE AT WORK

When you have studied this chapter, you should be able to:

➡ List some expectations that employers have of employees

➡ Describe what workers can reasonably expect from their employers

➡ Discuss what co-workers expect of each other

Vocabulary Words

Contract

Flextime

Compensation

Occupational Safety and Health Administration (OSHA)

Severance pay

Workplace politics

In Chapter 11 you learned that a qualified applicant who displays an enthusiastic, positive attitude has a good chance of being hired. Those attitudes will not only help a person find a job, but also will help him or her succeed in it. Attitudes tell employers what they can expect of someone if he or she is hired.

All employers have expectations of workers. As you learned in Chapter 5, you also should expect certain things from an employer. For example, the Johnsons hired Bill as a babysitter because he seemed reliable, honest, and interested in the children. He wanted to work for the Johnson's because they promised to pay him a specific amount at the end of each work assignment and because he liked the children. The Johnsons still give Bill all their babysitting work because he has lived up to their expectations. Bill still works for the Johnsons because they keep their promise.

What an Employer Expects

When an employer and an employee agree to an employment arrangement, they are entering into a **contract**. A contract is a legal agreement between two or more people. Some contracts are written by lawyers and signed by the people involved. Many employers do not use written contracts. They make a verbal agreement when they hire someone. No matter what kind of agreement you have with employers, they will expect you to have a cooperative attitude and responsible work habits.

Willingness to Work

Employers expect employees to do their job as well as they can. They expect workers to be cheerful and courteous at work, no matter what their mood is. Employers do not want personal problems to affect an employee's work.

Bill was upset one afternoon because he had argued with a friend. He was not looking forward to going to the Johnson's to babysit. However, he had made a commitment to watch the children that day, and he is expected to show up unless he is ill. He also is expected to be watchful and kind, no matter how he feels. Bill kept the problem to himself at the Johnson's and decided to talk to his friend when he went home. Before long, he even found that being with the kids helped him feel better.

Willingness to Learn

If you accept a job, you agree to do your work the way your employer wants you to do it. Once you learn the employer's procedures for work, you should follow them, even if you would

Employers expect the people they hire to be pleasant and cheerful.

rather do the work another way. An employer usually has reasons for wanting a particular job done a certain way. For example, your boss may want you to use a certain method so your work can be coordinated with someone else's.

Once you have learned your employer's way of doing the work, you can tell your employer about your method if you still think it is better. If your employer disagrees, however, drop your argument and use the employer's method. If, however, your employer asks you to use a procedure that seems unsafe, point this out to him or her. Except where safety is involved, your employer has the final word on how a job should be done.

Willingness to Follow Rules

Employers have rules that workers must follow. Those rules vary from one company or business to another. Employers have reasons for their rules, although the reasons may not always be clear to employees. When Bill babysits for the Johnsons, he may not have visitors. The Johnsons have this rule because they do not want strangers in their home while they are away. As a rule, workers at the local restaurant must request schedule changes in advance so managers can make sure they have enough help. Whether or not you like your employer's rules, you must observe them, because there are reasons why the rules were made.

Most employers have rules to assure safety. They also may have rules about vacation time and how often you can miss work because of sickness. Also, most businesses ask workers to give at least two weeks' notice before leaving jobs.

Most employers have rules about working hours, too. Many offices are open only from 9 A.M. until 5 P.M., so their employees must work between those hours. A manufacturing plant, on the other hand, may operate around the clock, with employees working in eight-hour shifts that start at different times.

The local restaurant has a **flextime** plan that allows workers to set their own schedules within limits. Jessica asked to work from 5 P.M. to 8 P.M. on Tuesday, Wednesday, and Thursday evenings and from 7 A.M. to 2 P.M. on Saturdays. This schedule gives her time for schoolwork and household chores, as well as for fun with her friends. Now that she has set this schedule at work, Jessica must stick to it every week. If she wants to change her hours or her days, she must request the change at least two weeks ahead of time. She also could try to get another employee to trade working times with her, providing her supervisor approves.

Loyalty and Fairness

Employers expect workers to be fair. If you have a complaint, talk to your supervisor about it. Do not talk to another employee or someone outside the business behind your employer's back. Jessica, for example, saw a mouse in the food-storage room at work. Reporting the restaurant to the health department or gossiping about it to her friends would have hurt the business's reputation. Instead, Jessica told her supervisor, who called an exterminator. By

Most employers have rules that must be followed to assure safety. These workers must wear masks and special clothing.

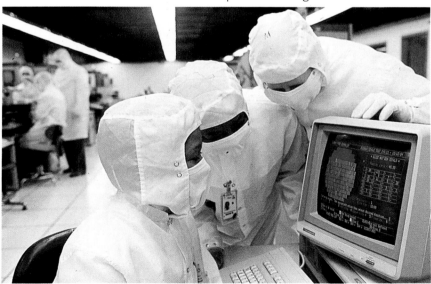

**Review
Questions** _____

1 ▶ What should you do
if an employer asks
you to do a job in a
way that makes no
sense to you?

2 ▶ What do most
businesses ask
workers to do
before leaving their
jobs?

3 ▶ If you have a
complaint at work,
what should you
do?

telling the supervisor and not other employees or outsiders about the mouse, Jessica was a loyal and fair employee.

Employers also expect workers to be honest. Because most people take honesty for granted, an employer may never bring up the subject. Honesty, however, is a requirement for any job. It means telling the truth and not taking or abusing an employer's property. Honesty also means being prepared to do a full day's work for a full day's pay—arriving and leaving work on time, and doing the best job you can do each and every day.

What Workers Can Expect

In the agreement or contract between you and your employer, your expectations are just as important as your employer's. Any employee has a right to expect certain things from a job. If you discover that your expectations are not met, you should discuss it with your employer, manager, or supervisor.

Regular Wages

Your most basic right as an employee is to receive the pay that you have earned. You deserve to be compensated promptly for your work. **Compensation** includes money plus any other fringe benefits you receive. Those benefits may be vacations, insurance, or other things. You also deserve to have the same compensation as co-workers who have the same classifications. Beyond these basic rights, compensation agreements depend on the job.

Flannery has a special arrangement with Ms. Kolton, whose house she cleans every Saturday. Ms. Kolton pays Flannery the same amount no matter how many hours she works. On some Saturdays, when the floors need waxing or the windows need washing, Flannery works longer hours. On other Saturdays, she finishes all her work in only a few hours. In the long run, Flannery is paid fairly, and Ms. Kolton gets her work done.

A business usually pays employees different amounts, depending on their experience and their responsibilities. Towne Hardware, where Nicole works as a clerk, distributes paychecks every Friday. Some employees receive the same amount in each paycheck. Others receive a different amount in each paycheck because

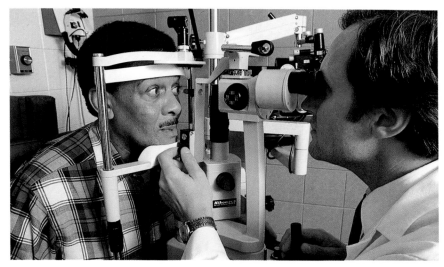

Optometrists examine people's eyes to diagnose and treat vision problems and eye diseases. They are part of Health Diagnosing and Treating Practitioners.

they receive commission in addition to salary. Nicole and the other part-timers are paid by the hour, so the amount of money they earn depends on the number of hours they work.

A Safe Workplace

You also are entitled to work in a clean, safe environment. In restaurant kitchens or other areas where spills are common, floors should have nonslip surfaces or floor mats, and they should be cleaned regularly. Businesses of all types must have clearly marked fire exits. Workers who are exposed to dangerous chemicals should be required to wear protective clothing. Businesses must keep machinery in safe running condition. They also need to provide adequate protective gear to workers who use those machines.

Tim spends summers working as a carpenter's helper. His employer is responsible for keeping ladders, power tools, and other equipment in safe operating condition. When Tim uses a power saw, one of his employer's rules is that Tim must wear safety goggles. Tim's employer cares a lot about safety.

If you encounter hazards on your job, point them out to your employer, manager, or supervisor. If he or she fails to correct the dangerous conditions, you can complain to the **Occupational Safety and Health Administration (OSHA)**. OSHA is a federal agency that sets and enforces standards for job safety. It can inspect job sites and order employers to correct safety hazards.

If a job requires skills you cannot get at school, your employer may help you get the training you need.

Training

Employers also are responsible for making sure workers are properly trained to do their jobs. That does not mean your employer should teach you math or spelling. You should learn those basic skills at school. However, if a job requires specific knowledge or occupational skills that you cannot get at school, your employer may help you get the training you need.

When Markham's Department Store hired Melissa as a checkout clerk, she had to attend training sessions for three days. There she learned how to operate the computerized cash register. She also learned how to find out the prices of unmarked items. The trainers did not teach her to count money, because Markham's expects their employees to have that basic math skill.

When employers buy new equipment, they often send workers to classes so they can learn how to use it. The company that makes the equipment may send trainers to the workplace. You also might get on-the-job training from a co-worker. When co-workers train you, you need to keep in mind that they also have other duties. When they are teaching you a procedure, pay close attention and take notes if necessary. That way you will not need to interrupt your co-worker later with questions.

Supervision

Employees need supervision to do their work well—especially if they are new on the job. You probably will have a supervisor who assigns work and explains how to do it. A good supervisor guides you in your work by pointing out problems, offering suggestions, and answering questions. A supervisor also evaluates your job performance frequently and tells you how you are doing.

Fair Treatment

Employers are forbidden by federal law to treat anyone unfairly because of race, religion, disability, or sex. Individual states and cities have laws against that, too. Experienced workers may earn more than new workers for the same job, but a business may not pay men more than women or white workers more than non-whites. Employees are entitled to equal opportunities for promotions and favorable assignments, as well as fair pay. Your advancement should depend on your job performance, not on your skin color, sex, disability, or religious beliefs.

Sometimes workers lose their jobs for reasons other than performance. Workers may be dismissed if a company is losing money or going out of business. Employees also may lose their jobs if a company is sold or if it relocates to a new town or city.

A large company that must dismiss employees who do not deserve to be fired may offer them **severance pay**, or money to make up for the job loss, if the company can afford it. The amount of the severance pay usually depends on how long an employee has worked for the company. A business may help workers find new jobs. It also may continue to provide health insurance or other fringe benefits for these workers. Not all companies offer such benefits, so workers should not expect to receive these courtesies if they lose their jobs due to uncontrollable circumstances.

Supervisors should discuss your work performance with you.

Review Questions

1 ▶ What is your most basic right as an employee?

2 ▶ What should you do if you encounter safety hazards on a job?

3 ▶ Are employers obligated to teach you all the skills you need to do your job?

In many jobs, even in technical ones, people must work together.

You and Your Co-Workers

Even though your contract is with your employer, your co-workers also will expect certain things of you. Getting along with them will help you succeed on the job. You will enjoy your work more, and your employer will respect your cooperative attitude.

Do Your Share

When Len began working at Hanratty's Home Center, he noticed that Sam did less work than the other stockroom employees. While everyone else in the stockroom was lifting boxes on and off shelves, Sam stood around and made jokes. Len also saw that his co-workers at Hanratty's resented Sam for not doing his share of the work. His behavior added to their work load, and they were angry about it. When Len recognized this, he made a point of doing at least as much work as everyone else.

Keep Confidences

Len thought about reporting Sam to the manager, but he decided against it. He knew that nobody respects a tattletale. Len made a good decision. If he told the manager about Sam, his co-workers might think he was trying to make himself look good.

If you are angry about a co-worker's behavior, it is better to voice your complaint to the co-worker first before going to your manager or supervisor. That way your co-worker will not only
(continued on page 226)

THE FIRST DAY

When I walked into the hospital, I got confused. All the corridors looked the same, and I could not figure out where to go. Luckily, the nurse I asked knew exactly where the recreation department was.

As I followed her directions, my mind raced. I told myself that I just had those "first day at a new job jitters," but that did not ease my fear that I would never be able to handle the work. What in the world had made me think that my "sunny disposition" and "warm and fun-loving nature" could get me through a summer job in a hospital? When I found the door marked "REC," I took a deep breath and walked in.

Ms. Reed, the recreation director (and the person who hired me), welcomed me. As we talked in her office, I realized why I had taken this job. Ms. Reed radiated all those qualities I had been told I possessed, and she gave me the confidence that I could use those qualities to help others.

After being introduced to the staff, I was told I would be working with Stacey. We would spend the morning visiting patients, Stacey said, as she filled a box with decks of cards, books, magazines, embroidery hoops, and other recreational items requested by or intended for patients.

"Nervous?" Stacey asked. I nodded. I had never been with hospital patients before. Would they accept and like me?

Mrs. Williams' room was the first one we visited. She was an elderly woman with a broken hip. When Stacey introduced me, Mrs. Williams told me how brave and wonderful it was for a "young thing" like me to want to work in a hospital. She was so friendly that before long, we were talking and laughing. Mrs. Williams made me promise to visit her every day.

As the day went on, I felt more comfortable. I saw that just by smiling and being friendly, I could give the most to the patients I visited. By the end of the morning, I knew I could handle the job, and the corridors seemed as friendly as the patients.

During lunch, Stacey confirmed my feelings by telling Ms. Reed how well I had done. I knew I still had a lot to learn, and I knew that not all patients were as friendly as Mrs. Williams. I felt secure, though, because the staff was so supportive.

That afternoon at bingo, I met dozens of patients. Several made "dates" with me for the following day—there was playing checkers with Mr. Upton, reading to Ms. Sanders, teaching Mr. Lewis how to crochet, and lots more. I think that this is going to be the best summer job I ever had. ■

know why you are upset, but you will be giving him or her a chance to change the behavior that is bothering you.

Many people, even adults, find it difficult to express anger directly. It usually is easier if you use a humorous approach, although if you do, the other person might think you are just kidding. Another helpful approach is to limit your complaint to specific behavior and to phrase it in a positive way.

One day when everyone but Sam was stocking shelves, Len said, "Hey, Sam, how about giving us a hand?" Sam answered with a wisecrack, but then he pitched in. His response probably would have been very different if Len had said, "Sam, you are lazy and inconsiderate and I am sick of it." By expressing his feelings in a friendly way, Len got a friendly response.

Workplace Politics

Even though all employees are entitled to fairness, some supervisors let their feelings influence their treatment of employees. The stockroom manager at Hanratty's, for example, is a friend of Sam's father. He enjoys Sam's joking manner. Because he likes Sam, he does not notice that Sam is not doing his share of the work. In fact, the manager has recommended Sam for a promotion. Arlene, who works harder than Sam and has been employed at the store for just as long, thinks she should get the promotion. She may be right. However, losing her temper and accusing her manager of favoritism would only harm her ability to get along with him. She could,

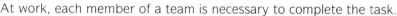
At work, each member of a team is necessary to complete the task.

Telephone company operators help customers with calls that require assistance. Their jobs can be very hectic and stressful.

however, approach her manager and ask to talk to him about her own chances for promotion in the future.

In any organization, **workplace politics**, or favoritism and personality clashes, may influence how workers are treated. Racial, sexual, and religious discrimination are illegal under antidiscrimination laws, but a boss who favors certain personalities is not breaking the law, even though this may be unfair. If you encounter workplace politics, you may want to talk to your supervisor or manager to point out your accomplishments. Be sure, however, not to accuse him or her of favoritism.

Review Questions

1 ▶ What should you do if a co-worker is doing something that makes you angry?

2 ▶ Is it against the law for a supervisor to offer a promotion to a favorite employee who does not deserve it?

3 ▶ What should you do if you are not busy and a co-worker is?

Support Your Co-Workers

Do you remember Melissa from Markham's Department Store? She waits on customers as quickly as she can while still being friendly. As a result, the lines in front of her cash register move quickly. If a co-worker has a line of customers and Melissa has none, she asks some of the customers to come to her register. This gives the customers faster service and takes pressure off Melissa's co-workers. When Melissa has a long line at her register, her co-workers are likely to return the favor.

Doing your own work well and offering help to others when it is needed is the best way to get along with co-workers. Supervisors usually will notice how well you interact with others, too. A cooperative, supportive attitude can help you have good relationships with co-workers, as well as success on a job.

Summary

- [ ] All jobs depend on agreements between employers and workers. They may be based on written and signed contracts or on verbal agreements.

- [ ] Employers have certain expectations of workers.

- [ ] By accepting a job, you agree to do what your employer asks you to do. You also agree to follow your employer's guidelines regarding safety, attendance, and other concerns.

- [ ] Employers expect workers to act in the employer's interest by not discussing business problems with outsiders.

- [ ] Workers are entitled to be paid what they have earned at the promised time.

- [ ] Specific compensation agreements vary from job to job.

- [ ] Federal law requires that employers provide safe, clean workplaces. It also forbids them to discriminate against people because of race, sex, disability, or religion.

- [ ] Employers are responsible for making sure that workers are properly trained to do their jobs.

- [ ] A good supervisor points out problems, offers suggestions, and answers questions.

- [ ] To get along with co-workers, employees should do their share of the work, avoid tattling to the boss, and offer help when it is needed.

Vocabulary Exercise

True or False?

1. Flextime means you work only when you want to.

2. Jobs depend on contracts between workers and employers.

Complete the sentences below with the best word from the following list.

compensation

Occupational Safety and Health Administration

severance pay

workplace politics

3. _____ can include fringe benefits as well as wages.

4. Favoritism is an example of _____.

5. If your workplace is unhealthy, you can complain to the
_____.

6. _____ is money that an employer may offer to compensate a worker for the loss of a job.

Discussion Questions

1. Suppose you suspect that your supervisor is stealing supplies from the company. Should you tell someone about this? Why or why not?

2. If a company is moving to another state, what could it do to help its employees? Will offering this help benefit the company? Explain your answer.

3. If you are a woman or a member of a minority group, how can you be sure an employer is treating you fairly?

Thinking Further

1. (Reading) At the library, find out as much as you can about federal and local laws against discrimination. What kinds of discrimination are illegal where you live? What happens to employers who are accused of discrimination?

2. (Math) Real estate agents make most of their salary in commissions. They often make 3 percent or 6 percent of the total selling price of the home. If you were an agent, and you could choose to make only one of the following deals, which one would you choose? Three percent of $128,000 or 6 percent of $61,000? How much would you earn on that deal?

3. (Listening) Invite a supervisor to speak to the class. Ask him or her to explain the give-and-take between employer and employee at his or her company. Ask students to listen and think about whether the supervisor mentions points that were not covered in this chapter.

4. (Reading) Read the following feature to learn more about jobs.

WHO CARES FOR THE SICK?

If you were badly injured or became seriously ill, you would need to go to the hospital. You might need to stay there for several weeks. During this time, many skilled professionals would take care of you.

Health care professionals work as a team to help patients get well. Perhaps the most familiar members of the team are the registered nurses, or R.N.'s. Registered nurses, such as Ann, carry out the doctor's plan of treatment for each patient. In larger hospitals, nurses take care of groups of patients with similar needs. Ann, for example works with cardiac patients.

Ann monitors her patients' progress, keeps records, and administers medicine. Sometimes she bathes her patients or gives them back rubs. These routine tasks, however, usually are performed by licensed practical nurses, orderlies, or nurse's aides. Much of Ann's time is spent supervising these hospital employees.

Laura, the hospital dietitian, plans nutritious meals for patients. Oftentimes, a patient must have a special diet. Laura consults with the doctors and nurses to make sure her menus fit with the patient's treatment. Laura also supervises the kitchen employees who prepare the food.

Dennis, the hospital pharmacist, dispenses the medicine used to make patients well. He advises the health care team on which drugs to prescribe, and he recommends proper dosages. Dennis monitors the effects of various drugs and makes sure the drugs are used efficiently and safely.

Therapists are other important members of the health care team. Howard is a physical therapist. He helps patients regain muscle strength and flexibility following an illness or an injury. To loosen stiff joints, Howard stretches and manipulates patients' arms and legs. Howard also shows patients how to do various exercises to

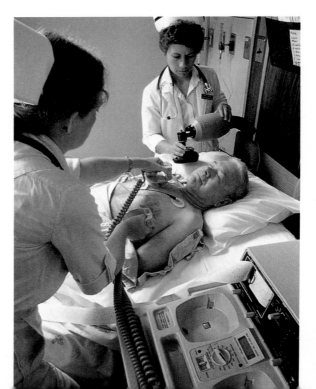

strengthen their bodies. Physical therapy can take a long time and patients often continue treatment after leaving the hospital.

Sue is an occupational therapist. She works with patients whose mental abilities have been damaged because of a stroke or head injury. Sometimes these patients must be taught to read and write again. They may need help with daily living skills, such as getting dressed or feeding themselves.

Registered nurses, dietitians, pharmacists, and therapists must have a great deal of training. They must study subjects such as biology, chemistry, anatomy, and psychology. In all states, registered nurses, physical therapists, and pharmacists must be licensed. To obtain a license, they must complete an approved program of study, which lasts from four to six years, and then they must pass an examination. In the future, as medical technology becomes more complex, even more training may be required.

Health care professionals must have empathy for other people and want to help them with their problems. They must be able to work with all types of patients.

Of course, health care professionals work in a number of other places besides hospitals. Many of them work in nursing homes, outpatient clinics, doctors' offices, community centers, and private homes.

These professionals also teach people preventive care so they do not get sick or injured in the first place. The primary responsibility of many health care professionals is to teach people good nutrition, hygiene, prenatal care, and safety. Other health care professionals work in clinics where they screen people for high blood pressure, diabetes, poor vision, and other ailments and provide treatment.

There are a large number of job opportunities in health care. More people are needed to care for patients whose lives are being saved or prolonged by medical technology. In particular, there is a great demand for nurses in the United States. Here are just a few more occupations in the Registered Nurses, Pharmacists, Dietitians, Therapists, and Physician Assistants cluster of the *Occupational Outlook Handbook*:

❏ athletic trainer

❏ industrial nurse

❏ physician assistant

❏ recreational therapist

❏ respiratory therapist

❏ speech-language pathologist

UNIT 4

YOU AND THE ECONOMY

AMERICA'S ECONOMY

When you see money, what comes to mind? More than likely, you think about the items you can buy.

Money and merchandise are available to you because of the type of economic system the United States has. That system, called a free enterprise system, allows people the freedom to choose how they want to earn money and how they want to spend it (above).

Economic conditions in other countries are very different from those in the United States. Many people do not enjoy the freedom, prosperity, and technological advances that Americans have (right).

People's income in the United States is determined by the economy. That is why trade unions are a part of many industries. They help workers in related jobs to negotiate for wages and better working conditions. Union representatives do this by meeting and talking with management (above).

Prices in a free enterprise system are regulated by supply and demand. This means that items, such as tickets, that are in great demand but limited supply can command a high price because many people want them (left).

235

Stores commonly compete with one another by offering merchandise on sale. They hope that new and regular customers will be attracted to their store because of those sales (right).

Stores are not the only settings where you can buy merchandise. Sometimes you can find better prices and quality by shopping at farmer's markets, flea markets, bazaars, or yard sales (above).

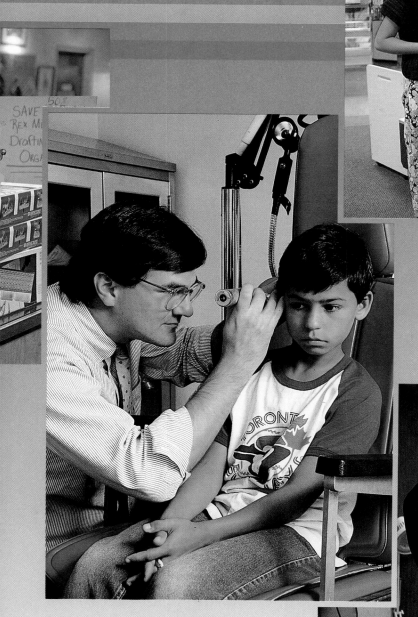

In most stores people can choose from a wide variety of items. That is why you should comparison shop, or compare the price and quality of similar items, when you buy anything (above).

In a free enterprise system, service businesses, such as health care businesses, compete for customers, too. Do you think quality is more important than price when seeking services (above)?

Learning to manage your money involves making choices about spending and saving. If you have a budget, it will be easier to decide how much money you can spend on any one purchase (above).

Most financial institutions offer a wide variety of services. You can use those services to help you manage your money (right).

Successful businesses are a cornerstone of the free enterprise system. They provide jobs and keep money flowing through the American economy (left).

When people want to purchase a large item, such as a house or car, they often go to a financial institution for a loan. They are evaluated by the institution based on the likelihood that they will be able to repay all the money they borrow (above).

Small businesses and entrepreneurs contribute to the American economic system by offering a wide range of products and services (left).

In the United States people are free to buy and sell shares of ownership in corporations. They do that in a place called a stock exchange (above).

CHAPTER

13

Earning an Income

When you have studied this chapter, you should be able to:

➡ Describe the most common methods of calculating workers' pay

➡ Explain how to use financial institutions to help you manage your money

➡ List the typical items in an adult's budget

➡ Discuss the responsibilities of an adult in American society

Vocabulary Words

Check

Wage

Tip

Piecework rate

Interest

Loan

Budget

Income tax

Boycott

Suppose you have a part-time job. You can spend the money you earn in many ways. You can buy necessary items, such as food or clothing. You can save the money for the future, or you can spend the money buying items you want, such as new compact discs. There probably will be times when you have trouble deciding how to spend your money. You may not know whether to spend or save it. The decisions you make about spending money will affect many parts of your life, especially when you are an adult.

Types of Income

Income, or money people earn from their jobs, can be calculated in many ways. A worker may be paid by the hour or by the week. In addition to money, a worker's income may include any fringe benefits the employer provides.

Money Income

Most people receive the majority of their earned income as cash or by **check**. A check is a written order directing a financial institution to pay money to someone. Employers use a variety of methods for calculating the money they pay their employees.

Some workers are paid a **wage**, which is an hourly rate of pay. Some of you may be familiar with that form of payment from babysitting. Part-time workers also earn wages in other kinds of jobs. When Hannah went to work at Ronnie's Music Store, for example, the owner agreed to pay her $5 an hour. If she works five hours a week, she earns $25. If she works eight hours, she earns $40. Full-time workers also may earn a wage.

Some workers earn **tips**, called a gratuity, in addition to their wages. A tip is a small amount of money that a satisfied customer leaves for a worker. Customers generally tip hairdressers and barbers, taxi drivers, servers, and hotel employees. Many of these workers earn the majority of their income from tips. Customers usually decide whether they want to tip and, if so, how much. Some restaurants and hotels, however, automatically add 15 or 20 percent to customers' bills for tips.

People who receive tips often share them with co-workers who assist them but do not receive tips. For example, restaurant customers do not usually tip Terry for clearing and setting the tables, but because his prompt table setting and cleaning helps the servers earn tips, the restaurant's policy is to have them share the money they earn in tips with Terry.

Sunshine Togs pays Nick at a **piecework rate**, which is a set amount for each piece of work he does. Nick's job is to sew labels

REGULAR HOURS	OVERTIME HOURS	RATE	REGULAR EARNINGS	OVERTIME EARNINGS	OTHER PAY				PAY PERIOD
					BASIS	RATE	AMOUNT	DESCRIPTION	2
40	0	13.45	538.00	00.00					

TOTAL GROSS
538.00

DEDUCTIONS THIS PAY PERIOD				
FED. WITH.	SOC. SEC.	STATE WITH.	CITY WITH.	
75.02	49.98	13.00		

TOTAL DEDUCTIONS
138.00

EMPLOYEE INFORMATION	TOTALS YEAR-TO-DATE		
	FED. WITH.	SOC. SEC.	STATE WITH.
	150.04	99.96	26.00

NET PAY
400.00

GARLAND STATE BANK

ORANGE, TEXAS

DATE	CHECK NO.	AMOUNT
03/01/91	5779239	400.00

PAY
TO THE
ORDER
OF

Stacy DiMeglio

Lorretta P. Sherry

Paying piecework rates benefits the manufacturer because it encourages people to work faster. It also is a way to recognize workers who put in more effort.

into shirts. Instead of paying him by the hour or by the week, the company pays him according to the number of labels he sews.

A salesperson usually works for a commission, or a percentage of the sales that person makes. For example, Glenn sells automobiles at a car dealership. The more cars he sells, and the more expensive those cars are, the more money he earns. For instance, if he sells a $7,000 car and receives a 5 percent commission, he earns $350. He would make $500 if he sold a $10,000 car. Some salespeople receive a basic salary as well as commissions, whereas others receive only commissions. However, basic salaries for commissioned salespeople usually are very low. Either way, the more sales they make, the greater their incomes.

An office worker may receive a salary, which is a weekly, monthly, or yearly rate of pay. Salaried employees often work 8 hours a day and 40 hours a week, but sometimes they may work fewer or more hours. Workers on salary are paid the same amount for each pay period regardless of how many hours they have worked. The most common pay periods are for one week, two weeks, or one month of work. Most salaried employees are paid for a specific number of days for vacations and a specific number of days when they miss work because of sickness. However, they also may work extra hours without getting any extra pay, especially if they are supervisors or managers.

1 Control number				
8P3	**00095**	OMB No. 1545-0008		

2 Employer's name, address, and ZIP code	3 Employer's identification number **89-228-5675**	4 Employer's state I.D. number **44-45-460**
The Pink Moon Tea Shop **400 West 16th Avenue** **Port Fine, IL 98779**	5 Statutory employee ☐ Deceased ☐ Pension plan ☐ Legal rep. ☐	942 emp. ☐ Subtotal ☐ Deferred compensation ☐ Void ☐
	6 Allocated tips	7 Advance EIC payment

8 Employee's social security number **100-100-1000**	9 Federal income tax withheld	10 Wages, tips, other compensation **$12,000**	11 Social security tax withheld **$700.00**
12 Employee's name, address, and ZIP code		13 Social security wages **$12,000**	14 Social security tips
Yvonne Leonard **7596 North 21st Street** **Port Fine, IL 98777**		16	16a Fringe benefits incl. in Box 10
		17 State income tax **$205.00**	18 State wages, tips, etc. **$12,000**	19 Name of state **Illinois**
		20 Local income tax	21 Local wages, tips, etc.	22 Name of locality

Form **W-2 Wage and Tax Statement**
Employee's and employer's copy compared ☐

Copy 1 For State, City, or Local Tax Department

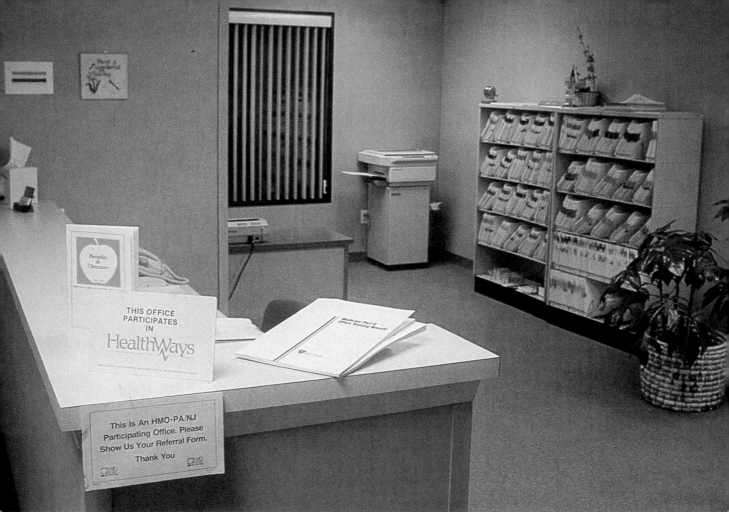

Fringe benefits make up part of the income you are paid for doing a job.

Review Questions

1 ▶ Which kinds of employees usually are paid for vacations and sick time?

2 ▶ What can a worker's income include in addition to money?

3 ▶ What are three fringe benefits that workers may receive from their employers?

Fringe Benefits

Even though fringe benefits are not part of the money people get paid for doing a job, they make up an important part of most people's incomes. Many large companies provide about $35 worth of fringe benefits for every $100 they pay in wages and salaries to full-time employees. Some part-time employees receive fringe benefits, although most people who work part time in after-school and weekend jobs do not receive any benefits.

Common fringe benefits include paid vacations and holidays. Many employers pay part of the cost of health insurance for their workers, too. They also may contribute to pension plans, which provide income for employees after they have retired. Other fringe benefits may include money for job-related classes and child care for workers' children. A company also may offer employees its products at a discount, or a reduced price.

Handling Your Money

Knowing how to manage money is just as important as knowing how to earn it. Financial institutions such as commercial banks, savings and loan associations, mutual savings banks, and credit unions offer a wide range of services to help you manage your income. Since most financial institutions charge fees for a lot of these money management services, the first step in managing your money is deciding which services you need to have.

Using Financial Institutions

The most common financial institutions are commercial banks and savings and loan associations. They vary in the financial services they provide and in the fees they charge.

After Natalie started a lawn care service in her neighborhood, her father suggested that she open a savings account at a local bank. That way, she could save her money for special purposes, such as a new bike or radio. Her money would grow as she earned **interest**. Interest is money that people or institutions earn when they allow someone else to use their money.

When Natalie and her father went to the bank to open a savings account, Natalie discovered that there are several other ways to save money. Some banks offer other savings accounts, such as money market accounts, in which you can earn more interest than a regular savings account. She also learned that banks offer certificates of deposit that also earn greater interest than savings

Financial institutions usually offer a wide range of services to people.

SHARON D. FRANCES
2785 Collier Blvd.
Queenston, CT 11116

14—18
2000

No. 119

Feb 23 19 91

PAY TO THE
ORDER OF   *Hubnal's Emporium* $ 20.00

Twenty and 00/100   DOLLARS

First Bank of Ivy Ridge
Queenston Ivy Ridge Hwy., Ivy Ridge, CT 11117

Memo *Acct.# 58-580-5522*   *Sharon D. Frances*

⑆ 2312711741⑆   19 303398 2⑈

accounts, because the bank keeps your money and you cannot use it for a specific amount of time. Money placed in savings accounts, on the other hand, can be withdrawn at any time.

Checking Accounts

When Natalie finished high school, she decided to continue building her flourishing lawn service. This time her father suggested they visit the bank with another purpose in mind—to open a checking account. Most people keep the money that they use for paying bills in a checking account. That account allows them to make payments and purchases without using cash.

A check authorizes the bank to give a specific amount of your money from your checking account to the person or organization whose name is written on the check. A check also gives you a way of proving that you have made a payment. Using a checking account is safer than carrying large amounts of cash or sending cash through the mail. Most adults keep money in checking accounts to pay for routine expenses.

To open a checking account, Natalie deposited money with her bank. She also filled out a card and signed it so the bank can verify the signature on the checks she writes. The bank then gave Natalie a supply of blank checks. It also gave her a check register in which she will record information about the checks she writes and the deposits she makes. This will help her keep track of the amount of money she has in her checking account.

(continued on page 248)

WHO IS KEEPING UP WITH WHOM?

The first job I got when I finished college was in an advertising agency. The job paid well, I loved the work, and my co-workers were terrific. They were a lot of fun in and out of work. They lived fast-paced, exciting lives. I was dazzled by them, and I wanted to be like them in every possible way.

After working for a few months, I applied for my first credit card. In four weeks I received approval from the bank and a $2,500 spending limit. A month later I moved to a new neighborhood to be near my friends from work. The rent there was high, but I felt I could handle it. I used my credit card to begin decorating and furnishing my apartment. In no time, I reached my $2,500 limit. I decided what I needed was another credit card—and I got it.

I kept spending—or rather charging. After all, I had to keep up with my friends. I shopped for clothes and jewelry where they did, and I went to all the same fancy restaurants and clubs.

As the months went by, I continued to get more preapproved credit card applications in the mail. I could not resist getting the cards or using them. Some banks even sent me checks for personal loans. That is when I decided that I needed to get a loan so I could buy a sports car. I made an appointment with a loan officer. He was very helpful, and he even showed me how I could take out a personal loan for a vacation. Before I left, he gave me the loan application forms to fill out at home.

I will never forget that night. I went over the figures three times because I could not

believe it was true. My monthly expenses—rent, food, transportation, credit card payments, entertainment, and other living costs—exceeded my income by $200 a month. I realized that I could not afford a new car or a vacation and that I might not even be able to pay my current bills.

The following day I called the loan officer and told him why I could not consider taking out a loan. He referred me to a financial counselor who helped me make up a budget, watched me destroy my credit cards, and advised me about living within my means.

It took me over a year to pay off my debts. Now I stick to my budget. I have taken out a loan, which I can afford, for a new economy car. I am saving to go to Mexico on vacation next spring. I think my lifestyle is great just the way it is. ■

On each check she writes, she will include the date and the name of the payee, which is the person or organization she is paying. She also will write the amount of the payment in longhand and in figures. Then she will sign her name the way it appears on her signature card. Checks also include a blank space to make a note of the reason the check is written.

Another service that many financial institutions provide is automated teller machines (ATMs). Customers can use these machines to make deposits and withdrawals at any time of the day or night. This way customers do not have to visit the financial institution during business hours and wait in line.

Financial institutions often charge fees for checking accounts. They may charge a certain amount for each check written and for each deposit or withdrawal made from an ATM. Some financial institutions charge monthly fees for accounts that have less than a specific amount of money in them. Some checking accounts that must have a greater amount of money in them pay interest. Policies on checking account fees and interest vary widely, so investigate them before you open an account.

Purchasing Insurance

Adults usually purchase insurance policies to protect themselves against unplanned expenses for which they cannot afford to pay. For example, Cheryl's parents have medical insurance to help pay hospitals and physicians in case they become ill. They also have car insurance that helps pay for repairs if they are involved in any automobile accidents. Home insurance would pay for repairs if their home were damaged in a fire or other mishap. Most people purchase insurance because a serious illness or accident could cost them more money than they have saved.

Getting a Loan

Even some planned expenses, such as house and car purchases, require more money than most people can save. Many adults pay for those costly items by obtaining **loans**, or by borrowing money from a financial institution and repaying it gradually. Frank's mother decided to borrow from a bank to buy a house. Like everyone who borrows from a financial institution, she filled out an application. On it, she provided details about her income, her expenses, money she owed to anyone, and her employment history. This information helps the creditor, the institution loaning the money, evaluate whether an applicant is likely to repay the loan. Loans are granted or refused based on that evaluation.

IMPERIAL CARD

Mr. Carl Schumann
6000 Aloe Court
Green Run, FL 99922

Box 8080 Pelican Creek, FL 99684

TRANSACTION DATE	REFERENCE NUMBER	TRANSACTION DESCRIPTION	PURCHASES/ CHARGES	PAYMENTS/ CREDIT
04/29	985JRK666	Pendleton's, Fargate sportswear	15.00	
04/30	240000392	Payment—Thank you		35.00
05/16	33335XX97	Soundsonics, Roland Ave. stereo equipment	20.00	
05/20	52113896PR8	Wilmer and Kelley, 8th St. gourmet department	4.25	

PREVIOUS BALANCE	PAYMENTS	FINANCE CHARGES	NEW BALANCE
35.00	35.00	00.00	39.25
		Please pay balance on time to limit any FINANCE CHARGES	

BILLING DUE	DATE DUE	MINIMUM PAYMENT DUE	ACCOUNT NUMBER
05/22	06/15	5.00	923 45 3977

LINE OF CREDIT	AVAILABLE CREDIT	*NOTE IMPERIAL CARD'S NEW POLICY ON FINANCE CHARGES. SEE PAGE 3 OF THIS STATEMENT.
500		

The bank lent Frank's mother $47,000 to purchase a house. Over the course of 30 years, she must pay the bank $423 each month. Her payments will add up to far more than $47,000, because they also include the interest the bank is charging her. She is willing to pay the interest because it enables her to buy a house for more money than she has been able to put aside.

Many adults use credit cards to pay for smaller purchases. When you use a credit card, the company that issues the card pays for your purchase and sends you a bill later. Some companies require cardholders to pay their entire bills each month, whereas others allow people to pay only part of what they owe. Credit card companies, like other creditors, charge interest. Credit card interest rates often are very high, and they can add up to a lot of money if

Taylor's Monthly Budget		Taylor's Parents' Monthly Budget	
Monthly Income	$180.00	*Monthly Income*	$2,100.00
Fixed Expenses		*Fixed Expenses*	
Bus Fare	$32.00	Food	$630.00
		Rent	$525.00
		Transportation	$250.00
Savings	$18.00	Savings	$210.00
TOTAL	$50.00	TOTAL	$1,615.00
Flexible Expenses		*Flexible Expenses*	
Movies	$28.00	Clothing	$210.00
Snacks	$40.00	Medical Expenses	$168.00
Books & Magazines	$28.00	Luxury Spending	$57.00
Camera Supplies	$24.00	Education	$50.00
Other	$10.00		
TOTAL	$130.00	TOTAL	$485.00

Review Questions

1 ▶ What are the differences between a savings account and a certificate of deposit?

2 ▶ What does a check authorize a bank to do?

3 ▶ What is the danger in using credit cards?

bills are not paid in full each month. Credit cards offer a convenient way of making purchases, but they must be used cautiously. Because they are so easy to use, many people buy without thinking about how much they are spending. Credit card users can quickly find themselves owing more money than they can afford to repay.

Budgeting Your Money

Managing money well requires a **budget**, which is a plan for spending and saving your income. Budgets that adults make must include money for necessities. The remaining money may be put aside for the future, or it may be spent on luxuries.

Purchasing Necessities

The largest part of most adult budgets is spent on necessities. Everyone needs food, clothing, and shelter as well as transportation, personal items, and medical care. Some people also have expenses for education and health care.

The biggest items in most household budgets are food and housing. Financial advisors suggest that a family spend no more than 30 percent of its income on food. People usually spend about 25 percent of their incomes on housing, although this varies according to where they live. In some areas, especially big cities and their suburbs, housing may represent a bigger part of a family's budget. In areas where housing costs are relatively low, housing may take up only 15 percent of a family's budget.

Transportation may represent 10 to 20 percent of a family budget. A smaller part of the budget, usually around 10 percent, should be allocated for clothing. Personal and medical expenses generally account for another 7 to 20 percent of a family budget.

The costs of necessities, and the percentage of the budget that is spent on them, differ from one household to the next. For example, a family with six children probably will spend more on education than a family with one child. A person who must wear suits to work will need to spend more on clothing than someone else who can wear jeans to work. It is very important that a budget be based on a realistic estimate of each person's or family's spending needs. That is the only way it will be accurate.

Paying Taxes

Most adult workers, and some teens, must pay **income taxes**. Income taxes are portions of people's income that must be paid to the federal government. Most states and some cities also tax peo-

Form **W-4** Department of the Treasury Internal Revenue Service	**Employee's Withholding Allowance Certificate** ▶ For Privacy Act and Paperwork Reduction Act Notice, see reverse.		OMB No. 1545-0010 **1991**

1 Type or print your first name and middle initial   Last name
Johnathan Xavier Underwood

2 Your social security number
555-45-9298

Home address (number and street or rural route)
27 Boar's Head Circle

3 Marital status

☒ Single   ☐ Married
☐ Married, but withhold at higher Single rate.

Note: *If married, but legally separated, or spouse is a nonresident alien, check the Single box.*

City or town, state, and ZIP code
Olde Nook, SD 88881

4 Total number of allowances you are claiming (from line G above or from the Worksheets on back if they apply) . . **4** *1*

5 Additional amount, if any, you want deducted from each pay . . . . **5** $ —

6 I claim exemption from withholding and I certify that I meet **ALL** of the following conditions for exemption:
  • Last year I had a right to a refund of **ALL** Federal income tax withheld because I had **NO** tax liability; **AND**
  • This year I expect a refund of **ALL** Federal income tax withheld because I expect to have **NO** tax liability; **AND**
  • This year if my income exceeds $500 and includes nonwage income, another person cannot claim me as a dependent.

If you meet all of the above conditions, enter the year effective and "EXEMPT" here   ▶ **6** 19

7 Are you a full-time student? (**Note:** *Full-time students are not automatically exempt.*) . . . . **7** ☐ Yes ☐ No

Under penalties of perjury, I certify that I am entitled to the number of withholding allowances claimed on this certificate or entitled to claim exempt status.

Employee's signature ▶ *Johnathan X. Underwood*   Date ▶ *June 21,* 19 *91*

8 Employer's name and address (**Employer:** Complete 8 and 10 **only if sending to IRS**)
Harver, Sills, and Carney
503 Castle Street
Chad, SD 88924

9 Office code (optional)

10 Employer identification number
85-4010223

The clothing choices you make will not only affect the way you look, but also what else you can afford to buy.

ple's income. Many employers automatically deduct the money for taxes from their worker's pay. People who run their own businesses also pay taxes on their incomes. They generally are responsible for making payments every three months toward what they expect their tax bills to be for the year.

These taxes help pay for public education and public services such as fire fighters and police. Governments also need tax money to fund programs for helping poor people. In addition, taxes pay for roads, armed forces, and medical care. Earning an income enables you to pay your share of these costs through taxes, which is one of your adult responsibilities.

Review Questions

1 ▶ What are the two biggest items in most family budgets?

2 ▶ What do governments do with the taxes they collect? (continued on page 253)

Savings

After purchasing necessities and paying taxes, you can use the money you have left over in any way you wish. Financial advisors recommend that workers save at least 10 percent of their incomes for unexpected expenses and future needs. Many people also choose to spend some of their extra money on luxuries.

The more money you save, the less you will need to spend on borrowing money. Lisa, for example, always set aside part of her earnings from her newspaper route. Over the years, she saved $2,500. When she got her first full-time job, she bought a car for $7,500. Because she could use her savings to help pay for the car, Lisa only had to borrow $5,000. As a result, her monthly payments on the loan were much lower than they would have been if she had borrowed the entire $7,500.

3 ▶ How much of its income should a family save for the future?

Income and Responsibility

When you earn an income you are free to make a number of choices. Along with those choices, you will have some new responsibilities. This chapter has discussed two of those responsibilities—purchasing necessities and paying taxes.

Responsibility as a Worker

As you learned in Chapter 12, workers have responsibilities to their employers. They are responsible for doing their jobs as well as possible and for being loyal to their employers. In addition, workers

An adult has many responsibilities as a worker, a consumer, and a voter.

Being sure that your purchases please you helps to ensure that good products stay on the market.

also have certain responsibilities to society. If they are to fulfill those responsibilities, they must believe that the work they do is worthwhile and important to society.

When Dominic finished business school, he received job offers from several companies. The two most attractive offers came from a tobacco company and an insurance company. Although the tobacco company offered Dominic a higher salary, he took the job with the insurance company. Dominic believes that tobacco products are harmful. Even though he would not be making the products, he still would be supporting the success of those products. Dominic knew he would not feel right helping to produce any of those products. By working for an insurance company, on the other hand, Dominic feels that he helps create something people need. He feels that his job is worthwhile, not just for the income it provides him with, but for its importance to society.

Everyone has a different opinion on which products and services are useful and which ones are harmful. Most people need to examine their values and form an opinion when choosing a job. To do their best work, they need to have a positive feeling about the value of their employer's business to society.

Responsibility as a Consumer

Just as you help a business by working for it, you help it by spending your money on its products or services. When people buy or use certain products or services, they are acting as consumers. As a consumer, you may choose to spend money only on products or services that you consider worthwhile. Before Lisa bought a car, for example, she researched the models she liked. She purchased one that had a record for safety and reliability. Such responsible spending encourages companies to continue making good products and to stop making bad ones.

Many consumers also choose to deal only with companies whose policies they support. Jeff learned that the manufacturer of the shampoo he used had a record of polluting natural resources. He decided to switch to a brand made by a company that had a record of keeping the environment clean.

Sometimes consumer organizations organize **boycotts**. A boycott is a plan to influence an organization by refusing to buy its products or services. The purpose of boycotts is to persuade a company to improve its products or to change its policies.

Responsibility as a Voter

American adults have the power to influence government policies by voting responsibly. Adults can use their votes to support politicians who act in society's best interest—and to defeat those who do not. People differ in their opinions about what is best for society, of course, and that is why voting is important. With voting power comes a responsibility to stay informed about political issues and to form opinions about them. Responsible voters know which politicians represent them nationally and locally, and they know those politicians' positions on important issues.

With their votes, adults influence taxes and other economic policies. A voter may support a candidate who calls for spending more money on education and less on weapons, or vice versa. The next chapter includes a broader discussion of economic issues and how they affect both workers and consumers.

Review Questions

1 ▶ How are employees responsible to society for the work they are doing?

2 ▶ How can consumers act responsibly?

3 ▶ How can a responsible adult show disapproval of government policies?

Summary

- ❑ A worker's income includes money as well as fringe benefits.

- ❑ Employees may be paid wages, tips, piecework rates, commissions, or salaries.

- ❑ Financial institutions pay interest to their customers for the use of their money, such as that in savings accounts.

- ❑ Checking accounts allow you to make payments with checks rather than with cash. By writing a check, you authorize your financial institution to give a person or business a certain amount of money from your account.

- ❑ Most people purchase insurance policies to help protect them against large, unexpected expenses.

- ❑ People often apply for loans for major planned purchases such as houses and cars. They repay what they have borrowed gradually. Because of interest charges, their payments add up to more than the amount they borrowed.

- ❑ Credit cards offer a convenient way to pay for smaller purchases. However, using them carelessly can result in overspending and high interest charges.

- ❑ Adult budgets must include money for food, clothing, housing, and other necessities. Money that is left over can be saved or spent on nonessentials.

- ❑ The biggest items in most household budgets are food and housing. Financial advisors suggest that workers spend no more than 30 percent of their incomes on food, 25 percent on housing, and 20 percent on transportation.

- ❑ Financial advisors recommend that workers set aside at least 10 percent of their incomes for the future.

- ❑ Adults have social responsibilities, including doing work that benefits society, spending money on worthwhile products and services, and electing politicians who will work for the good of society.

Vocabulary Exercise

check	piecework rate	budget
wage	interest	income tax
tip	loan	boycott

Complete the sentences that follow with the best word from the list above.

1. _____ is the money you earn when you allow a bank to use your money.

2. A _____ authorizes a bank to give someone money from your account.

3. _____ are small amounts of money left for workers by satisfied customers.

4. A plan for saving and spending is called a _____.

5. An employee whose pay depends on how many pairs of shoes he packs into boxes is being paid at a _____.

6. An employee who receives pay by the hour earns a _____.

Discussion Questions

1. Which way of calculating pay would you like to have on your first full-time job? Why?

2. What would you do if you learned that your employer was polluting the air?

3. Which responsibility to society do you think is the most important? Why?

Thinking Further

1. (Listening) Obtain information from two banks about their interest rates and fees. Find out how much interest they pay on savings accounts and certificates of deposit. Also, find out what fees they charge for checking accounts and whether they pay interest on checking account balances.

2. (Speaking) Report to the class on your findings from the previous activity. Explain how the banks' policies differ and say which bank you would choose and why.

3. (Math) Suppose you are a single adult who earns $400 a week after your taxes are deducted. Your rent costs $425 a month and your transportation costs amount to $150 a month. Create a budget that shows how you will spend the money.

4. (Reading) Read the following feature to learn more about jobs.

WHO PROVIDES SERVICES FOR DAILY LIVING?

You already have worked in the service industry if you have delivered newspapers or have cared for children. Cutting lawns and walking dogs are other common service jobs for young people.

Workers in the service industry perform tasks for others. These usually are routine tasks that people do not have the time or the resources to do themselves.

Many teenagers find their first jobs in the service industry because they are plentiful and require little or no training or experience. These types of jobs, such as that of cashier at a restaurant, frequently can be performed on a part-time basis.

The service industry can be divided into several segments. One of the most important is protective services. Protective service workers guard people and their property. They also keep streets and highways safe by enforcing traffic laws.

Patrol officers probably are the most familiar protective service workers. Vicki and her partner, Eddie, are police officers who patrol a specific neighborhood. They look for anything unusual or suspicious. If anyone in the neighborhood is in trouble, Vicki and Eddie respond to the call for help. To be accepted for training as police officers, Vicki and Eddie both had to pass difficult physical examinations.

When Vicki and Eddie began their training, they expected to learn how to use firearms and how to handle emergencies. They were surprised that their training also included spoken and written skills. These skills are important, though, because police officers have to communicate effectively with citizens. Furthermore, police officers must write reports that often are referred to in court cases or other legal action.

Another major segment of the service industry is food service. These workers prepare and serve meals for people. They work in a variety of settings. The food service segment is expanding rapidly, because more people are eating meals out.

Many jobs in food service are for unskilled workers. One job that requires a lot of skill and experience is that of a chef or

cook in a restaurant. Darrin, for example, is the executive chef of a hotel restaurant. The restaurant attracts many customers because of his reputation for excellence.

Darrin started out in the food service business as a kitchen worker. He enjoyed cooking so much that he enrolled in a cooking course at a vocational school. Then he served an apprenticeship sponsored by a restaurant association. Over the years Darrin worked his way up the ranks—from short-order cook to vegetable and sauce cook to bread and pastry baker to his present position.

As executive chef, Darrin supervises the other cooks and kitchen workers. He develops menus for the restaurant, calculates the size of servings, and orders the food and other kitchen supplies. Darrin also is responsible for seeing that the kitchen maintains a high standard of cleanliness and sanitation.

Another important segment of the service industry is personal service and cleaning. Personal service workers perform tasks that help people look and feel better. For example, Davis and Cece are cosmetologists who operate their own unisex salon. In addition to cutting and styling hair, Cece and Davis give perms and color hair. They also give manicures and facial treatments. To become cosmetologists, Davis and Cece attended cosmetology school for one year and then passed a state licensing exam. Cece and Davis are much in demand because of society's emphasis on appearance.

The demand for home-cleaning services also has increased. Because of busy work schedules outside the home, more people are hiring others to do their housework. Jodie works for an agency that sends workers to clean people's homes. She dusts and polishes furniture, vacuums carpets, and scrubs floors. She also cleans ovens and refrigerators and washes windows. Jodie has not had any special training for her job.

As you might imagine, the tasks that service industry workers perform for other people are almost endless. Here are just a few more examples of jobs in the Service Occupations cluster of the *Occupational Outlook Handbook:*

- ❏ child care worker
- ❏ FBI agent
- ❏ fire fighter
- ❏ flight attendant
- ❏ janitor
- ❏ nursing aid
- ❏ security guard
- ❏ waiter or waitress

14

Understanding Our Economic System

When you have studied this chapter, you should be able to:

➡ Explain why profit and competition are important in a free enterprise system

➡ Discuss how prices are affected by supply and demand, and by inflation and deflation

➡ Give examples of how a basic understanding of these economic concepts can affect a worker's job choices and voting choices

Vocabulary Words

Free enterprise system

Enterprise

Competition

Supply

Demand

Inflation

Deflation

Prime interest rate

Trade union

Imagine living in a nation where you do not have freedom to pursue the career you want or to apply for the job you want. Instead, you must take a job that the government selects for you. Now suppose that there is almost no choice for consumers in the stores. You would certainly not be living in the United States. The United States has what is called a **free enterprise system**—its laws and traditions favor giving everyone as much freedom as possible and allowing them to run their own lives.

Many people think the United States has become the richest nation on earth because it has this type of economic system. In recent years, other nations, which used to have very different economic systems, have begun trying to make their own economies more like a free enterprise system. One reason they are doing this is because their own economies have been far less productive than the American free enterprise economy.

What principles lie behind a free enterprise system? How does it function? How will knowledge about the free enterprise system and answers to these questions affect you, now and when you are older? This chapter discusses these issues so that you will understand the impact of the free enterprise system on your own life.

Principles of a Free Enterprise System

A free enterprise system gives all citizens in the country as much freedom as possible. These systems reward and depend on people who show **enterprise.** Among its many meanings, enterprise means clever or bold inventiveness. Enterprise also is another word for a business. Thus, a nation with a free enterprise system encourages people who come up with clever ideas to invent products and solve problems. It also allows them great freedom to start, and profit from, businesses founded on such ideas.

Profit

Profit, as you have read, means the amount of money the owners of a business make after all expenses are deducted. It is the reward for risk, for turning a clever idea into real products or services, and for trying to keep producing them so that others can benefit. As long as consumers want the products or services, the business will be able to make a profit. When people no longer need or buy them, the business will cease to be profitable.

Every day Craig buys 50 copies of the *Lincoln Ledger* for 10 cents each and delivers them for 20 cents each. When he collects from his customers at the end of the week, he calculates his profits. He receives $1.40 from each customer (20 cents × 7 days), making a total of $70 ($1.40 × 50 customers). He also receives $10 in tips,

Trading goods is a common form of exchange for children. Because our society is so complex, money is commonly used for this purpose.

raising his total income to $80 per week. However, he pays the newspaper company $35 (10 cents × 50 copies × 7 days). So his profit is $45 ($80 minus $35). This is what encourages him to get up early every morning to deliver the paper.

If Craig gets lazy, however, and delivers the newspaper during his lunch hour instead of in the morning, there will be fewer people in his neighborhood who subscribe to the paper. This will affect his profit. It also will affect the amount of money he pays to the newspaper company, which may start looking for a more reliable delivery person. The consumers in Craig's neighborhood are protected in any case, because both Craig and the newspaper want to make a profit. If the service Craig provides is inadequate, both his and the newspaper's profits will suffer. Craig will then have to choose between providing better service or losing his job.

Competition

Profit is one feature of the free enterprise system, but it is not the only one. When Craig found he had fewer homes on his delivery route, you might ask, could he raise his prices and sell his newspapers for $1 each? This would make his delivery route profitable again. Even if he only had seven people left on his route, he now would be making 90 cents on each newspaper sold ($1 minus 10 cents). Forgetting about tips this time (he probably would not get any tips at that price anyway, especially with lunchtime delivery), the new, higher price would lead to a profit of $44.10 each week (90 cents × 7 people × 7 days). That is a fairly good profit for delivering only seven papers, four hours late.

This is where **competition** comes in. In economics, competition means almost the same as it does in other fields. When you try to gain a place on a baseball team, you are competing with other people who want the same thing. If you make the team instead of those you are competing against, your competitors will be disappointed. Similarly, in economics, if two businesses are both trying to sell a product or service, they are in competition with each other. The one that makes its product or service most attractive to consumers' needs or wants will almost always win.

Businesses can compete in several different ways. The product a business provides may be more attractive because it is made better, or it may be more attractive because it is less expensive. By selling newspapers at $1 each, Craig is opening himself up to competition. If there is a rival newspaper, and the delivery person for

One of the more obvious ways that stores compete is in price. Do you know how else they can compete?

Demand is made up of the number of customers who buy a product or service.

Review Questions

1 ▶ In a free enterprise system, how are people encouraged to risk converting clever ideas into real products and services?

2 ▶ What prevents businesses from raising their prices if they are growing less profitable?

3 ▶ Name two different ways in which businesses can compete.

that newspaper promises delivery before breakfast for 25 cents, this would be an offer no customer could refuse. Craig would soon have no customers. His competitor would have beaten him and driven him out of business.

The same kind of thing would happen on a large scale if the *Lincoln Ledger* started to publish news that offended its readers in some way. *The Lincoln Telegraph*, a competitor, would begin to win more readers, and might even drive the *Ledger* out of business, unless it responded to its readers' complaints.

In a free enterprise system, competition helps assure people of products and services that are up to the standards of quality they expect. Competition also prevents businesses from overcharging for their products. Higher quality and lower priced products and services are two very important benefits to the consumer.

How a Free Enterprise System Functions

As you could perhaps see from the story about Craig, prices are affected by more than competition and the desire for profit. They also are influenced by other forces. When Craig started delivering the *Ledger* at lunchtime, he lost customers even though the *Telegraph* had not yet begun to deliver newspapers in his territory. Even if the *Telegraph* had not existed, by raising his price to $1 Craig most certainly would lose most of his customers. In a free enterprise system, prices are not only controlled by competition, but they also affect and react to **supply** and **demand**.

What skills and aptitudes do you think this worker needs to have?

Supply and Demand

In economics, supply has a special meaning. It means the amount of a product or service suppliers will provide at a particular price. Suppose Rebecca and two of her high school friends are operating a car wash service one day a week. They charge $6 per car and can handle 12 cars in a day. If they washed any more cars, they would be too tired the next day. Thus, the supply they can handle is 12 cars per week, or 48 cars per month.

They easily can find people willing to pay their price. In fact, they have a list of 48 regular customers, each of whom wants his or her car washed once a month. In addition, there are at least three times as many people who want to get onto their list of regular customers. However, they only can handle these people's cars occasionally, when a regular customer is out of town.

The number of customers who are ready to buy a product or service at a particular price makes up the demand. It seems that, at a price of $6 a wash, there are at least 192 people (48 customers × 4) who would like Rebecca's group to wash their cars. Rebecca and her friends are known for the care they take when washing the cars, and for their fair price, that is way below the $10 price charged by a local automatic car wash.

Rebecca wonders what would happen if she raised her prices. In fact, one of the neighbors, who is not on her list of regular customers, said he would be willing to pay $9 to have his car washed. Rebecca does not want to spoil her relationship with her regular customers. She is sure she would lose some of them if she raised her prices and offered no additional services. What should she do? Should she lose some of her customers and begin charging the $9 her new neighbor is offering? Because her car washing service is in demand, she now has the option to raise her prices.

However, as word gets out that neighbors are willing to pay $9 for a car wash, Rebecca realizes that other groups of teenagers probably will start car washing operations of their own. As they begin to offer their services, the supply of car washing in the neighborhood will increase. Soon, there may be two or three groups willing to wash cars, which between them could handle 36 cars each weekend, or 144 per month. That is getting close to the 192 customers Rebecca knows about. Rebecca has realized if the price goes up, the supply of car washing services will go up too, adding a lot of competition she did not have before.

Suppose at the higher price some of the customers decide to have their cars washed only once every two months. In that case, as the price goes up, demand will come down. Then how many cars will there be to wash each month? Perhaps there will be even fewer than 144. Demand for car washes would be *lower* than supply. What would happen to the prices then?

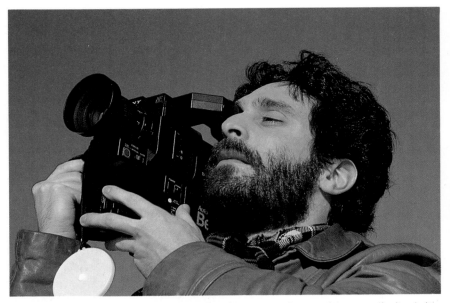

When an item, such as a camcorder, is new and quantities are limited, it commands a high price. However, when its supply is greater than its demand, the price will fall dramatically.

The neighbor who offered Rebecca $9 now has other groups who can wash her car. If Jordy's group offers a car wash for $8.50, who is likely to get more business? Obviously, Jordy is. If Ned says he will wash cars for $8, Jordy's business will be his. Perhaps Rebecca can keep her customers by doing a better job than the competition, but most of the neighbors may be satisfied with Jordy's and Ned's work. Rebecca will need to bring her prices down again if she is to keep earning the profits she wants.

In general, if the demand from consumers is greater than the supply from producers, prices tend to rise. This is one reason why gold is so expensive—only a limited supply is available. If, however, the demand from consumers is lower than the supply from producers, prices will fall. This might happen if people stopped wanting so much gold. Suppliers would have to bring the price of gold down to find enough customers who wanted to buy it. The price of gold also might become lower if the supply of gold suddenly increased. Once again, because supply would be larger than demand, prices would begin to come down.

Inflation and Deflation

When your parents or guardians were younger, they may tell you, they could buy about a dozen candy bars for $1. Today, $1 will buy only two or three candy bars. Does this mean that the
(continued on page 268)

CHANGING TO KEEP UP WITH THE TIMES

Two years ago I had a thriving dry cleaning store. I handled the cleaning, my wife handled the customers, and I employed six people to help. We were doing very well.

Then last year our landlord announced that she was raising the rent. When she told us she planned to triple our rent, we knew we could not pay that much and still stay in business. I tried to bargain with the landlord, but she insisted that the storefront was worth a "luxury" price.

When the initial shock wore off, I met with my employees and told them to start looking for new jobs. That night my wife convinced me to look for ways to keep the business without the store. For weeks I thought of nothing else. Then one day while I was at work the idea struck me.

I began by buying a new business suit and printing business cards and brochures. Then I set out to "sell" my new business. I talked to hospital administrators, restaurant owners, airline personnel, and heads of other businesses where employees wore uniforms. I offered them a competitive price for door-to-door dry cleaning services. Many places hired me on a trial basis.

I told my employees to stop looking for new jobs. A week later I applied for and got a bank loan. I bought two delivery vans. Then I moved my equipment to warehouse space I had rented. My wife still dealt with the customers, but now she did it on the phone from our home.

I did not want to lose our regular customers, so I arranged to pick up and deliver their

dry cleaning at their homes or offices. They suggested I advertise my dry cleaning delivery service in the local paper. The response was overwhelming.

Today I employ 20 workers who help me with the cleaning and pickups and deliveries. Working people are so busy nowadays that they appreciate the convenience of our home and office delivery service.

We have been very successful because we have adjusted our business to fill a need and because we save people time. Very often time is money for our customers. ■

demand for candy has increased more than the supply? No, it does not. Another reason that prices change is **inflation.**

Inflation refers to a general rise in prices that occurs when businesses increase the prices of their goods and services to cover the increased cost of production. Workers may ask for higher wages because prices have risen. Those wages, in turn, add to businesses' production costs. As you can see, this is a circular phenomenon. It is often called the wage-price spiral. Though it appears to raise both prices *and* wages, its overall effect is neither of these. Instead, it simply lessens the value of money.

Suppose when your parents were young a particular job paid $2 an hour. Someone in that job could buy a ticket to a movie for one-half hour of work, or $1. Today an hour's work in that job earns $10, but how long would it take to earn the cost of a movie ticket? The answer is still one-half hour. Not much has changed over the years except for the value of the dollar.

Does the dollar's value decrease evenly? No, it does not. In some years, prices and wages edge up slowly. This is a good sign. It means the economy is healthy. In other years, however, wages and prices move very fast, with wages not quite keeping up with prices. People have more money because their wages are increasing, so they buy products. Because prices also are increasing, however, people may find themselves borrowing heavily to pay for all the products they buy. This can lead to a sudden change in the economy as people realize how large their debts have become.

In fact, the opposite of inflation may occur. This is called **deflation**, and it happens during times when the economy is very inactive. Consumers, feeling they do not have much extra money, spend less. Then the demand for goods and services decreases. Because businesses do not need to produce as much, they need fewer workers. As a result, some people lose their jobs. Because people are out of work, even less money is spent on products and services. Although this may lead some businesses to lower their prices, it also may lessen their profits and force them to lay off still more workers. Fortunately, deflation has been relatively rare in recent times. It can, however, have a very destructive effect on an economy if it continues for a long period of time.

Also fortunate is the fact that the Federal Reserve System of our government can control deflation and excessive inflation to some degree. If you follow news reports on the **prime interest rate**—the interest rate banks charge their biggest business customers—you can see which way experts think the economy is headed. If there is danger that inflation will cause people to go into debt, the prime rate will be increased. This discourages borrowing and encourages saving. If, however, there is risk of deflation, the prime rate will be reduced. This encourages companies and businesses to use their money to create more jobs and more products.

Review Questions _____

1 ▶ What economic concept means the amount of a product or service that businesses will provide at a given price?

2 ▶ If the demand for a service increases, what effect is this likely to have on the fees people charge for it?

3 ▶ What happens to the value of the dollar in times of inflation?

Economic factors influence every part of a person's life. Do any of these factors affect your life now?

Economics and Your Job

Inflation, deflation, and other economic factors may sound abstract but they do affect prices and jobs. Economics influence every worker's ability to find a job and keep it. The principles of economics help to determine how much money workers earn from their jobs, as well as how much they can buy with their money. Understanding the basic principles of economics can help you choose your future occupation wisely.

The Demand for Special Skills

When Amanda accepts a job, she is selling her time, knowledge, and skills to the company that will employ her. The company pays wages—her income—for her time, knowledge and skills. The amount she is paid depends in part on the economic ideas discussed earlier in this chapter—competition, supply, and demand.

If many businesses want her particular skills—skills not many workers have—she will earn a high salary. The demand for her skills exceeds the supply. Earlier in this chapter, you read how the scarceness of gold contributes to its high price. Amanda's skills are gold on the job market. On the other hand, if many people with the same skills are competing for only a few jobs, the people who get those jobs usually earn low incomes.

Many specialized jobs, which require a lot of talent and training, command high wages because there are few people with the necessary qualifications.

Trade Unions

Until this century, most American workers competed individually for jobs. Because many workers had the same skills, individuals often would accept low wages, or work long hours in order to get and keep a job. As a result, many employers were able to pay low wages and offer few fringe benefits because there was such a large supply of workers. This resulted in big profits for the businesses and little competition from other businesses.

Late in the 19th century, however, workers began banding together in **trade unions** to negotiate for wages and better working conditions. A trade union is generally made up of workers in related jobs. The Teamsters Union, for example, negotiates for truckers, and the Newspaper Guild negotiates for news reporters and editors. Workers in a trade union agree not to offer their work for lower wages. They will work only at the rate the union has negotiated. To get what they think are fair rates, union representatives talk with management in collective bargaining. If unions do not get what they bargain for, they sometimes organize strikes and other kinds of protests. By negotiating through unions rather than individually, workers in many industries have obtained better wages and working conditions.

The influence of unions has diminished in the last decade or two in the United States because union growth has slowed. However, unions still are very powerful in some industries. In such industries, many companies have union shops, where workers must pay union dues even if they do not support the union. Dues are required payments. Union supporters say union shops are fair because all workers benefit from the unions' efforts. Other workers, however, disagree with this and other union policies.

You and Economics

Understanding economic principles can help you better plan your life. Your understanding of competition, supply, and demand can help you identify those occupations that are most likely to pay well. If you can acquire the education and skills required for one of these occupations, you may be able to earn a comfortable income throughout your working life or until you retire.

Most workers, however, change jobs from time to time. In fact, workers today are likely to change careers several times. An understanding of economics can help you choose the best time to change jobs or careers. Newspaper stories about increased consumer spending, or about a decrease in the prime interest rate, may tip you off that businesses will be hiring more workers. Stories about

Workers in unions can use a strike as a bargaining tool—as long as they all stick together.

Review Questions

1 ▶ How can the principles of supply and demand affect how much you earn from a job?

2 ▶ What is the purpose of a union?

3 ▶ Why is an understanding of economic principles important to a worker?

deflation, on the other hand, should encourage you to hold on to the job or career that you have.

Staying informed about economic trends also will help you vote more responsibly. Develop your own views on economic issues such as trade unionism. You will be better able to vote responsibly if you understand how these issues affect workers, businesses, and the economy in general.

An understanding of economic principles also is essential for anyone who starts a business. As you will learn in Chapter 15, successful entrepreneurs must make careful choices. They must decide what businesses to pursue, where to get the money they need, and when to begin. The more an entrepreneur knows about economics, the better his or her choices are likely to be.

Summary

- ❑ The American free enterprise system has enabled this country to become one of the richest nations in the world by making its citizens free to control their own lives.

- ❑ Excessive profits are controlled by competition between businesses that try to win the consumers' dollars.

- ❑ Supply and demand regulate prices in a free enterprise system.

- ❑ During periods of inflation, prices and wages increase continuously, with the effect that the dollar loses value.

- ❑ Deflation occurs when consumers slow down their spending.

- ❑ Both inflation and deflation can have destructive effects on society if they continue for a long period of time.

- ❑ By acquiring skills that are in great demand but short supply, you can improve your chances of earning a comfortable income.

- ❑ To improve jobs where the demand for workers is less than the supply, many workers join trade unions.

- ❑ Understanding basic economic issues can help you make more responsible career choices.

Vocabulary Exercise

Match the terms on the left with the definitions on the right:

1. supply
2. deflation
3. demand
4. inflation
5. competition

A. The number of consumers who want to purchase a product or service at a particular price

B. An upward spiral of prices and wages

C. The effort by several people or businesses to obtain something they cannot all have

D. The availability of an item or service at a particular price

E. An economic trend in which consumers spend little, so producers sell less, and many workers lose their jobs

True or False?

6. In a free enterprise system, businesses have freedom but people do not.

7. Enterprise means business, and it also means clever inventiveness.

Discussion Questions

1. The chapter says profit is a reward for risk. Does it seem fair to you that the owners of businesses are the ones who make the profit and that workers usually earn a fixed wage? What if the business fails to make a profit? Do you think that employees should go without their wages?

2. What signs of competition do you see within your own town or community? Do you think that competition affects price more often than it affects quality, or vice versa? Explain your answer.

3. Important jobs for which the supply of workers is limited are often highly paid. However, it frequently happens that such jobs become less desirable after some years have passed. Why should this be?

Thinking Further

1. (Writing) From newspapers, magazine articles, and encyclopedias, find out as much as you can about the economic system of a communist or socialist country. Write a report for the class in which you discuss the roles of competition and profits in that country. Include your own opinions about the advantages and disadvantages of such economic systems.

2. (Speaking) If you have a job that you work at fairly regularly, calculate the money you make each month. Do you have any expenses you must pay? How does competition affect the job(s) you have and your ability to get new jobs? Is the supply of people with your skills less than the demand, or is it greater? Prepare and give an oral report to your class about these matters.

3. (Listening) Interview two or three people who work in the same field. Find out how much their company charges for the products or services it provides. Are their prices close to each other? Try to account for the similarity or differences.

4. (Reading) Read the following feature to learn more about jobs.

WHO EDUCATES THE STUDENTS?

You probably are familiar with the jobs people have at your school, but you may not realize how many things they do as part of their jobs. Let us take a closer look.

First, there are your teachers. You know they devote several hours a week to teaching your class. Are you aware of what they do the rest of the week? Mrs. Christensen, for example, has three classes of math and two classes of life science. She supervises a homeroom and a study hall. After school, she coaches girls' gymnastics and tennis.

She also meets with other staff members to discuss students' progress once a week, and she takes time to prepare lessons and correct papers. She often does this work at home at night or on weekends.

Mrs. Christensen's reports are shared with Mr. Adams and Ms. Garcia, the school counselors. You probably know the counselors at your school because they help you choose classes and arrange schedules. They also give achievement tests. After scoring the tests, they add the information to the students' permanent records.

Mr. Adams and Ms. Garcia also organize school activities. Mr. Adams is the student council advisor. Ms. Garcia leads a Junior Great Books discussion group.

The most important job the counselors do is help the students with their problems. A student might be having trouble getting along with a teacher, or a student might be getting poor grades in one class. In situations like these, counselors often give students advice and encouragement.

Another person who is vital to the school is Mr. Maxey, the librarian. You probably have asked for help from your school librarian. Helping students find information in the library is a school librarian's main job. In addition to doing that, Mr. Maxey teaches a

unit to every English class on how to use the library. He keeps track of all the books, magazines, and other library resources. He also does all the ordering for the library.

He often calls the library a media center because, in addition to books, they have tapes, records, and films there. Some media centers even have computers.

School teachers, counselors, and librarians must have bachelor's degrees from accredited colleges. To maintain their teaching licenses, teachers must continually update their knowledge and skills by attending workshops, college classes, and seminars. Many states require counselors to have a master's degree in counseling plus several years' teaching experience. More and more school systems are only hiring librarians with a master's degree in library science.

It takes special abilities to be a school teacher, counselor, or librarian. They must know their subject area very well and be able to communicate it in a clear and interesting way. They must be able to work with students of varying ability levels. They must be patient, understanding, and able to inspire confidence. Above all, they must enjoy working with young people. Oftentimes, the most important parts of the job are helping young

people feel good about themselves and helping them get along with others.

In the years ahead, dedicated and skillful teachers, counselors, and librarians will be needed more than ever. Children will need more education to live in a complex society. Schools will be expected to help solve the problems of American society. Even today, schools are including more topics in their curriculum, such as drug education.

You know that teachers, counselors, and librarians are employed by public and private schools. There also are many other places where people with this kind of training can work. Here are just a few of the related careers in the Teachers, Librarians, and Counselors cluster of the *Occupational Outlook Handbook*:

❏ college or university librarian

❏ employment counselor

❏ mental health counselor

❏ public librarian

❏ rehabilitation counselor

❏ special librarian

WHO HELPS PROFESSIONALS?

When you go to the public library, a library assistant may help you find a book. If someone in your family needs legal advice, a paralegal might do much of the paperwork. When your school was built, construction workers followed a blueprint drawn by a drafter. If you fly on an airplane, air traffic controllers must assist the pilot in getting the plane safely in and out of airports.

These workers belong to a group who assist, or support, the work of professionals. They perform their jobs under the supervision of professionals. The workers in this cluster do not have as much education or training as professionals, and they usually do not have as much responsibility.

One of the workers in this group is Bruce. He is a library assistant at a branch library. He assists the librarian in ordering and processing new books, magazines, and tapes, and in keeping materials organized on shelves and in filing cabinets. Bruce also helps library patrons find information and operate library equipment.

Bruce earned an associate of arts degree in library technology at a local junior college. The two-year course of study included library organization, operation, and automation, as well as liberal arts courses.

Harold is a paralegal for a law firm. Har-

old helps lawyers find out how similar situations were handled in previous cases. Harold uses a computer to search for cases. He studies the information and summarizes his findings in a report. Harold also helps the lawyers by preparing legal documents such as contracts, mortgages, and divorce papers.

Harold works in a medium-size law office handling general legal matters. Paralegals also can work for large law firms with specialized departments such as bankruptcy, real estate, and family law. They also can work for corporations, the government, or community legal services.

Most paralegals must complete formal training before working. Harold got his job after completing a two-year program in legal assistance at a local business school.

Georgina works for an architectural firm. As a drafter, she turns the architects' rough sketches of office buildings and houses into detailed drawings. The drawings show the exact dimensions of the buildings and specify the materials and procedures to be used.

Georgina does her drawings manually. She uses a drawing board, compasses, protractors, and triangles. Georgina learned drafting fundamentals by taking a two-year course at a vocational-technical institute.

Juan, Jarrod, and Katie are air traffic controllers. They control when and where planes land and take off. During a flight, several controllers—each with a different responsibility—assist the pilot.

Juan, Jarrod, and Katie work in the control tower at a metropolitan airport. Planes are constantly landing or taking off in all directions. The air traffic controllers use radar—and visual observation—to monitor the position of each plane. When a plane is ready to leave the airport, Juan directs the plane to an open runway. Jarrod informs the pilot about weather and wind conditions and gives the okay for takeoff. Katie guides the plane out of the airport's airspace.

Air traffic controllers work as a team to bring planes safely in and out of airports. They must be able to speak clearly and to make quick decisions. This job requires tremendous concentration.

To be accepted for training as air traffic controllers, Juan, Jarrod, and Katie had to be 31 or younger and have four years of college or three years of work experience. They had to pass a written aptitude test and physical and psychological exams.

Formal training for air traffic controllers lasts about four months. They also receive on-the-job training. Air traffic controllers do not become fully qualified until they have had several years of work experience and additional classroom training.

Library assistants, drafters, paralegals, and air traffic controllers offer valuable assistance to professionals. Other workers in the Technologists and Technicians, Except Health cluster in the *Occupational Outlook Handbook* include the following:

- ☐ broadcast technicians
- ☐ computer programmers
- ☐ engineering technicians
- ☐ science technicians
- ☐ tool programmers

15
Becoming an Entrepreneur

When you have studied this chapter, you should be able to:

▶▶ Explain what entrepreneurs do

▶▶ Describe important characteristics of successful entrepreneurs

▶▶ Discuss the role of entrepreneurship in the American economy

Vocabulary Words

Venture

Agent

Market research

Collateral

Franchise

Business plan

Innovation

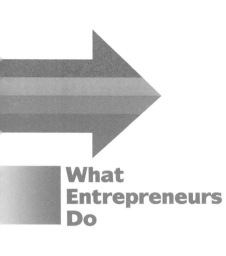

What Entrepreneurs Do

Courtney has been videotaping parties and special occasions for friends and relatives for years. She dreams about starting her own business after she finishes high school. Courtney knows that being an entrepreneur involves many risks. She probably will have to invest a lot of time, effort, and money in her new business. She also will have to plan carefully, but she feels the rewards of entrepreneurship outweigh the risks.

In the American economic system, entrepreneurship is a career option for everyone, but one few people choose. In Chapters 5 and 10 you learned why entrepreneurs start businesses and the traits they must have to succeed. This chapter expands on what you already know by providing you with information about what specific entrepreneurs do to start their businesses. It discusses the risks they take, how they judge an idea's chances of success, and how they organize the resources they need.

Entrepreneurs: The Risk Takers

Entrepreneurs represent the spirit of the American free enterprise system. Many entrepreneurs are living proof of the American dream that even a person who was born in poverty can grow up and succeed in the world of business.

An entrepreneur can build a business on any of three foundations. Some entrepreneurs base their **ventures** on their own ideas or inventions. A venture is a task or job that involves risk. Others purchase existing businesses, then contribute their own ideas in hopes of making those businesses more successful. The third alternative is to act as an **agent**, forging deals between people with ideas and people with money to invest in them. For example, many authors hire agents to present story ideas to book publishers and to negotiate contracts with those publishers.

Whatever their products or services, entrepreneurs are people who take risks. Their ventures may make them incredibly wealthy, or they may leave them with huge debts. Many entrepreneurs risk their lifetime savings to start businesses. Others risk homes they have worked hard to purchase. At the very least, entrepreneurs run the risk that the long hours of hard work they spend on a venture will be lost if the business fails.

An entrepreneur starts to build a business by perceiving a need for a new product or service, or for an improvement on a product or service that already is available. Next, the entrepreneur must create a profitable means of filling the perceived need. This involves organizing the necessary resources and building a business organization—both of which pose risks.

Some entrepreneurs build their ventures on creative inventions or artwork.

Perceiving a Need

For an enterprise to succeed, there must be a demand for the products or services it is selling. As Chapter 14 explained, demand determines how much a business can charge for a product or service. If the number of people who want the product or service is too small, the business will fail. How do entrepreneurs determine if a demand exists for what they want to sell?

Some follow hunches based on their own observations. In this chapter we are going to take a look at some real examples. Two New York women, Sophia Collier and Connie Best, saw a need for soft drinks made without artificial colors or preservatives. In 1977 they founded American Natural Beverage Corporation, which makes Soho Sodas. At first, they mixed and bottled soda in Collier's kitchen and sold it to local stores from her car. Store managers responded enthusiastically, which confirmed their hunch. In 1978, Collier and Best sold 72,000 bottles of soda. Nine years later, their company sold $30 million in soda.

Most successful businesspeople rely on more than their instincts. Most do **market research**, which consists of studies to determine who will buy a product or service and how much people are willing to pay. Market research reduces an entrepreneur's risk by helping to predict whether a venture will succeed. If that research shows success is unlikely, the entrepreneur may drop the idea before risking a great deal of time or money on it. On the other hand, if the market research points toward success, the entrepreneur probably will go ahead with the idea. Market research also can help persuade investors to lend an entrepreneur money to help fund a venture. In fact, an entrepreneur is more likely to do market research if the venture he or she is starting will require other people to make a large investment.

Putting Together a Deal

Starting a business requires money, but that does not mean entrepreneurs need to be wealthy. The less money entrepreneurs have, the more energetic and imaginative they have to be to succeed. Most entrepreneurs risk money of their own on their ventures. Those without much money often take risks to get the funds they need for starting businesses. Entrepreneurs who borrow money

Robert DeKraft and Michael Lancaster are two former technicians who bought their boss's Lawn Doctor franchise in 1975. A few years ago they had a 20 percent profit and were winners of back-to-back awards for image and professional standards.

Judi Sheppard Missett's success as an entrepreneur began when she started the Jazzercise corporation.

from financial institutions to start businesses, for example, often are required to use their homes as **collateral**. Collateral is a valuable possession that a borrower uses to guarantee repayment of a loan. If a venture fails, and the owner cannot repay the loan, the financial institution recovers its money by selling the collateral.

Some entrepreneurs act as agents, helping other entrepreneurs find financial backers. The backers may lend money, much as a bank does. More frequently a backer gives money to an entrepreneur in exchange for shares of the venture's profits.

Agents do not risk their own money on the business ideas of others. (They do risk the money they spend on their own offices, telephones, and other business necessities.) They must show enterprise, however, in finding people with good ideas for products or services and in promoting those ideas to investors.

Agents provide an important service to the many entrepreneurs who know little about how to attract investors. Without an agent's business skills, even an inventor with a brilliant idea for a product might fail in business. For acting as a go-between in a business deal, an agent may charge a percentage of the money invested—or a percentage of the new venture's profits.

Entrepreneurs whose businesses succeed and expand can sometimes sell **franchises** to other entrepreneurs. A franchise is the right to sell a company's goods or services and use its name in a certain area. Purchasing a franchise is one of the least risky and least expensive ways to become an entrepreneur. The person who purchases a franchise risks money to purchase it, but the business idea already has been profitable in other market areas.

Jazzercise, Inc. has grown dramatically because of Judi Sheppard Missett's franchising strategy. As founder and president of the aerobics corporation, she sells franchises for a low start-up fee of $500. This allows a lot of people to buy a franchise. Then, the people who purchase the franchise must pay the Jazzercise corporation 20 percent of the money they earn. In this way, the company makes a profit. Today Missett has revenues of $13 million with 3,800 franchises operating worldwide.

Many national fast-food restaurant chains are franchise operations. So are other kinds of businesses, from car repair services and lawn care services to real estate dealerships.

Creating an Organization

A new business may have only one or two workers, the owner or partners who founded it. Business ventures succeed when the demand for their services or products increases. When this happens, the founders may no longer be able to handle all the work themselves. Then they need to hire other qualified people to help make the products or provide the services.

A growing business also may need to hire people who have skills that its founders lack. An entrepreneur with basic math skills can keep simple financial records, but as a company grows, its records become more complex. The founders may need to hire or contract with someone who is skilled at keeping complex financial records. Eventually, a growing business also will need workers with other specialized, technical skills. Whenever a business succeeds, its continued growth depends on hiring trustworthy workers with the necessary skills, knowledge, and experience.

When adding employees to a new business, an entrepreneur needs a good sense of timing as well as judgment about people. If the entrepreneur hires too many employees too soon, their salaries could exceed the venture's income and put it out of business. When entrepreneurs are too slow to hire help, they may fail because they cannot keep up with the demand for their products or services. Entrepreneurs also risk failure as their businesses grow if they hire people who turn out to be unreliable.

Review Questions

1 ▶ Describe three foundations on which an entrepreneur can build a business.

2 ▶ What do entrepreneurs risk?

3 ▶ What must an entrepreneur do after perceiving a need for a product or service? What does this involve?

The failure rate for new businesses is high. It is estimated that at least one-fourth of new ventures will fail within the first three years of operation. Of those that stay in business, most will achieve only modest success. It usually takes at least five years for a new venture to become profitable. A few entrepreneurial businesses will grow into companies that make their founders extremely wealthy and provide jobs for many people.

Many entrepreneurs who fail in their first business ventures go on to found new ones. Their persistance eventually may reward them. If you decide to start a business, its success will depend on careful planning, organization, hard work, patience, and your willingness to accept help from others.

Be Well Organized

Successful entrepreneurs have well-thought-out plans for their ventures. Those plans are based on solid information. An entrepreneur applying for a loan from a financial institution must present a written **business plan**. Individual investors usually require a business plan, too, before deciding whether to back a venture. A business plan includes information about how many customers the venture can expect to have and how the owners arrived at those figures. It also states how the entrepreneur will let potential customers know about the business. Some of the other questions that must be answered in a business plan are:

- [ ] How much will the venture charge for its product or service?
- [ ] How much will it cost to provide the product or service?
- [ ] How will the business expand if demand for the product or service increases?

Entrepreneurs do not always prepare written business plans, especially for very small businesses that do not require loans. Every entrepreneur, however, should have a clear plan in mind, if not on paper, before risking time and money to start a business.

Work Hard and Patiently

Any entrepreneur must be prepared to work very hard to make his or her venture succeed. Entrepreneurs often work many more hours than people who are employed in organizations, especially when the entrepreneurs' businesses are new. They may work a lot of evenings and weekends in addition to normal working hours.

(continued on page 286)

THERE IS MORE THAN ONE WAY TO RUN A BUSINESS

Five years ago I inherited enough money to open my own woodworking store in town. I had studied woodworking since I was 14 years old. I wanted to run my own business and sell the handmade furniture I had designed and made over the years.

After I received the inheritance, I rented a shop. I moved my furniture into the store and carefully arranged it in groupings. I waited for customers to come.

I did not make any sales for a few months until the summer tourists arrived. They were the only people who could afford to buy my furniture. I charged a lot, since it took me a long time to make each piece. I made a few sales to tourists and hoped for better luck next year.

All winter I designed and made new pieces. I only opened the store on weekends. I made one sale that winter. Business improved that summer because of the tourists, but by October I was broke.

When I gave up the store and put my furniture in the attic at home, it was the lowest point in my life. Before too long, my depression ended. I decided that I was going to find a way to run my business successfully. This time, though, I did a little research first.

I started by contacting organizations for furniture makers, cabinetmakers, and woodcrafters. Then I read books about marketing and spoke to marketing professionals. A new kind of business took shape in my mind.

To maintain year-round customers, I would make and sell inexpensive but well-crafted wooden household utensils, toys, and gifts. I contacted local woodworkers who made items like that and offered them an outlet for their goods in my store.

Then I created a store out of the two front rooms of my house. This saved me a fortune in rent. I hired a part-time salesperson who could handle the customers while I continued to make the merchandise. I advertised in the local papers.

By having a wide range of products with varying prices, I have attracted many people. I now have many regular local and seasonal customers. I am glad I did not give up. I just got business sense instead. ∎

When entrepreneurs first start a new business, they usually have to do the work of many people.

Their socializing may be linked to the new business's success, too, such as when they entertain prospective clients.

When Marshall Rinker started his cement business he worked 12-hour days, which is not unusual for an entrepreneur. Rinker started his business in the 1930s with one dump truck and a shed. He built his company into Florida's largest cement producer. A few years ago, he sold it for $515 million.

In most new businesses, the founders put in long hours doing *all* the work, not just the parts that interest them most. The founders of an advertising agency, for example, may be interested primarily in writing and designing ads. Before they can do that, however, they must sell their services to clients—even if they dislike sales work. They also may handle their own correspondence and maintain their own financial records. Of course, the founders can pay other people to perform these services, but hiring people costs money that many entrepreneurs do not have. Even if they borrow from banks or investors, entrepreneurs often do all the work themselves at first. They may continue to do everything until their businesses grow too large for them to handle everything.

Entrepreneurs need patience because they may face setbacks from time to time. They may not make profits as quickly as they hoped. Customers they counted on may not buy. Business costs may increase more than expected. A fire, flood, or other disaster may destroy supplies or a batch of a product. Even an entrepreneur who plans well, makes responsible decisions, and acts carefully can encounter bad luck. Some entrepreneurs give up on their businesses when they encounter setbacks. Others, including some of the most successful people in business, have continued working in spite of extreme difficulties.

Sophia Collier and Connie Best made a $1 profit the year after they founded American Natural Beverage Corporation. That might have discouraged many people, but Collier and Best persisted to build a multimillion dollar, nationwide company.

Lynn Moore had tried other careers before she started her own business in her mid-20s. She had saved $15,000 when she started her public relations business in 1982. By the end of the year, she had spent her savings and was $50,000 in debt, but she refused to give up. She invited some former Western Electric bosses to lunch, borrowed a mink coat to appear well-off, and got the executives to invest $30,000 in her business. A few years ago, Moore International earned $1.3 million and was debt free.

The Small Business Administration provides many services that entrepreneurs can use. Here a retired executive provides advice to someone planning to start her own business.

Accept Help That Is Available

Review Questions ———

1 ▶ What kinds of information does a business plan include?

2 ▶ Why do people who start businesses usually do all the work themselves at first?

3 ▶ How does the Small Business Administration help entrepreneurs?

People who start businesses may not be able to hire help at first, but some kinds of help are available at no cost. Many organizations have an interest in helping new businesses succeed. A city government, for example, may offer tax breaks and other help to a business that will eventually provide jobs. A bank that lends money to entrepreneurs also wants them to succeed, so the entrepreneurs will do more business with the bank. Because of this, bankers may offer free financial advice to their business customers. Experienced entrepreneurs, too, often are willing to share what they have learned with people who are starting businesses.

Another source of help for new enterprises is the Small Business Administration (SBA). The SBA was established by the federal government for the purpose of helping entrepreneurs. The SBA gives loans to businesses and provides expert advice to new business owners. It also publishes dozens of pamphlets on topics of interest to entrepreneurs, which it sells at very low prices.

Entrepreneurs and the American Economy

Government policies also encourage new businesses—that is part of what distinguishes the American economic system from foreign economic systems. The government encourages new business ventures because the businesses provide jobs and help to keep money flowing throughout the system. Entrepreneurs also bring other benefits to consumers and businesses.

Entrepreneurs and Innovation

An **innovation** is a new idea. The invention of a physical object is an innovation, but so is an idea for a product or service that solves an old problem in a new way. Many entrepreneurs base their new businesses on innovations. As innovators, entrepreneurs contribute to the wide range of goods and services that are available to American consumers and businesses.

Brooke Knapp started her charter airline company, Jet Airways, Inc., to solve two problems. While having dinner with a group of businesspeople, she learned that they were having difficulty getting flights from one city to another and that they also were having to pay too much money in taxes for travel. In 1979, Brooke organized Jet Airways as a luxury charter company and as a tax shelter for the people who used it. In six years, she expanded her company to 9 planes and 19 pilots.

Trish Cronan combined her love of the sea and her business sense into a profitable venture—a glamorous yacht-chartering company named Ocean Escapes, Inc.

Entrepreneurs and Employment

When entrepreneurs succeed, their businesses grow and they cannot handle all the work themselves. They must hire people to help them meet the demand for their products or services. Successful new companies soon need skilled workers. A business also may hire researchers to develop additional products. As a business organization becomes larger and more complex, it needs managers to keep its departments or divisions running smoothly.

A venture started by one entrepreneur can grow into a company that employs many people. Berkley & Co., an Iowa corporation that manufactures fishing tackle, is an example. Berkley Bidell started the company in his parents' home when he was 15, in the 1930s. A few years ago, it was selling $60 million worth of tackle a year and providing jobs for 900 people.

Some entrepreneurs must pruchase expensive equipment before they can start their own businesses. Can you think of other pieces of equipment entrepreneurs might need to buy?

Repeat Entrepreneurs

Many successful entrepreneurs are satisfied with starting one business. Those who love their work often stay with their companies even after they become wealthy. Other successful entrepreneurs sell their companies and retire on the profits.

For some entrepreneurs, however, the challenge of starting a new business is irresistible. No sooner have they sold one successful business than they feel the urge to start another.

Michael S. Dell is one entrepreneur who seems to love starting businesses. Dell started a mail-order stamp business when he was 13 and earned $2,000 in a few months by selling stamps he had collected. At 16, he began a new business selling newspaper subscriptions one day per week. That business earned him $18,000 in little more than a year. After enrolling at the University of Texas, Dell began selling personal computer parts from his dormitory room. Before he finished his first year, Dell was selling $80,000 worth of parts each month. This business became the Dell Computer Corporation. Today the Houston company's sales exceed $159 million a year, and it employs about 650 people.

Richard Bernstein failed in his first venture as a real estate agent in New York. Then he persuaded a group of Maryland investors to back him in a new venture. He offered to manage an apartment building for them without pay in exchange for a share of their profits. They agreed. Bernstein used his earnings to make more real estate deals. In the 1970s, he returned to New York. Few people wanted to buy New York real estate at that time, so Bernstein bought several buildings at low prices. He left the real estate business in 1981. The buildings he had purchased in the 1970s were worth seven or eight times what he had paid for them. Instead of retiring, though, he used his real estate earnings to go into a new industry. He purchased a publishing company that was losing money. Five years later, thanks to the business know-how Bernstein had gained in his earlier ventures, the publishing company was making a $60 million annual profit.

Steven Jobs, the founder of Apple Computer Corporation, is another example of a repeat entrepreneur. Apple made Jobs fantastically wealthy. When he left the company at age 30, he had made enough money to retire in luxury. Almost immediately, though, Jobs began another new venture in computers.

Entrepreneurs like Dell, Bernstein, and Jobs are a constant source of new ideas—and employment. Their business ventures help keep the American economy alive and growing.

Review Questions ___

1 ▶ Why does the federal government encourage entrepreneurs?

2 ▶ What does innovation by entrepreneurs add to the American economy?

3 ▶ Why do some successful entrepreneurs continue starting businesses even after they become wealthy?

The organization that manufactures the Apple Macintosh computer began less than 20 years ago with two people working together in a garage.

Summary

❑ Some entrepreneurs base their businesses on their own ideas or inventions. Others buy existing businesses and contribute their own ideas to make those businesses more successful. Still others act as agents, matching inventors with people who have money to invest in their inventions.

❑ Many entrepreneurs risk their own savings or homes to found businesses. All entrepreneurs take risks by putting long hours of hard work into their ventures.

❑ The first step in starting a business is to perceive a need for a product or service.

❑ Many entrepreneurs conduct market research to measure the demand for the products or services they plan to offer.

❑ Most entrepreneurs risk money of their own on ventures. Those without much money often borrow from banks. They may be required to use things they own as collateral.

❑ One of the least risky ways to go into business is to purchase a franchise.

❑ In most new businesses, the owners do all the work themselves. As their business grows, they may hire other people to help them.

❑ The failure rate for new businesses is high. Many entrepreneurs remain optimistic, however, and those who fail often go on to other ventures that are more successful.

❑ Innovative entrepreneurs contribute to the wide range of products and services Americans can purchase.

Vocabulary Exercise

venture   collateral   business plan

agent   franchise   innovation

market research

Complete the sentences below with the best word from the list above.

1. _____ can help an entrepreneur measure the demand for a product or service.

2. If you borrow money from a bank to start a business, you may have to use your home as _____.

3. Purchasing a _____ is one of the least risky ways to go into business.

4. An _____ forges deals between people with business ideas and people with money to invest in them.

5. An entrepreneur seeking money from financial institutions or investors must present a _____.

6. If you start a job that involves risk, you are starting a _____.

Discussion Questions

1. What do you think would be the best foundation for a business of your own? Why?

2. If you needed money to start a business, how would you attempt to obtain it? Why?

3. Would you like to own your own business? Why or why not?

Thinking Further

1. (Writing) Think of a product or service you could provide at a profit, and suppose you needed money to go into that business. Write a business plan that would persuade investors to back your business. Be sure to include information about how much you will charge, how you will find customers, and what your expenses will be.

2. (Speaking and Listening) Interview the owner of a small business in your community. The business can be a store, a catering service, or any other small venture owned by an individual. Find out when the owner started or acquired the business. What products or services does the business sell? How has the business changed over the years?

   Ask what risks the owner faced in going into the business. Did the owner work long hours at first? How many hours does he or she work now per week?

   Does the owner plan to stay in this business until retirement? Would he or she consider starting another business? What advice does this entrepreneur have for a young person who is thinking about starting a business?

3. (Reading) Find an article in a newspaper or magazine about a successful entrepreneur. See how his or her story compares with those in this chapter. How are they alike or different?

4. (Reading) Read the following features to learn more about jobs.

WHO TRANSPORTS PEOPLE AND GOODS?

Transportation workers move people and goods from place to place. You may not realize how much you depend on these workers. For example, bus drivers may take you to and from school every day. Truck drivers bring manufactured goods from factories and warehouses to stores. Without these workers, you could not buy your favorite jeans, compact discs, or shampoo.

Jerry is a transportation worker. He flies passenger jets. Along with the co-pilot and flight engineer, Jerry operates the controls, monitors the instrument panel, and calculates the plane's speed, altitude, and direction. Jerry's 747 also transports some cargo—primarily lightweight electronic components for computers.

T.J. drives a panel truck. She picks up packages at the airport and delivers them to factories and businesses. At each stop, T.J. has the customer sign a receipt for the goods. One of T.J.'s customers is CBT Manufacturing, where she delivers the components from Jerry's flight.

At CBT Manufacturing the electronic parts are assembled into personal computers. Bart, a long-distance truck driver, delivers the personal computers to stores and warehouses in the Midwest.

Bart is a senior trucker. He and his trucker's helper, Drew, often are on the road for

weeks at a time. Bart drives the 18-wheeler most of the time, but Drew sometimes drives for a few hours so Bart can rest.

Tammy is a local transit driver. Five days a week, her bus makes several round trips to take people from the suburbs to downtown and back. Tammy collects fares, hands out transfers, answers questions about schedules and routes, and announces stops.

Although airline pilots, truck drivers, and bus drivers operate different vehicles, there are similarities in their responsibilities. Before leaving the terminal or warehouse, they must plan, or be familiar with their route. Jerry checks his plane's engines, con-

trols, and instruments to make sure they are functioning properly. He also checks his cargo. T.J., Bart, and Tammy also inspect their vehicles before starting out. They check the tires, brakes, windshield wipers, lights, oil, fuel, water, and safety equipment.

On reaching their destination or at the end of the day, pilots, truck drivers, and bus drivers must do some paperwork. Jerry completes records describing the flight. Bart completes reports about the trip and the condition of the truck. Tammy must fill out a daily trip report. Another similarity is that pilots, truck drivers, and bus drivers are expected to maintain a schedule.

While there are similarities in the responsibilities of these workers, there is a great difference in the education and training required for these jobs. Jerry had to fulfill extensive requirements to become an airline pilot. In addition to earning a regular pilot's license, he had to earn a flight engineer's license and an airline transport pilot's license. Each license involved accumulating a minimum number of hours of flying experience and passing difficult written and in-flight tests. To be hired by the airline, he also had to have a college degree. To maintain his license, Jerry still must pass periodic physical exams and tests of flying skills.

By contrast, T.J., Bart, and Tammy only

needed to be 21 years of age and in good physical health, possess a commercial motor vehicle operator's license, and pass a written examination on driving regulations. Some trucking companies, such as Bart's, require that a new driver be at least 25 years old and experienced. T.J. took a truck driving course at a vocational school to prepare for her job. T.J., Bart, and Tammy received further instruction in routes and regulations after being hired at their jobs. All three have taken courses in automobile mechanics so they can deal with minor roadside repairs.

The number of jobs for transportation workers goes up and down with the economy. When the nation's businesses are thriving, there are more goods to move and more people with money to travel. Here are some other jobs in the Transportation and Material Moving Occupations cluster in the *Occupational Outlook Handbook*:

- ☐ ambulance driver
- ☐ bulldozer operator
- ☐ chauffeur
- ☐ crane operator
- ☐ taxi driver
- ☐ tractor driver

16

Deciding For Yourself

When you have studied this chapter, you should be able to:

➡ Summarize the reasons why self-knowledge and understanding of jobs are important for making career decisions, and how you can develop these skills

➡ List key steps in decision making and explain how to apply them to career decisions

➡ Explain how a broad view of the world of work is valuable for tomorrow's citizens

Vocabulary Words

Stress

Initiative

Outcome

Compromise

Where do you go from here? Now that you have learned how to begin planning your career, what is the next step? In other words, how do you start to use all the information you have learned, and how do you put it into motion?

Let us take a look at how Russ and his friends start planning their careers. They will show you what steps you need to take and how you can begin to take them.

Planning

Russ knows that the first thing he needs in order to choose a career direction is a plan. He begins to develop one by learning about himself and his options. The plan may involve one specific occupation or it may be more general, so it allows him to try many different fields. A general plan usually is better because it allows a person to adapt to changing employment trends. The more Russ learns about options that interest him, the better the chance he has of choosing career goals that are right for him.

Knowing Yourself

Everyone needs food, clothing, and shelter, and Russ knows that an occupation must provide him with money to pay for these. Russ also would like to make enough money so he can travel. He has visited much of the United States, but he hopes to travel to many foreign countries when he is older. He needs to keep this priority in mind when he chooses a career.

People have emotional needs and wants as well as material ones. Everyone needs a feeling of self-esteem and a sense of security and acceptance. Beyond that, each person has different emotional priorities. For example, Russ enjoys being around other people and showing people how to do things. His work can help satisfy many of his nonmaterial needs and wants.

The work you choose should suit your principles, interests, preferences, and overall personality. For example, Russ's friend, Leslie, enjoys exercising and being outdoors. She might enjoy working as a tree surgeon. On the other hand, tree surgery would be a poor career choice for Russ because he prefers being indoors and reading to physical activity. He will take into consideration how he reacts to **stress,** or continuous pressure and crises, because some jobs are more stressful than others. Russ likes fast-paced environments, so he probably would react well to stress.

Russ identifies his aptitudes because he knows it will help him choose work he can learn to do well, without too much difficulty. To identify his natural talents, he thinks about his hobbies, his scores on aptitude tests, and how well he does in particular classes

The work you choose should suit your principles, interests, preferences, and personality.

at school. He also asks himself which classes he prefers the most and why. Using computers always has been easy for Russ, and he enjoys learning new computer programs. With that aptitude, ability, and knowledge, he might be suited to a career as a computer programmer or a computer trainer.

Identifying and Narrowing Your Choices

Before Russ decides on a career, he needs to know what his options are. Guidance counselors, teachers, and other adults help him identify occupations for which he might be well suited. He also obtains valuable information at the library. He learns some important facts about various occupations from printed materials. One such resource is the *Occupational Outlook Handbook* (*OOH*), published by the United States Department of Labor. The *OOH* discusses working conditions, wages, employment prospects, and other important points about many kinds of work.

Russ thinks he might enjoy doing many kinds of work, so he wonders how to choose among them. He narrows his choices by thinking in terms of clusters of jobs that require similar skills. He uses the Labor Department's *OOH* and *Dictionary of Occupational Titles* (*DOT*), which group jobs in 20 clusters. Grouping occupations into clusters makes it easier for people to decide which clusters include the types of jobs that interest them.

To begin narrowing his choices, Russ lists all the career clusters that he thinks might interest him. Then he browses through the *OOH* and some other printed career resources at the library. He reads about a few occupations in each cluster he has listed. He crosses off any clusters that do not interest him after all or that require aptitudes he lacks. Finally, Russ narrows his list to two clusters. They are Natural, Computer, and Mathematical Scientists, and Teachers, Librarians, and Counselors.

Next Russ focuses on details of specific jobs in order to narrow his choices further. He looks at the tasks each job involves as well as the salary and fringe benefits it provides. For each job he asks himself, "Will it require me to travel much of the time? Will I be working closely with people? What will my promotion prospects be? Will I be reasonably secure in this career, or are jobs in this field shrinking?" The answers to those questions help him choose among the occupations within his two clusters.

He learns more about specific jobs by talking to adults who have those jobs as well as by doing library research. Russ plans to find a part-time job when he turns 16 that will enable him to observe people in jobs that interest him.

Review Questions

1 ▶ What needs and wants can you expect your career to fulfill?

2 ▶ How can you identify your aptitudes?

3 ▶ Where can you find out about career options that might be suitable for you?

Goals and Strategies

Understanding yourself and your career options helps you determine a specific career goal. The next step Russ takes is developing a plan of action. He starts to do this by setting long-term and short-term goals. Then he plans how to reach his goals.

Setting Specific Goals

After all his researching, Russ decides that his career goals are to work with computers and people. His specific career goal is to work as a trainer for a software company, teaching people to use computers in their jobs. Russ has divided his long-term goal into a series of short-term goals. One of his short-term goals is to take computer classes in high school. Another is to find a part-time job in an office where he can use his computer skills.

By breaking a long-term goal into short-term goals as Russ did, you give yourself tasks that are easier to accomplish. These short-term goals prepare you for the long-term goal and lead naturally

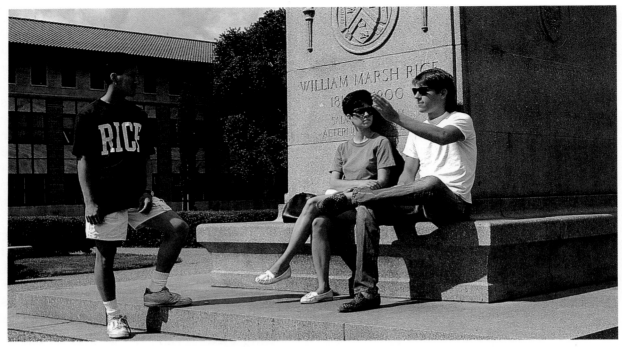

Even if your long-term goals are not clear yet, you can set short-term goals, such as going to college. This will keep your options open and allow you to explore a variety of fields.

toward it. To set short-term career goals, you need to find out the requirements for success in the occupation you want to pursue. You can learn about those requirements by doing library research and by talking with adults who work in that occupation.

After setting short-term goals, develop strategies and schedules for reaching those goals. Russ, for example, has developed the following strategy and schedule for reaching his short-term goals. First, he plans to take an introductory computer course in the ninth grade. In tenth grade he wants to take courses to learn how to use different kinds of computer software. After passing those courses, he will apply for part-time jobs where he can use the computer skills and abilities he has acquired. He plans to save some of his earnings from his part-time job to help pay for further education. Each time Russ reaches one of these short-term goals he has set for himself, he will be closer to his long-term goal.

Building Your Qualifications

Every job has a set of qualifications that applicants must meet. To qualify for a job as a software trainer, for example, Russ must have certain qualifications. Once you have set a long-term career goal for yourself, take steps toward acquiring the qualifications you need.

You can build qualifications for jobs in many of your high school classes.

Begin working toward short-term goals now, even though your long-term goal is many years away.

The first step Russ takes toward his career goal is strengthening his basic skills in language and math. To do any job well, you must know how to read and write, speak correctly, listen, and apply basic mathematical principles. If the career you want requires advanced math or language skills, you can begin taking classes—now or in high school—so you can acquire these advanced skills. If your career goal requires an associate or bachelor's degree, take high school classes that will prepare you for postsecondary education. You also can acquire skills and job qualifications outside school, through part-time jobs, volunteer work, recreational activities, or even household chores.

Russ's friend, Crystal, plans to become a chef. Except for home economics, which she already has taken, Crystal's school does not offer any classes in food preparation. Even so, she has begun building her qualifications. She knows that a chef must calculate amounts of ingredients when working with recipes, so she works hard at developing math skills. A chef needs language skills to communicate with co-workers and others, so Crystal concentrates on English classes, too. She also has begun reading about the admission requirements of postsecondary schools that train chefs. This will help her decide what classes to take in high school.

Crystal is building career qualifications outside school, too. By helping with the shopping and cooking for her family, she is learning about recipes, ingredients, and the economics of cooking. Crystal has a work permit and hopes to find a part-time job busing tables. Crystal will not do any cooking on the job, but it will give her restaurant experience—and a chance to observe chefs and other restaurant employees at work.

By beginning to prepare for a career while she is a teenager, Crystal is demonstrating her interest in and commitment to the career. When you are committed to a goal, you work hard to achieve it. Crystal also is demonstrating her **initiative** by setting her own goals and starting herself on the path toward achieving them. You have initiative if you start a task or project on your own. Employers will be impressed by Crystal's initiative and by her early commitment to becoming a chef.

Making the Most of Work Experience

In looking for work, Crystal and Russ face two major challenges. First, they must identify places that might have jobs to offer in their fields. Then they must convince the person who does the hiring that they will be competent and reliable workers.

What expectations do you think this babysitter's employer has of her?

When Crystal is ready to apply for a job, she looks for help-wanted signs in restaurant windows. She also checks the classified advertisements in the newspaper for job listings. She lets her friends and acquaintances know she is looking for work, too, because they may know about job openings. In addition, she signs up with a placement service that helps teenagers find jobs.

When she applies for jobs, Crystal will try to make good impressions on the people who interview her. She will show up on time for appointments. She will dress carefully and conservatively, too, even though bus persons usually wear uniforms. She will take special care with her grooming because that will help her create the impression she is neat and dependable.

When Crystal goes on job interviews, she will take notes listing details such as the names and addresses of schools she has attended. She may be asked to provide such information on applications. When her interviewers ask questions, she will answer them clearly and directly. She also will ask questions of her own—about job duties, the work schedule, wages, and what fringe benefits she will receive. She is more likely to be hired if her questions and answers convey her positive, enthusiastic attitude.

After Crystal is hired, she will have to live up to her employer's expectations. Employers expect workers to do their jobs as well as they can, and to do them the way the employers want them done. Employees must follow their employers' work schedules, safety regulations, and other rules. Employers also expect loyalty and honesty from the people who work for them.

Workers, on the other hand, expect to be paid promptly, and to be paid the same amount as others with the same qualifications. They are entitled to clean, safe working conditions, too. In addition, they expect employers to show them how to do their jobs according to the employers' procedures. Employees also are entitled to adequate supervision and evaluation of their work. Federal and local laws require that employers treat workers fairly, without regard to race, sex, disability, or religion.

Workers have expectations of each other, too. When Russ gets a job, his co-workers will expect him to do his share of the work, avoid gossip, and offer to help them when he can. Russ will do

There are lots of ways that you can learn how to work as part of a team while you are in school.

those things because he knows that working well with co-workers will contribute to his success on any job.

Maintaining Flexibility

No matter how committed you are to a goal, you must maintain the flexibility to make changes when necessary. Even when you plan carefully, you cannot always predict the **outcome** of your efforts. The outcome is the result. Develop alternate plans in case your original strategies do not work out. Suppose, for example, when Russ goes to high school he finds that some of the software courses he had planned to take are not offered. As an alternative, he could take a summer class on the software at a local vocational school. By doing that, Russ is **compromising.** To compromise is to acknowledge that you cannot have exactly what you want and to find an acceptable alternative. People need to be able to compromise, because sometimes their plans are affected by economic trends and other forces they cannot control.

Review Questions _____

1 ▶ How can you make a long-term goal easier to achieve?

2 ▶ How can a person your age begin acquiring job qualifications?

3 ▶ What are some of the expectations employers have of workers?

Taking a Broader View

When Russ and Crystal finish with their education and training and obtain full-time jobs, they will earn incomes. Those incomes will enable them to pay for food, clothing, shelter, and other products or services they need or want. In addition to knowing how to get jobs to earn money, it is important that Russ and Crystal also know how to handle money. The more they understand about money and economic principles, the better able they will be to manage their money responsibly. Knowing how the American economic system works also will help them make better career decisions.

Understanding Money

Banks and other financial institutions offer a wide range of services that will help Russ and Crystal manage their money. These include checking and savings accounts as well as credit cards and loans. Russ and Crystal will earn interest on most of the money they deposit with financial institutions. When they borrow money from financial institutions, they will have to pay interest. Credit cards also carry interest charges, which often are quite high.

To manage money well, Russ and Crystal each will need a budget. Their budgets must include money for necessities. They can spend the rest of their income on nonessentials, although they should put some aside as savings for the future. Food and housing

(continued on page 306)

IT IS NEVER TOO LATE TO ADJUST PLANS

I was finally in New York, the financial capital of the world. Even though I was just starting out, I knew it would only be a matter of time before I would be in the big leagues. Because of my economics grades, I had an internship with a big brokerage house on Wall Street. I was watching deals being made that were worth millions of dollars. I felt like I was on my way to making my life-long ambition come true.

At first my enthusiasm and energy were boundless. I went to the office early, did my work, and asked for more. I pushed myself to learn as much as I could. I always had seen myself as a financial wizard—now I would prove it. I saw my Wall Street internship as my first step in my well-thought-out career plan. After a few months, my energy and enthusiasm began to slip. I could not understand why I felt differently.

Then one day I saw things clearly for the first time. That day the stock market had been very unstable, and it kept going up and down like a roller coaster. When I walked into the trading room after lunch, the scene was unbelievable. People were screaming into phones, "Buy this, sell that," as they stared at green numbers flitting across electronic screens. They were keying their computers frantically, then making phone call after phone call. The noise was incredible, and the atmosphere was total chaos.

I realized that I did not want to work under those high pressure conditions. I did not want to deal only with computers, phones, and electronic numbers. I wanted to work more closely with people.

When I returned to school after my internship ended, I told a few of my teachers I was considering giving up economics. One professor listened to my story and then suggested that I try financial and investment planning. She said I could still use my economics skills, but in situations where I would be dealing directly with people.

The next summer I got a junior level job doing financial and investment planning at an insurance company in New York. I was back in the Big Apple working in finance. Even though I am not wheeling and dealing millions of dollars every day, I am doing what I love and I am helping other people, too. I am looking forward to next fall when I will be working at this job full time. ■

Sometimes you may have to adjust your strategy because of a change. For example, if a course you planned to take is not offered at your school, you might sign up to take it during the summer at a local community college.

are the biggest items in most household budgets. Other big items are transportation, medical expenses, and clothing.

Budgeting is not the only responsibility that comes with earning an adult income. Russ and Crystal also will be responsible for doing work they believe is worthwhile. As voters, they will be responsible for electing politicians who they believe act in society's best interests and favor sound economic policies. As consumers, they will have a responsibility to spend their incomes only on goods and services they consider worthwhile.

Competition for profits distinguishes the free enterprise system from other types of economic systems. Supply and demand play important roles in a free enterprise system. A continuous increase in consumer demand for goods and services can lead to inflation. When inflation is rising, wages grow but prices grow more. This encourages consumers to borrow money. On the other hand, low consumer demand can lead to deflation. Both inflation and deflation are destructive to society if they continue for too long. The federal government attempts to control these problems by influencing interest rates on savings accounts and loans.

Inflation, deflation, and other economic factors affect jobs. They influence employment prospects. They also help determine how much Russ and Crystal will earn and how much they will be able to buy with their incomes. Understanding supply and demand will help them choose a career that gives them a satisfactory income. Russ and Crystal probably will earn high salaries if they have skills that are in great demand. If Russ or Crystal were to change jobs or open a business of their own, an awareness of economic trends would help them choose the right time.

Throughout your life, you probably will wear many different ''hats'' at work.

Understanding Entrepreneurs, Managers, and Workers

Throughout their careers, Russ and Crystal will work with people who hold many different roles in the working world. Some will be their co-workers who will have responsibilities similar to their own. Others will be supervisors who oversee Russ's and Crystal's performance. They also may work with managers, who have more responsibility than supervisors. Some of their colleagues at work may be entrepreneurs who are building new businesses or working in older enterprises that have grown in complexity.

The work people perform in each of these roles is vitally important to their employers and to the American economy. When people in these roles work together smoothly, they help themselves as well as their employers and society in general. The American economy depends on entrepreneurs who are willing to take risks and start businesses that create jobs. Entrepreneurs, on the other hand, depend on workers to help their businesses grow and succeed. As a business becomes more complex, it needs supervisors to coordinate the work of other employees and help them do their jobs well. Eventually, it needs managers to see that projects and departments run smoothly and stay within their budgets. If employees perform well in all these jobs, their employer generally continues to succeed. An employer's continued success means secure jobs for workers.

Russ and Crystal may hold many of these roles throughout their careers. At first, they probably would be one of many employees, responsible for only their own work. Later, they may become

This chemist works at a laboratory in private industry. She does research and develops new products.

Where you go from here is all up to you.

Review Questions

1 ▶ When do financial institutions pay interest? When do they charge interest?

2 ▶ What must a household budget include?

3 ▶ How do inflation, deflation, and other economic trends influence jobs?

supervisors or managers, with responsibility for the productivity of many people. Most people spend their entire lives as employees, while some may become entrepreneurs. Russ and Crystal one day may start businesses of their own. In the beginning, their businesses may depend solely on their own efforts.

Regardless of your role in the workplace, how well you do your job will affect the quality of your life. Your job performance also will reflect your contribution as an adult member of society. Working enthusiastically and productively will help you earn a satisfactory income and build self-esteem. It also will help ensure the continued success of the American economy.

Summary

- [ ] To begin planning your career, you need to identify your own abilities, aptitudes, preferences, and personality traits. You also need to know what kinds of jobs might be available to you. This information will help you choose the career option most suitable for you.

- [ ] Your performance in school and the activities you choose outside school can give you important information about your aptitudes. Information about career options is available from guidance counselors and other adults as well as from printed materials you can find in a library or guidance office.

- [ ] After you select a career objective, you can set specific goals. You can break a long-term goal into a series of short-term goals.

- [ ] Even though your long-term career goal is several years away, you can begin to build your qualifications for it now. The first step is to acquire basic skills, and perhaps more advanced skills, in school. You also can acquire job qualifications through after-school work and other activities.

- [ ] You must be flexible and willing to compromise in your career planning, because you cannot always predict the outcomes of your strategies.

- [ ] From the income you earn as an adult, you must provide for your needs.

- [ ] Continued increases in consumer spending can lead to inflation, continued decreases can lead to deflation. Inflation, deflation, and other economic trends influence how many jobs are available, how much people earn at those jobs, and how much they can buy with their incomes.

- [ ] People hold many different roles in the workplace. Some are responsible only for their own work, but others are supervisors, managers, and entrepreneurs.

Vocabulary Exercise

True or False?

1. Flexibility is important because you cannot always predict the outcome of your plans.

2. By doing only what you are told to do, you show initiative.

3. A compromise is an acceptable alternative to something you want but cannot have.

4. All jobs have about the same amount of stress.

Discussion Questions

1. Have you ever shown initiative? If so, how? If not, why do you think that is so? Do you think it is a worthwhile trait to have when planning a career? Why or why not?

2. You have read about the importance of flexibility in career planning. Is flexibility important on the job, too? Can you think of situations where it might be necessary to compromise with employers or co-workers?

3. Suppose you are an adult who earns $500 a week. After paying your taxes, rent, transportation, food, and clothing expenses, you have no money left to spend or save for the future. Why might this be so? What can you do so that you will have money to spend or save?

Thinking Further

1. (Reading) At the library, find the *Occupational Outlook Handbook* or some other reference book that gives information about career options. Find a job that looks interesting to you. Then develop a list of short-term goals you could set that would help you become qualified for this job.

2. (Writing) Find the file you labeled Career Plans at the beginning of this course. Do the exercise again and include any new material. Then explain how what you have learned in this course can help you create a career plan.

3. (Speaking) Study your local newspaper for articles that mention politicians' viewpoints on economic issues. Using information from these articles, compare and contrast the views of two politicians. Give a report to the class in which you discuss the differences and similarities in their views. In the report, include your own opinion about which politicians' views are in the best interest of voters. Explain your opinion.

4. (Reading) Read the following feature to learn more about jobs.

WHO INFORMS AND ENTERTAINS PEOPLE?

Most Americans spend several hours each week in front of the television set. As you watch television, you may not think about all the people who put a program together. For example, consider the news broadcasts of local television stations. You are probably familiar with the newscasters, sportscasters, and meteorologists. Let us meet some of the people you may not be familiar with—the people who work off camera.

Stuart is program director for Channel 7's news at 6 and 10 P.M. He plans the content of each newscast and supervises its preparation. Stuart assigns topics or specific locations to writers and reporters.

Ann, one of Channel 7's reporters, gathers the information for news stories. Ann sometimes can get a story by making a few telephone calls, but most of the time she must go on location to observe events and interview people. She prepares commentary for her filmed reports and sometimes appears on camera during a newscast to introduce her stories. Ann often must report "live" from the location of an important, late-breaking news story. In this situation, she must compose her story as she speaks to the television audience.

Teong is a camera operator. He works as part of a team that includes a reporter and other technicians. The team travels in a

Channel 7 van to the locations of news stories. Teong uses a special electronic news-gathering camera to capture events on videotape. The images also can be transmitted via satellite back to the newsroom.

Back at the station, Jana and Theresa use information supplied by wire services or reporters to write news items for broadcast. Since Channel 7's reporters generally write the stories concerning local and state news, Jana and Theresa concentrate on national and international stories. They also put together and edit all the news stories in a script for the newscasters to read.

Marcy and Adam are production assistants. They help reporters and writers by

doing background research and by checking the accuracy of facts, dates, and statistics. Marcy and Adam also check news scripts for correct grammar. If necessary, they add or rearrange sentences to make their meaning clearer. The job of production assistant is an entry-level position in the newsroom.

Nancy, the staff artist, charts and produces graphs, maps, and other visuals for use on the air. Nancy is known as a graphic artist because she uses her artistic talents for commercial, or business, purposes.

Jennifer and Perry are Channel 7's popular co-anchors. They read accounts of the day's news stories and introduce videotaped news or live transmissions from on-the-scene reporters. Although both Jennifer and Perry have extensive journalism experience and prepare many of their own stories, they were chosen to be co-anchors also because of their attractive appearance and pleasing personalities.

To be hired at Channel 7, reporters, writers, newscasters, and production assistants must have college degrees in journalism, communications, or liberal arts. Camera operators can learn through on-the-job training, although course work in photography at a junior college or vocational school will be helpful in getting a job. The most important qualification for a staff artist is an impressive

portfolio or examples of the artist's work. Most newsrooms offer internships or work-study positions to college students who want to learn about broadcast news.

Newsrooms usually are hectic as the staff rushes to have the news ready by airtime each day. People who work in television news must be able to concentrate among confusion, and they must be creative under pressure. They also must be curious about events and persistent in digging up the facts.

Television is not the only medium that informs and entertains people. Books, newspapers, magazines, movies, plays, and radio shows also inform and entertain. People who work in these media have jobs similar to people who work in television news. The following jobs are included in the Writers, Artists, and Entertainers cluster in the *Occupational Outlook Handbook*:

❑ disc jockey

❑ fashion designer

❑ fine artist

❑ interior designer

❑ movie director

❑ performing artist

❑ photographer

Career clusters are designed to group occupations of a similar nature. Several cluster systems have been developed, but two of the more popular and useful ones are those developed by the United States Office of Education and the United States Department of Labor. The Office of Education uses a 15-cluster classification. The Department of Labor uses a 20-cluster classification. The following charts show how the two compare. The numbers after each of the 15 clusters in the top chart are correlated to the 20 clusters listed in the bottom chart.

UNITED STATES OFFICE OF EDUCATION
15 OCCUPATIONAL CLUSTER CLASSIFICATIONS

Agribusiness and Natural Resources ②	Hospitality and Recreation ⑯
Business and Office ① ⑩ ⑱	Manufacturing ④ ⑩ ⑫ ⑭
Communications and Media ⑱ ⑳	Marine Science ② ⑬ ⑱
Construction ③ ⑤	Marketing and Distribution ⑪
Consumer and Homemaking ⑮ ⑯	Personal Services ⑯
Environment ② ⑬ ⑱	Public Services ⑧ ⑨ ⑰
Fine Arts and Humanities ⑨ ⑳	Transportation ⑲
Health ⑥ ⑦	

UNITED STATES DEPARTMENT OF LABOR
20 OCCUPATIONAL CLUSTER CLASSIFICATIONS

① Administrative Support Occupations, Including Clerical	⑪ Marketing and Sales Occupations
② Agriculture, Forestry, Fishing, and Related Occupations	⑫ Mechanics, Installers, and Repairers
③ Construction Trades and Extractive Occupations	⑬ Natural, Computer, and Mathematical Scientists
④ Engineers, Surveyors, and Architects	⑭ Production Occupations
⑤ Handlers, Equipment Cleaners, Helpers, and Laborers	⑮ Registered Nurses, Pharmacists, Dietitians, Therapists, and Physical Assistants
⑥ Health Diagnosing and Treating Practitioners	⑯ Service Occupations
⑦ Health Technologists and Technicians	⑰ Teachers, Librarians, and Counselors
⑧ Armed Forces	⑱ Technologists and Technicians, Except Health
⑨ Lawyers, Social Scientists, Social Workers, and Religious Workers	⑲ Transportation and Material Moving Occupations
⑩ Managerial and Management-Related Occupations	⑳ Writers, Artists, and Entertainers

Glossary

A

achievement test A test that measures a person's skill and knowledge in certain subject areas. (4)

agent A person who makes deals between people with ideas and people with money to invest in the ideas. (15)

alternative Another possible choice. (8)

applicant A person who is applying for a job. (11)

application form A form that an employer asks an applicant to fill out to supply information about himself or herself. (11)

apprenticeship A formal system of on-the-job training for teaching people skills. (8)

aptitude A natural ability or talent. (4)

aptitude test A test that measures a person's ability to learn something. (4)

attitude The way a person typically thinks and feels. (3)

B

bachelor's degree The type of degree earned after completing a four-year program at a college or university. (9)

body language Any of the messages you send through your mannerisms, such as facial expressions. (11)

bonus Extra money given to employees at the end of a profitable year or a successful project. (7)

boycott An organized consumer plan to influence a company by refusing to buy its products or services. (13)

budget A plan for spending and saving income. (13)

business plan An outline of an entrepreneur's goals for a venture and the ways the entrepreneur intends to reach those goals. (15)

C

career A planned sequence of jobs. (1)

career ladder The standard path an employee can follow when moving into positions of greater responsibility. (5)

check A written order directing a financial institution to pay money to someone. (13)

cluster A group of similar occupations. (6)

collateral A valuable possession that a borrower uses to guarantee repayment of a loan. (15)

commission A set percentage of money from total sales that a person receives as payment for a job. (7)

compensation The money and fringe benefits a person receives as payment for work. (12)

competition When businesses sell the same product or try to do better than each other. (14)

compromise To acknowledge that one cannot have exactly what one wants and to find an alternative. (16)

consumer Any person who buys and uses products. (2)

contract A legal agreement between two or more people. (12)

cooperative education A program in which teachers place students in jobs. (6)

courtesy The ability to be thoughtful and considerate of others. (3)

D

deadline A date by which a task must be completed. (8)

deflation A situation in which less money is spent on products and services. (14)

delegate To assign work to others. (5)

demand The number of customers who are ready to buy a product or service at a particular price. (14)

E

employment agency A business that helps people find suitable jobs. (6)

employment trend An indication of which jobs are becoming more in demand and which jobs are declining in employment opportunities. (6)

enterprise Another word for a business. It also can mean clever or bold inventiveness. (14)

entrepreneur A person who starts his or her own business. (5)

evaluate To judge the worth of a particular thing. (8)

extrovert An outgoing person who focuses on other people and activities. (3)

F

flextime A type of plan that allows workers to set their own schedules within limits. (12)

franchise The right to sell a company's goods or services and use its name in a certain area. (15)

free enterprise system An economic system in which laws and traditions favor giving everyone as much freedom as possible and allowing them to run their own lives. (14)

freelancer A self-employed professional person who does short-term work for companies. (5)

fringe benefit Payment for a job in a form other than money, such as in the form of health insurance and vacation. (7)

G

goal An aim that a person is willing to make an effort to achieve. (1)

H

habit A behavior pattern that a person frequently repeats. (3)

help-wanted advertisement A notice placed in the classified advertising section of a newspaper by an employer who wants to have a job opening filled. (10)

I

implement To carry out a plan. (8)

income tax A portion of a person's income that must be paid to the federal government. (13)

inflation A general rise in prices that occurs when businesses increase their prices to cover the cost of production. (14)

initiative Starting a task or project on one's own. (16)

innovation A new idea. (15)

interest Any activity that a person especially likes. (1) Money a person or institution earns when they allow someone else to use their money. (13)

interview A formal meeting between an employer and a job applicant. (4)

introvert A quiet person who often enjoys being and working alone. (3)

J

job A position that a person holds to earn a living. (1)

job shadowing When a person spends time with a worker in a particular occupation in an attempt to get firsthand information. (7)

junior volunteer Any person who volunteers to help patients in a hospital or nursing home. (10)

L

lifestyle The particular way a person chooses to live. (2)

loan Money borrowed from a financial institution to be repayed gradually. (13)

M

major A course of study in a particular field. (9)

manager A person who coordinates the efforts of many employees so that a business is able to function efficiently. (5)

market research Studies that determine who will buy a specific product or service and how much people will be willing to pay for it. (15)

N

need An item a person cannot do without, like food or shelter. (2)

networking The process of exchanging job-related information with a group of people. (7)

O

objective (adj) To be able to look at a situation without emotion. (1)

occupation The work a person does to earn a living. (1)

occupational ability pattern A set of abilities that represents several hundred different occupations in all fields. (4)

Occupational Safety and Health Administration (OSHA) A federal agency that sets and enforces standards for job safety. (12)

outcome The result of an action. (16)

overtime A higher hourly wage paid to employees if they work more than their regular hours per week. (7)

P

pension A provision for an income after a person retires. (7)

personality The individual qualities that make you act differently from everyone else. (3)

personnel department People in a company who interview all applicants and decide which ones are good employment prospects. (11)

piecework rate A rate of payment in which people are paid a set amount for each piece of work they do. (13)

placement service A business that gathers information about which jobs are available, as well as about people who want to work. A placement service tries to match job seekers with employers. (10)

postgraduate degree A degree earned after a bachelor's degree by any person who finishes graduate school. (9)

postsecondary education Training beyond high school. (9)

preference One of a person's basic likes or dislikes. (2)

prime interest rate The amount of money banks charge their biggest business customers for borrowing money. This is lower than the consumer rate. (14)

principle A basic belief that helps people make decisions by setting standards for their behavior. (2)

private job A job in which a person works for an individual or a family rather than for an organization. (10)

producer A person who contributes to society and earns money. (2)

productivity The amount of work a person can produce per hour. (5)

profit Any of the money a business has left over after bills are paid. (5)

prospective To be likely or expected to come about. (11)

qualification Any characteristic, skill, or knowledge that enables a person to do a job. It is also any award, degree, or activity that shows a person has appropriate skills or knowledge for a job. (9)

reference A person who can tell an employer about an applicant's character and quality of work. (11)

resume A written account of a person's previous jobs and skills that is given to a potential employer. (4)

salary A fixed amount of money an employee is paid. (7)

self-esteem A healthy confidence that people have in themselves and in their abilities to achieve their goals. (2)

severance pay Money paid to an employee in an attempt to make up for the loss of a job. (12)

situation-wanted advertisement A notice placed in the classified advertising section of the newspaper by a person looking for a job. (10)

skill A developed ability. (4)

stress Continuous pressure and crises. (16)

stress interview A formal meeting in which an employer creates stress to see how the applicant behaves. (11)

supervisor A person who gives employees work orders, answers many of their questions, and checks their work. (3)

supply The amount of a product that suppliers will provide at a price. (14)

tip Money that a satisfied customer usually leaves for a service worker. (13)

trade union A group of workers who band together to negotiate for wages and better working conditions. (14)

transferable skill Any developed ability that can be used in, or transferred to, different jobs. (6)

values Principles or qualities that people consider important in their lives, such as friends, security, and education. (1)

venture A task or job involving risk. (15)

volunteer A person who works without pay. (2)

wage An hourly rate of pay. (13)

want An item that a person would like to have but could live without. (2)

work permit Work certificate. (10)

workplace politics Business practices including favoritism and personality clashes. (12)

work-study An opportunity for students to apply classroom learning in an actual job setting. (9)

Further Readings

Alexander, Sue. *Finding Your First Job.* New York: E. P. Dutton, 1980.

Anema, Durlynn. *Get Hired! 13 Ways to Get a Job.* Hayward, CA: Janus Books, 1980.

Ashmore, M. Catherine. *Risks and Rewards of Entrepreneurship.* St. Paul, MN: EMC Publishing and the National Center for Research in Vocational Education, 1988.

Biegeleisen, J. I. *Job Resumes: How to Write Them, How to Present Them, Preparing for Interviews.* New York: Grosset & Dunlap, 1982.

Borchard, David C., et al. *Your Career: Choices, Chances, Changes.* Dubuque, IA: Kendall/Hunt Publishing Co., 1984.

The Bottom Line: Basic Skills in the Workplace. Washington, D.C.: U.S. Department of Labor and U.S. Department of Education, 1988.

Bruton, Elsa. *Be Credit-Wise: A Guide to Credit.* Hayward, CA: Janus Books, 1984.

Building a Quality Workforce. Washington, D.C.: U.S. Department of Labor, U.S. Department of Education, U.S. Department of Commerce, 1988.

Campbell, Richard. *Working Today and Tomorrow.* St. Paul, MN: Changing Times Education Service, EMC Publishing, 1987.

Caple, John. *The Right Work: Finding It and Making It Right.* New York: Dodd, Mead & Co., 1987.

Career Briefs series. Largo, FL: Careers, Inc.

Career Information Center. 4th ed. 13 vols. Encino, CA: Bennett & McKnight/Glencoe, 1989.

Career Planning and Decision-Making for College. Encino, CA: Bennett & McKnight/Glencoe, 1986.

Career Summary series. Largo, FL: Careers, Inc.

Career World: The Continuing Guide to Careers. Highwood, IL: Curriculum Innovations, current since 1971. Available monthly during the school year.

Cetron, M., and Appel, M. *Jobs of the Future: The 500 Best Jobs—Where They'll Be and How to Get Them.* New York: McGraw-Hill Book Co., 1985.

Clawson, James G., et al. *Self-Assessment and Career Development.* Englewood Cliffs, NJ: Prentice-Hall, 1985.

Concise Occupational Reference Handbook. Scottsdale, AZ: Associated Book Pubs. Inc., 1983.

Crowell, Caleb, and Mosenfelder, Don. *You and Your Money.* New York: Educational Design, 1983.

Dianna, Michael A. *Career Education for Elementary Grades.* ERIC Document Reproduction Service, 1984. (ED248404)

Dictionary of Occupational Titles. rev. ed. U.S. Department of Labor. Washington, D.C.: U.S. Government Printing Office, 1977.

Didsbury, Howard F., Jr., ed. *The World of Work: Careers and the Future.* Bethesda, MD: World Future Society, 1983.

Directory of Internships, Work Experience Programs and On-the-Job Training Opportunities. 2 vols. Santa Monica, CA: Ready Reference Press.

Douglas, Martha. *Go For It! How to Get Your First Good Job.* Berkeley, CA: Ten Speed Press, 1983.

Egelston, Roberta Riethmiller. *Career Planning Materials: A Guide to Sources and Their Use.* Chicago: American Library Association, 1981.

Elsman, Max. *How to Get Your First Job: A Field Guide for Beginners.* New York: Crown Pubs., 1985.

Exploring Career Decision-Making. Encino, CA: Bennett & McKnight/Glencoe, 1986.

Farr, Michael; Gaither, Richard; and Pick-nell, R. Michael. *The Work Book: Getting the Job You Want.* Encino, CA: Bennett & McKnight/Glencoe, 1986.

Figler, Howard. *The Complete Job-Search Handbook.* New York: Holt, Rinehart & Winston, 1982.

Gale, Barry, and Gale, Linda. *Discover What You're Best At: The National Career Aptitude Test.* New York: Simon & Schuster, 1982.

Gothard, W. P. *Vocational Guidance: Theory and Practice.* New York: Methuen, 1987.

Gourley, Pamela. *Careers to Think About: A Young Person's Guide to Future Job Opportunities.* Danville, CA: Tech West Publications, 1987.

Graham, Lawrence. *Jobs in the Real World: The Student Job Search Handbook.* New York: Grosset & Dunlap, 1982.

Hall, Robert B., and Nixon, Regina. *Youth Employment in American Industry.* Washington, D.C.: The National Urban League, 1984.

Hoffman, Gloria, and Graivier, Pauline. *Speak the Language of Success.* New York: Grosset & Dunlap, 1983.

Hollenbeck, K. "Employer Recruitment and Selection of Young Workers." *Journal of Industrial Teacher Education* vol. 23, no. 4 (1986), pp. 43–44.

Hopke, William E., et al., eds. *The Encyclopedia of Career and Vocational Guidance.* 6th ed. 3 vols. New York: Doubleday & Co., 1984.

Investing in People: A Strategy to Address America's Workforce Crisis. Washington, D.C.: U.S. Department of Labor, 1989.

Jackson, Tom. *The Perfect Resume.* Garden City, NY: Anchor Press, 1981.

Jones, Ilene. *Jobs for Teenagers.* New York: Ballantine Books, 1983.

Keirsey, David, and Bates, Marilyn. *Please Understand Me: Character and Temperament Types.* Del Mar, CA: Prometheus Book Co., 1984.

Kent, Calvin A., ed. *Encyclopedia of Entrepreneurship.* Englewood Cliffs, NJ: Prentice-Hall, 1982.

Kimbrell, Grady, and Vineyard, Ben S. *Entering the World of Work,* Encino, CA: Bennett & McKnight/Glencoe, 1986.

———. *Succeeding in the World of Work.* Encino, CA: Bennett & McKnight/Glencoe, 1986.

Klein, J. Ken, and Unterman, Celia. *Career Aptitude Tests.* New York: Arco, 1984.

Kostecka, Andrew. *Franchising in the Economy, 1986–1988.* Washington, D.C.: U.S. Department of Commerce, 1988.

———. *Opportunity 2000: Creative Affirmative Action Strategies For a Changing Workforce.* Indianapolis, IN: Hudson Institute, 1988.

Kurfman, Dana G., ed. *Developing Decision-Making Skills.* Washington, D.C.: National Council for the Social Studies, 1981.

Landau, Elaine. *The Smart Spending Guide for Teens.* New York: Messner, 1982.

Landy, Marc. *Positive Career Paths: A Self-Directed Career Counseling Guide.* Tacoma, WA: Landy & Associates, 1987.

Lewis, Diane, and Carroll, Joe. *The Insider's Guide to Finding the Right Job.* Nashville, TN: Thomas Nelson Pubs., 1987.

Littrell, J. J. *From School to Work.* South Holland, IL: Goodheart-Willcox Co., 1984.

Lobb, Charlotte. *Exploring Apprenticeship Careers.* rev. ed. New York: The Rosen Publishing Group, 1985.

———. *Exploring Careers Through Part-Time and Summer Employment.* New York: The Rosen Publishing Group, 1982.

Matching Yourself with the World of Work. Washington, D.C.: U.S. Government Printing Office, 1984.

McHugh, John. *Finding a Job.* St. Paul, MN: Changing Times Education Service, EMC Publishing, 1981.

———. *Getting Ready to Work.* St. Paul, MN: Changing Times Education Service, EMC Publishing, 1981.

———. *Interviewing for Jobs.* St. Paul, MN: Changing Times Education Service, EMC Publishing, 1981.

———. *Keeping and Changing Jobs.* St. Paul, MN: Changing Times Education Service, EMC Publishing, 1981.

———. *Practical Job Skills Series.* St. Paul, MN: Changing Times Education Service, EMC Publishing, 1981.

———. *Starting a New Job.* St. Paul, MN: Changing Times Education Service, EMC Publishing, 1981.

National Guide to Educational Credit for Training Programs. Washington, D.C.: American Council on Education, 1982.

Neufield, Rose. *Exploring Non-Traditional Jobs for Women.* New York: The Rosen Publishing Group, 1986.

The 1988–89 Job Outlook in Brief. Washington, D.C.: U.S. Department of Labor, 1988.

Northwest Regional Educational Laboratory. *Counting Money and Making Change: Making a Budget.* New York: McGraw Hill, 1980.

Occupational Outlook series. Washington, D.C.: U.S. Government Printing Office. Briefs, separately published.

Occupational Outlook Handbook. U.S. Department of Labor. Washington, D.C.: U.S. Government Printing Office, revised biennially.

Occupational Outlook Quarterly. Washington, D.C.: Occupational Outlook Service, Bureau of Labor Statistics, current since 1956. Quarterly.

Ratliffe, Sharon, and Herman, Deldee. *Self-Awareness.* Skokie, IL: VGM Career Horizons, 1982.

Rettig, Jack L. *Careers: Exploration and Decision.* Belmont, CA: Pittman Learning, 1986.

Ruggeberg, Rand, ed. *Summer Employment Directory of the U.S.* rev. ed. Cincinnati, OH: Writer's Digest Books, 1988.

Schein, Edgar. *Career Anchors: Discovering Your Real Values.* San Diego, CA: University Associates, 1985.

Schrank, Louise Welsh. *Life Plan. A Practical Guide to Successful Career Planning.* Lincolnwood, IL: National Textbook Co., 1981.

Schwartz, Lester, and Brechner, Irv. *The Career Finder: Pathways to Over 1500 Entry-Level Jobs.* New York: Ballantine Books, 1983.

Semi-Skilled Careers Kit. Largo, FL: Careers, Inc.

Shilling, Dana. *Be Your Own Boss: A Step-by-Step Guide to Financial Independence Through Your Own Small Business.* New York: William Morrow & Co., 1983.

Snelling, Robert O., and Snelling, Anne M. *Jobs! What They Are . . . Where They Are . . . What They Pay!* New York: Simon & Schuster, 1985.

SRA Occupational Briefs series. Chicago: Science Research Associates.

Starting and Managing a Business from Your Home. U.S. Small Business Administration, vol. 102. Washington, D.C.: U.S. Government Printing Office.

Stossel, John. *Shopping Smart.* Chicago: Regnery, 1980.

Straub, Joseph T. *The Job Hunt: How to Compete and Win.* Englewood Cliffs, NJ: Prentice-Hall, 1981.

Vineyard, Ben S., and Vineyard, Katharine. *Choosing the Right Career.* Encino, CA: Bennett & McKnight/Glencoe, 1986.

Vocational School Manual. Moravia, NY: Chronicle Guidance Publications, revised annually.

Whittlesey, Marietta. *The New Freelancer's Handbook: Successful Self-Employment.* New York: Simon & Schuster, 1988.

Workforce 2000: Work and Workers for the 21st Century. Indianapolis, IN: Hudson Institute, 1987.

Working Smarter. Fortune Editors. New York: Viking-Penguin, 1982.

Wright, Dick. *Hardball Job Hunting Tactics.* New York: Facts on File, 1983.

Index

industrial and construction clusters,
109–110
people-serving clusters, 107–108

U

Unions, trade, 270
United States armed forces jobs, 116–117
United States Department of Labor, 103,
106, 176, 298, 299
Unskilled laborers, 74–75, 214

V

Value of money, 268
Values
choosing one's job and, 254–255
defined, 17
Ventures, 279, 280, 281
See also Entrepreneurship
Vocational school, 167–168
Volunteer, defined, 37
Volunteer work, 177–178
Voter, responsibility as, 255, 271

W

Wage-price spiral, 268
Wages
defined, 241
demand for special skills and, 269
of retail sales worker, 173
trade union negotiations for, 270
workers' expectations of regular, 220–221
Wants, 29–33
defined, 29
emotional, 32
material, 30–32
Wholesaler, 172
Willingness to follow rules, 218–219
to learn, 217–218
to work, 217
Woodworking business, 285

Word processors, 24
Work, attitude toward, 45, 217
Work environment, 122, 124, 128–129
Worker
attitudes expected of, 217–220
expectations from job, 220–223, 303
responsibility as, 253–255
understanding, 308–309
Work experience
dependence of wages on, 220–221
making most of, 301–304
qualifications gained by, 169
Working hours
of entrepreneurs, 286–287
rules about, 219
Working Woman, 127
Work permits, 175–176
Workplace
politics in, 226–227
safety in, 52, 218, 221
Work skills, essential, 66–69
Work-study programs, 165, 167
Writers, Artists, and Entertainers cluster,
108, 312–313
Written language skills, 63, 160–162

Photo Credits